Ásura

in Early Vedic Religion

WASH EDWARD HALE

MOTILAL BANARSIDASS PUBLISHERS
PRIVATE LIMITED • DELHI

First Edition: Delhi, 1986
Reprint: Delhi, 1999

ISBN: 81-208-0061-3

Also available at:

MOTILAL BANARSIDASS

41 U.A. Bungalow Road, Jawahar Nagar, Delhi 110 007
8 Mahalaxmi Chamber, Warden Road, Mumbai 400 026
120 Royapettah High Road, Mylapore, Chennai 600 004
Sanas Plaza, 1302, Baji Rao Road, Pune 411 002
16 St. Mark's Road, Bangalore 560 001
8 Camac Street, Calcutta 700 017
Ashok Rajpath, Patna 800 004
Chowk, Varanasi 221 001

PRINTED IN INDIA
BY JAINENDRA PRAKASH JAIN AT SHRI JAINENDRA PRESS,
A-45 NARAINA, PHASE I, NEW DELHI 110 028
AND PUBLISHED BY NARENDRA PRAKASH JAIN FOR
MOTILAL BANARSIDASS PUBLISHERS PRIVATE LIMITED,
BUNGALOW ROAD, DELHI 110 007

ACKNOWLEDGEMENTS

I wish to express my gratitude to Daniel H.H. Ingalls for serving as my advisor for this thesis, to Joki Schindler for spending many patient hours trying to help me understand the Vedic and Avestan texts, to Sheila Sylvester for typing the manuscript and being so pleasant to work with, to the Harvard Center for the Study of World Religions for providing such a pleasant atmosphere in which to work, to Harvard University for providing the facilities for study, and especially to my father without whose support my studies at Harvard would have been impossible.

ABBREVIATIONS

AB	Aitareya Brāhmaṇa
AV	Atharva Veda Saṃhitā (Śaunaka)
AVP	Paippalāda Saṃhitā (of the Atharva Veda)
GB	Gopatha Brāhmaṇa
JB	Jaiminīya Brāhmaṇa
KB	Kauṣītaki Brāhmaṇa
KpS	Kapiṣṭhala Kaṭha Saṃhitā
KS	Kāṭhaka Saṃhitā
MS	Maitrāyaṇī Saṃhitā
PB	Pañcaviṃśa Brāhmaṇa
RV	Ṛg Veda Saṃhitā
RVKh	Ṛg Veda Khila
ŚāmĀ	Śāṃkhāyana Āraṇyaka
ŚB	Śatapatha Brāhmaṇa
SV	Sāma Veda
Svidh	Sāmavidhāna Brāhmaṇa
TB	Taittirīya Brāhmaṇa
TS	Taittirīya Saṃhitā
VS	Vājasaneyi Saṃhitā (Mādhyandina)
VSK	Vājasaneyi Saṃhitā (Kāṇva)
Y.	Yasna
Yt.	Yašt

INTRODUCTION

A comparison between early Indic language and early Iranian language shows that both Sanskrit and Avestan developed from a common source. The religious ideas expressed in the early works in these two languages show many close similarities, but significant differences also appear. One particular group of developments has been especially interesting to those who have studied the early history of the religions in these two areas. In India the word *deva–* has meant "god" all through the Sanskrit literature, both Vedic and classical. However, in Iran the cognate word *daēva–* throughout the Avesta means "demon" (or perhaps "false god" in some Gāthic passages). The classical Sanskrit word *asura–* refers to a particular class of demons, but the Avestan cognate *ahura–* is part of the name of Zaraθuštra's God, Ahura Mazdā. This has led to much speculation by scholars on how this apparent double reversal of meanings of words came about. The key to unlocking at least part of this mystery seems to be the early Vedic literature, because in that literature *asura–* frequently appears as an epithet for various gods, that is, in a meaning much closer to the one found in Iran. The corpus of Vedic literature thus must contain whatever evidence there is to inform us what this word meant in its earliest Indic usage and how its meaning changed to that found in classical Sanskrit. I intend to examine this corpus of literature to trace the change in meaning of this word.

My method of conducting this study is very straightforward. I have examined every passage in which the word *asura–* or its derivative or compound appeared in all the Saṃhitās and all the Brāhmaṇas in Vedic literature. For the mantra portions of the Saṃhitās the original text was examined in each case. However, in the Brāhmaṇas and the brāhmaṇa portions of the Black Yajur Veda Saṃhitās the word seemed to be already established in its later meaning, so only translations were examined (when they existed) unless the passage seemed especially interesting.

In order to find out where this word occurred, I consulted the VVRI Index.* I did not look up passages there which were listed as repeats of passages from the RV. Every verse from the mantra portion of the Saṃhitās listed as containing *asura–* or its derivative or compound is quoted and translated in this work, although some of the actual text and verse numbers listed there are not found here since they were found to be repetitions of verses already quoted. Thus, for example, only one verse is quoted from the SāmaVeda since all the others containing *asura–* are also found in the RV.

Before presenting this study of the occurrences of *asura–*, I present in the first chapter a summary of all the theories accounting for the change in meaning of this word by previous scholars that I could find. Each summary is followed by a brief criticism. Of course, in many cases a thorough criticism could not be offered until all the passages in the texts were examined, but I did try to indicate what errors seemed to appear in each theory or what ideas could be accepted.

The passages from the mantra portions of the Saṃhitās (that is, the verses) containing *asura–* and its derivatives and compounds are presented in the next eight chapters. It appears that by the time of the composition of the last of these texts the word has already taken on the meaning "demon" or "anti-god." In the next three chapters I examine some words in this new semantic field (*rakṣas–*, *dasyu–*, *dāsa–*, and their derivatives) to see what sorts of evil beings were known to the Vedic people that could help guide us in understanding the change in meaning in *asura–*. It turns out that the new meaning of *asura–* seems to have much more in common with the human dasyus and dāsas than with the non-human rakṣases. Consequently, the verses which speak of human asuras seem to be of prime importance in this study.

Chapter thirteen traces the change in meaning of the word *asura–* through the brāhmaṇa period by examining the occurrences of the word in prose passages (Brāhmaṇas and brāhmaṇa portions of the Black Yajur Veda Saṃhitās). Unlike the previous chapters, this one does not refer to every relevant passage. Although every

*Vishva Bandhu, ed., *A Vedic Word Concordance*, 16 vols., second ed. of vols. 1, 7, and 8 (Hoshiarpur: Vishveshvaranand Vedic Research Institute), 1955–1973.

passage containing *asura–* was examined, only a few representative ones are actually cited.

The concluding chapter sums up what has been discovered in this study and suggests one implication of this study for future studies.

An appendix is added to discuss the use of the word *ahura–* in the Avesta. No attempt is made to reconstruct the developments this word underwent in the history of Iranian religion. The purpose of this appendix is merely to amass evidence from the Avesta to support the conclusions reached concerning the earliest Vedic meaning of *asura–*. Although this study of *asura–* has some implications for reconstructing the early history and prehistory of Iranian religion, the actual reconstructing of this history is beyond the limits of this study. One important implication of this study for the prehistory of Iranian religion is indicated in the Conclusion.

CONTENTS

CHAPTER I

PREVIOUS THEORIES ABOUT *ÁSURA*–

I shall precede a study of the word *ásura*– with a survey of the positions taken by various scholars on what this word meant in its earliest occurrences in the RV and how it came to be used with a pejorative connotation in later times. I tried to be exhaustive in this survey by discussing every article referenced under *ásura*– in Renou and Dandekar's *Vedic Bibliography*.[1] Unfortunately, a few of the articles listed there were not available to me. However, the survey is very nearly complete. The summary of each scholar's position is followed by a few critical remarks.

F. B. J. Kuiper

According to Kuiper the asuras "constitute the central problem of Vedic religion."[2] They were a special group of gods associated with the first stage of creation.[3] At first the world was an undifferentiated mass of water with a clod of earth floating on it, and the asuras were its gods. Indra enters into the second stage of creation. His creative activity is twofold. He rivets in place the primeval hill which floats on these waters and splits it open by killing Vṛtra, who is a personification of the resistance he encounters. Secondly, "he functions as a pillar in propping up the sky, which until then had been lying upon the earth. In doing so he creates the duality of heaven and earth."[4] The upper world becomes that of the devas and the underworld that of the asuras.[5] These devas are in fact a group of gods who enter the scene along with Indra.[6] The Vedic

1. Louis Renou, *Bibliographie Védique* (Paris: Librairie d'Amerique et d'Orient, 1931). R. N. Dandekar, *Vedic Bibliography*, 3 vols. (Poona: Bhandarkar Oriental Research Institute, 1946, 1961, 1973).

2. F. B. J. Kuiper, "The Basic Concept of Vedic Religion," *History of Religion* 15 (1975): 112.

3. *Ibid.*, p. 108.

4. *Ibid.*, p. 110.

5. F. B J. Kuiper, "Cosmogony and Conception: A Query," *History of Religion* 10 (1970): 105.

6. Kuiper, "Vedic Religion," p. 112.

poets must have considered this fight of Indra, "the chief and protagonist of the devas," against the dragon Vṛtra to be directed against the asuras.[7] After this fight some of the chief asuras went over to the side of the devas while the others took refuge in the underworld. "We owe it to the very archaic character of the Rigveda that a direct and clear trace of this split within the group of Asuras has been preserved. In this oldest text a distinction was still made between *devā́v ásurā*, 'Asuras who have become Devas,' and on the other hand, *ásurā ádevāḥ*, 'Asuras who are not Devas.'[7a] The Ādityas are in fact one group of asuras who became devas.[8] "As for the Rigveda, it is for special reasons only concerned with this second stage of the genesis of the world."[9] The first stage of undifferentiated unity ruled by the asuras must therefore be reconstructed mainly from later texts. And one must rely on these texts even though the RV is chronologically quite distant from all other texts.[10] The researcher must realize that the absence of a particular idea from the corpus of the RV does not necessarily mean that the idea was not in the mind of the poets who composed it. These ideas may simply have been irrelevant to what the poets wished to express in this corpus. Indeed "it cannot be doubted that the Asuras and Devas represent the two fundamentally contrasting moieties of a dualistic cosmos,. . . ." and this dualism goes back to the Indo-Iranian period.[11] The lack of mention of the struggle between devas and asuras in the RV is because the RV differs in style from the Brāhmaṇas.[12]

Criticism of Kuiper's Position

It is obvious that the Ṛgvedic poets had some ideas which they never expressed in their poems, but it is methodologically unsound to attempt to reconstruct these entirely from later data. Only those ideas which can be seen reflected in the hymns themselves can be

7. *Ibid.*, p. 112.
7a. *Ibid.*
8. F. B. J. Kuiper, "Ahura Mazdā 'Lord Wisdom?' " *Indo-Iranian Journal* 18 (1976): 39.
9. Kuiper, "Vedic Religion," p. 109.
10. Kuiper, "Cosmogony," p. 93.
11. F. B. J. Kuiper, *Varuṇa and Vidūṣaka: On the Origin of the Sanskrit Drama* (Amsterdam: North-Holland Publishing Company, 1979), pp. 5 and 8.
12. *Ibid.*, p. 12.

safely assigned to the period of their composition. It is the thesis of a primordial undifferentiated state in which the asuras ruled that I find questionable, and Kuiper has admitted that the RV is concerned only with the second state so that confirmation of this concept in the RV cannot be found. But we can examine what he offers. He suggests that the defeat of Vṛtra represents the defeat of the asuras. If Vṛtra does represent the asuras, it seems strange that he is never explicitly called asura in the RV. (He is first explicitly called asura in the brāhmaṇa portion of the MS.) He sees Indra's propping apart of heaven and earth as an important act of creation by the deva Indra. But other gods are also said to prop apart heaven and earth, including Varuṇa (RV 7.86.1), Soma (RV 9.101.15), the Maruts (RV 8.94.11), and Agni (RV 6.8.3). Three of these—Varuṇa, Soma, and Agni—are among the devas he considers "former asuras."[13] He cites as evidence of the split into two types of asuras the phrases *devā́v ásurā* and *ásurā ádevāḥ*. It is significant that the first phrase occurs only in the dual and not the plural—the plural use of *ásura–* for gods is quite rare, as we shall see later. The translation "Asuras who have become Devas" is erroneous. There is nothing in these words to suggest the idea of "having become." The second phrase is misquoted. It occurs only once in the RV (8.96.9), and the accent is on the last syllable of *adevā́ḥ*. An accent on the first syllable would be normal for a *karmadhāraya* compound, but an accent on the last syllable should indicate a *bahuvrīhi*.[14] It should therefore be translated "without devas" rather than "not devas," and the phrase would mean "asuras who do not worship the gods." We shall see later that this makes sense in the context. The most important objection I have to Kuiper's theory is that the asuras do not seem to form a special group of gods in the early Ṛgvedic period. But my reasons for suggesting this will have to be postponed until we have examined some texts. More generally, Kuiper seems to err by being too comparative. He tries to reconstruct for early Ṛgvedic mythology a cosmogony that is like those of other cultures such as Mesopotamia and Egypt. The cosmogony he thus reconstructs is not Indic, and it rests on a fundamental misunderstanding of the early meaning of *ásura–*.

13. Kuiper, "Ahura Mazdā," p. 34.

14. Jacob Wackernagel and Albert Debrunner, *Altindische Grammatik*, 3 vols., 1896 and 1930, reprint (Gottingen: Vandenhoeck & Ruprecht, 1957, 1954, 1975), vol. 2, part 1, p. 293.

W. Norman Brown

W. Norman Brown also makes the fundamental error of thinking that *ásura–* referred to a class of gods.[15] He says that there are two classes of divine beings in the RV —devas and asuras. Some gods are called both, but a few are not. However, *ásura–* can also be applied to malevolent beings. Thus the asuras themselves are subdivided into two classes. The "good" ones are called Ādityas and are led by Varuṇa. The "bad" ones are called Dānavas and are led by Vṛtra. The basic meaning of *ásura–* is something like "lord," but in usage it comes to mean "powerful, a creature of power" or especially "having the superhuman or magic power of *māyā*."[16] "In the Rig Veda the word *ásura* and its derivatives are used predominantly of Varuṇa, Mitrāvaruṇā, the Ādityas as a group, Indra, Agni, the Sun in several aspects, probably of Rudra a number of times, the gods, and the opponents of the gods."[17] "It is never used with the Aśvins or in a primary way with Uṣas .... It is twice used unequivocally of the god Dyaus...."[18] Uṣas, the Aśvins, and Dyaus are definitely devas. Thus, Brown concludes, "It is evident that the asuras are well differentiated from the devas."[19]

Criticism of Brown's Position

I agree with the basic definition of *ásura–* as "lord." Again, one might note that Vṛtra is not explicitly called asura in the RV. I find his conclusion that the devas and asuras are two clearly differentiated groups totally unacceptable just on the basis of the evidence he gives. All of the figures he cites as predominantly called asura are also called deva except the opponents of the gods. Few of these are Ādityas, and none are Dānavas except some opponents of the gods. But the fundamental reasons for denying that there was a group of gods called asuras will have to be given in a later chapter.

15. W. Norman Brown, "The Creation Myth of the Rig Veda," *Journal of the American Oriental Society* 62 (1942): 88-91.

16. *Ibid*., p. 89.

17. *Ibid.*

18. *Ibid.* An application of derivative of *ásura-* to Uṣas had to be explained away as secondary in a footnote.

19. *Ibid.*

Haug

Haug was apparently the first to propose the theory that the different developments of *ásura–* in India and *ahura–* in Iran came from a split in the religion of the Indo-Iranian people.[20] This theory introduced the idea that there was at some time in history a group of gods called Asuras and a cult of Asura worshippers. This theory has persisted in various modified forms up until the present day. Both Brown and Kuiper suggest that there was such a group of gods, although they do not say much about a possible cult devoted to them.

P. von Bradke

The most thorough study of the word *ásura–* was done by P. Von Bradke and is a revision of Haug's theory.[21] He made a careful study of all the verses in the RV in which the word occurs and also looked at later occurrences of it, but less thoroughly. The meaning of *ásura–* is easier to find in the usage of its adjectival derivative *asuryà–*. The latter meant "highest lordship" or "highest lordship of the gods."[22] *Ásura–* thus was an epithet of the highest god. Dyaus was the old Indo-European high god, and the devas formed his princely court.[23] Even the great god Indra had taken over the *vajra*, one of his main attributes, from Dyaus.[24] It was this great god Dyaus who was the original asura.[25] But as *dyáus–* was used more and more to mean the sky and not the god, the epithet *ásura–* was transferred first to Varuṇa and Indra, then to other gods. Thus most gods can be called asura.[26] This same Indo-Iranian Dyaus Asura developed into Ahura Mazdā in Iran.[27] Pejorative uses of *ásura–* begin to appear in the RV, and in the AV they are more frequent than its usage in connection with the gods. When *ásura–* is used for beings opposed to the gods it is usually

20. Arthur Berriedale Keith, *The Religion and Philosophy of the Veda and Upanishads*, 2 vols., Harvard Oriental Series, vols. 31 and 32, 1925, reprint (Delhi: Motilal Banarsidass, 1970), vol. 1, p. 231.

21. P. von Bradke, *Dyâus Asura, Ahura Mazdâ und die Asuras* (Halle: Max Niemeyer, 1885).

22. *Ibid.*, pp. 30, 32, and 40.

23. *Ibid.*, pp. 50 and ix.

24. *Ibid.*, p. xi.

25. *Ibid.*, p. 44.

26. *Ibid.*, p. 42.

27. *Ibid.*, p. 81.

in the plural, but most of its occurrences in connection with the gods are singular.[28] In the Brāhmaṇas only the plural of *ásura*– appears and always with an antigodly connotation.[29] When a single anti-godly being is referred to in the Brāhmaṇas, the derivative term *āsurá*– is often used.[30] Since this concept of asura equal to high god shows no indication of having changed into *asurā adevāḥ*, this latter pejorative concept must have entered from outside.[31] It resulted from a clash of the Indians with the Iranians. But this had to happen after the initial separation of these two peoples in order for the abrupt change in the meaning of *ásura*– in late Ṛgvedic times to make sense.[32] The Indians encountered the Iranians, who worshipped a god named Ahura Mazdā, recognized *ahura*– as their word *ásura*–, and concluded that the god of an enemy must be a demon. Thus *ásura*– took on the pejorative connotation of demon for the Indians. Thus von Bradke continued Haug's theory by explaining the degradation of *ásura*– as stemming from an encounter with the Iranians, but changed the time of this encounter to a period after their initial separation. His theory also differs from Haug's in not positing the existence of a group of deities called asuras for the Indo-Iranian period.

Summary of Reviews of von Bradke's Book

Not surprisingly this book evoked several reviews, mostly favorable. Kaegi wrote a favorable review with little criticism.[33] Barth pointed out one objection. Von Bradke says that *ásura*–was originally an epithet of Dyaus, but in the most ancient documents we have already have this word meaning "enemy of the gods" in some instances.[34] Hillebrandt agrees with von Bradke in rejecting the idea that *ásura*– was originally neither god nor demon.[35] He

28. *Ibid.*, pp. 21-2.
29. *Ibid.*, p. 86.
30. *Ibid.*, p. 91.
31. *Ibid.*, p. 106.
32. *Ibid.*, pp. 108-9.
33. Adolf Kaegi, "Review of *Dyâus Asura, Ahura Mazdâ und die Asuras* by P. von Bradke," *Deutsche Litteraturzeitung* 36 (1885): cols. 1268-9.
34. A. Barth, "Review of *Dyâus Asura, Ahura Mazdâ und die Asuras* by P. von Bradke," *Revue de L'histoire des Religions* 11 (1885): 47.
35. Alfred Hillebrandt, "Review of *Dyâus Asura, Ahura Mazdâ und die Asuras* by P. von Bradke," *Theologische Literaturzeitung* 22 (1885): col. 528. Here I disagree with both these authors.

finds the argument that *ásura–* meant "highest god" plausible, but not compelling. But he is convinced by the argument that it was originally an epithet for Dyaus. Meringer criticizes von Bradke's lack of skill in etymological matters.[36] In particular, he is not convinced that *asuryàm* should be translated by "höchste Gottesherrlichkeit." He says it can mean "highest lordship of the gods" in a few of its occurrences, cannot in three or four, and need not anywhere.[37] He also objects to the theory that the negative connotation of *ásura–* came from contact with the Iranians. Since the Iranians had become monotheists after Zaraθuštra's preaching, the Indians should only have developed a single demon asura and not demons in the plural.[38] Spiegel accepts von Bradke's argument that Ahura Mazdā developed from Indo-Iranian Dyaus Asura.[39] But he suggests that *ásura–* in the Aryan (i.e. Indo-Iranian) period seems to have been a title for the highest person, divine or human. He agrees that Dyaus was originally the highest god with the devas under him and that the devas overran him, but goes on to interpret this as a normal development in the evolution of the worship of nature-gods when the one sky begins to be analyzed into parts.[40]

Criticism of von Bradke's Position

I agree with most of the negative criticisms of these reviewers. But there is another fundamental problem with von Bradke's methodology that they did not point out. He concludes that because the RV so often repeats phrases, it is basically a reworking of a group of older hymns.[41] He then takes the occurrence of such repeated phrases as an indication of the lateness of a hymn.[42] This allows him to dismiss some otherwise problematical passages as

36. Rudolf Meringer, "Review of *Dyâus Asura, Ahura Mazdâ und die Asuras* by P. von Bradke," *Oesterreichische Monatsschrift für den Orient* 4 (1885): 96.

37. *Ibid.*

38. *Ibid.*

39. F Spiegel, "Review of *Dyâus Asura, Ahura Mazdâ und die Asuras* by P. von Bradke," *Berliner Philologische Wockenschrift* 5 (1885): col. 1078-9.

40. *Ibid.*, col. 1080. I cannot accept this explanation in terms of nature worship.

41 von Bradke, *Dyâus Asura*, p. 8.

42. *Ibid.*, pp. 3ff.

late.[43] The repeated phrases found in the RV would perhaps better be interpreted as a natural consequence of its being an oral composition.[44] The occurrence of such phrases cannot be used reliably for dating hymns. His theory that the pejorative connotation of *ásura–* comes from hostile encounters with the Iranians also suffers by having no evidence that there was ever any such contact during the period of the composition of the RV.[45] But in spite of the criticisms that can be made, this work remains an important contribution toward the understanding of *ásura–*. He collected the relevant passages from the RV and discussed them. He also scanned the later Vedic literature and discussed the development of the meaning of the word there. And he pointed out a number of important facts to consider in studying this word. There is an important semantic value associated with the number of the word—the singular usually has a good connotation and the plural a pejorative one.[46] *Ásura–* is sometimes used for people.[47] *Āsurá–* is normally used in Brāhmaṇas for a single demon.[48] Such observations are a helpful guide for future researchers.

Rudolf Otto

Rudolf Otto continues Haug's theory. He says there was an asura religion which arose before the separation of the Indians and Iranians.[49] In India deva religion absorbed asura religion, but in Iran asura religion was kept pure by the group from which Zaraθuštra later arose.[50] Varuṇa and his circle of deities were

43. See, for example, *ibid.*, p. 70.

44. For a discussion of oral composition one might look at Albert B. Lord, *The Singer of Tales* (New York: Atheneum, 1973, original publication in 1960). This book deals with oral composition of epics and not hymns, but some of his observations and conclusions could also be applied to other types of or alcomposition.

45. Hillebrandt made an effort to shcw that there was such contact, but the evidence he offered was insufficient. See Keith, *Religion and Philosophy* vol. 1, p. 232.

46. von Bradke, *Dyâus Asura*, pp. 21-2.

47. *Ibid.*, p. 68.

48. *Ibid.*, p. 91.

49. Rudolf Otto, *The Kingdom of God and the Son of Man*, trans. by F. V. Filson and B. L. Woolf (London: Lutterworth Press, 1938), p. 20.

50. Rudolf Otto, *Das Gefühl des Überweltlichen* (Munich: C. H. Beck'sche Verlangsbuchhandlung, 1932), p. 190.

asuras.[51] He and his circle of asuras and Ādityas were absorbed into the very different Ṛgvedic pantheon of devas.[52] These gods were of a more exalted nature than the devas. Varuṇa is the most substantial and exalted god in the RV, and much of what is said of him could be said of Yahweh in the Psalms. Thus the incorporation of these gods elevated the devas, but never to the heights achieved by the asuras.[53] These asuras include Bhaga, Aṃśa, Aryaman, Varuṇa, and Mitra.

> In nature they are alike, and originally the names mentioned were probably nothing but words current in different tribes for essentially similar numina. Tribal relationship, perhaps political alliance of tribes and the inner agreement of the differently named but essentially similar numina of the asuras, unite them in the cycle of the 'seven ādityas.'[54]

Varuṇa is the asura and the āditya *par excellence.*[55] He is called wise (*medhira*). **Asura Medhira* corresponds exactly with Iranian *Ahura Mazdā*, the name of the god of the Iranian branch of the Indo-Iranians before they split with the Indians. The word *ásura–* is derived from *ásu–* and means "possessing asu."[56] *Ásu–* means "life-power." Varuṇa is called asura because of his ability to heal.[57] This great deity actually arises from that category of deities who both send and take away disease.[58] But "asu-possessor" has a deeper meaning as well. Possessing life also has the implication of immortality as that which separates god from non-god.[59] While *ásura–* began as a designation for gods, its use could be extended to others who were not gods, but possessed numinous power, such as clan princes. Thus in later profane use it could simply mean "lord."[60] The use of the term to refer to demons came somewhat

51. *Ibid.*, p. 186.
52. *Ibid.*, p. 128.
53. *Ibid.*, p. 128.
54. Otto, *Kingdom*, p. 21.
55. *Ibid.*, p. 128.
56. *Ibid.*, p. 186.
57. Rudolf Otto, *Gottheit und Gottheiten der Arier* (Giessen: Alfred Töpelmann, 1932), pp. 93-4.
58. Otto, *Kingdom*, p. 20.
59. Otto, *Gefühl*, p. 188.
60. *Ibid.*, p. 187.

later—only after it was used for rivals of the devas as the asura religion had been a rival of the deva religion some time before.[61]

Criticism of Otto's Position

Otto seems more or less to equate asuras and ādityas in early RV. This does not seem to be substantiated by the texts. Other deities such as Dyaus, Savitṛ, Soma, and Agni are also called asura. Also, the theory that the asuras were absorbed into the pantheon of devas required postulating the existence of separate pantheons of asuras and devas in the Indo-Iranian period, and this seems to be unacceptable. His linguistic equation of *medhira–* with *mazdā–* is not quite accurate, although both words are derived from the same stem, and he is justified in noting a close relationship. It is also impossible to maintain on the basis of the texts that *ásura–* is used first of gods and later in an extended use for people. *Ásura–* is used of people already in the earliest parts of the RV, and *ahura–* is used to mean "lord" and not Ahura Mazdā already a few times in the Gāthās.[62] One should also note that this theory offers a very poor explanation for how *ásura–* came to mean demon. If we believe Otto here, the idea of rivalry between devas and asuras went completely underground for several centuries only to emerge at the end of the Ṛgvedic period in the use of *ásura–* for demon after the original asuras had been throughly absorbed into the pantheon of devas. This seems quite unlikely.

Emile Benveniste

Benveniste is among those who believe in an Indo-Iranian cult of asura worshippers. He says that the Avestan word *ahura–* represents an Iranian inheritance from this cult.[63] The name of Zaraθuštra's god Ahura Mazdā indicates that he is "a being of the family of Asuras."[64] This god was probably not new with Zaraθuštra, but was a god already known whom he exalted. The compounds *ahura-miθra–* and *miθra-ahura-* must also have been of

61. *Ibid.*, p. 191. I am interpreting Otto a bit here, but this seems to be what he is suggesting.

62. These occurrences in the Gāthās are discussed in an appendix.

63. Emile Benveniste and Louis Renou, *Vṛtra et Vṛθragna, étude de mythologie indo-iranienne* (Paris: Imprimerie Nationale, 1934), p. 44.

64. Emile Benveniste, *The Persian Religion according to the Chief Greek Texts* (Paris: Libraire Orientaliste Paul Geuthner, 1929) p. 40.

Indo-Iranian origin and refer to the same god as the Vedic compound *mitrā-varuṇā*.[65] The compound *ahura-δāta–* is used in opposition to *daēva-δāta–* and refers not to something created by Ahura Mazdā, but to something created by the ahuras.[66] These and a few other terms refer to a primordial opposition between devas and asuras, but only a few traces of this survive because the Mazdian reform changes the opposition to one between daēvas and Mazdā.[67]

Criticism of Benveniste's Position

This theory is in line with Haug's in positing an Indo-Iranian opposition between devas and asuras. A full criticism of the details of the theory is beyond the scope of this thesis since Benveniste is dealing only with the Iranian evidence and I am concerned with the Indic development. However, my later results will show how little the Vedic material supports the idea of an early opposition between a group of devas and a group of asuras. The Avestan material will also yield virtually no support for this idea in its use of the uncompounded word *ahura–*. Benveniste himself offers no evidence to support his translation of the compound *ahura-δāta–*. Consequently his translation is too interpretive and cannot be accepted.

Sten Konow

Sten Konow also believes there was an early opposition between devas and asuras. He says that the Aryan Indians in the oldest period used both *devá–* and *ásura–* for gods.[68] There is no indication of an asura cult before the Indo-Iranian period, but one did arise at that time. The asuras who were worshipped were patterned after Aryan kings and perhaps reflect Babylonian influence.[69] Although worship of asuras developed before the Indians and Iranians divided, it must not have become firmly established

65. Benveniste and Renou, *Vṛtra et Vṛθragna*, p. 46.
66. *Ibid.*, p. 47.
67. *Ibid.*, p. 48.
68. Sten Konow, "Zur Frage nach den Asuras" in *Beiträge zur Literaturwissenschaft und Geistesgeschichte Indiens, Festgabe Hermann Jacobi zum 75. Geburtstag*, edited by Willibald Kirfel (Bonn: Kommissionsverlag Fritz Klopp, 1926), p. 259.
69. *Ibid.*, p. 262.

then since it died out in India.[70] The fates of devas and asuras in India and Iran developed separately and are not the result of two earlier rival factions.[71] In India the devas became more prominent along with Indra as gods worshipped by warriors, and the asuras gradually became demons.[72] But in Iran the devas became demons much as the pre-Christian gods of Europe did when the Europeans became Christian. As for the etymology of *ásura*–, a borrowing of the word into Finno-Ugric as *ezoro*– with the meaning "lord" helps establish "lord" as its early meaning and thus relate it to Latin *erus*–.[73]

Criticism of Konow's Position

The existence of an Indo-Iranian asura cult is highly questionable, but the evidence against it cannot be presented until the early Vedic texts have been examined. It is to Konow's credit that he emphasizes the relationship of *ásura*– to kingship and that he sees the diverse development of *devá*– and *ásura*– in the two lands as independent. His suggestion that the asuras gradually became demons in India deserves careful attention. It is easy to reach such a conclusion from too hasty a look at the data. That is not in fact what happened. Not a single figure can be cited who was called asura in the good sense in early RV and was later called asura in the bad sense. Thus there was not a change in the character of a group of beings to whom this term was applied. The change was rather in the usage of the term. It began to be applied to a different group of beings. (This will be discussed in more detail later.)

V. K. Rajwade

According to Rajwade *ásura*– means "powerful" or "strong" and is only generic in character.[74] When the Indian Aryans and Zoroastrians split, the Indians came to regard Indra as the supreme deity while the Zoroastrians apparently transformed Indra into Angra Mainyu.[75] "Originally of one stock, they quarrelled and

70. *Ibid.*, p. 263.
71. *Ibid.*
72. *Ibid.*, p. 261.
73. *Ibid.*, p. 263.
74. V. K. Rajwade, "Asurasya Māyā in Ṛgveda," in *Proceedings and Transactions of the First Oriental Conference, Poona* (Poona: Bhandarkar Oriental Research Institute, 1920), p. ix
75. *Ibid.*, p. x.

parted irreconciliably. Worshippers of *asura* or Ahura, the Zoroastrians were nicknamed Asuras [by the Indians]."[76] Avestan "seems to be Sanskrit mispronounced. . . . The Grammatical forms are almost the same, only they are mispronounced either deliberately to make the cleavage permanent or because the speakers were uncivilized barbarians."[77] Thus the Sanskrit word *mahas–* appears as Zoroastrian *mazdā–*. "India was certainly not the home of the Ṛgvedic people. Words like *asura*, *paṇi* (Phoenician), and *dasyu* point to a domicile other than India."[78]

Criticism of Rajwade's Position

This article hardly deserves serious consideration. The author's use of *Zoroastrian* is anachronistic. Sanskrit *mahas–* is not Avestan *mazdā–*. *Paṇi* is not Phoenician. The author shows no understanding of linguistics and no understanding or appreciation of the Avestan material.

U. Venkatakrishna Rao

Rao also mistakenly equates *ahuro mazdā* with Sanskrit *asuro mahā*.[79] He says that the asuras were worshipped in former times and gradually turned against, but offers no reason for this.[80] But he does make the interesting observation that the Amarakośa lists *pūrvadeva–* as a synonym for *ásura–*.[81] This suggests that the later Indians interpreted *ásura–* as a term for an older class of gods.

R. N. Dandekar

Dandekar suggests that *ásura–* was originally used for a being who possessed the highest occult power.[82] It is derived from *asu+ra* and literally means one who possesses *asu*. *Asu* indicated life-power.[83] This *asu* was in the form of a supernatural fluid like

76. *Ibid.*, p. xi.
77. *Ibid.*, pp. xi-xii.
78. *Ibid.*, p. xii.
79. U. Venkatakrishna Rao, "The Romance of Words," *The Aryan Path* 14 (1943): 204.
80. *Ibid.*, pp. 204-5.
81. *Ibid.*, p. 205.
82. R. N. Dandekar, "Asura Varuṇa," *Annals of the Bhandarkar Oriental Research Institute* 21 (1941): 179.
83. R. N. Dandekar, *Der Vedische Mensch* (Heidelberg: Carl Winter's Universitätsbuchhandlung, 1938), pp. 24-5.

orenda or *mana*.[84] The unique power of an asura was called māyā, and was the secret power to create miraculously.[85] The rivalry between Indra and the asura in Vedic religion may have been accentuated by a confusion between the names *ásura–* and *Assyrians* resulting from folk etymology.[86]

Criticism of Dandekar's Position

The last suggestion is problematical because of a lack of evidence that the Aryans had any historical encounter with the Assyrians. (We shall soon see more theories relating *ásura–* to Assyrians.) It is also difficult to accept the suggestion that māyā was unique to asuras. In spite of these criticisms, Dandekar's article on "Asura Varuṇa" contains a useful summary of theories about Varuṇa and some good critical comments on these theories.

James Darmesteter

Darmesteter suggested that the Indo-Iranian language had three words to designate gods: *asura–*, **Yag̑ata–*, and **daiva–*. *Asura–* designated supreme god or gods and meant "lord." **Yag̑ata–* meant "one to whom one should offer sacrifice." **Daiva–*meant "the shining." In Iran *ahura–* came to designate the supreme god, and *yazata–* was retained for those deities who did not go by the special name Aməša Spəntas. But *daēva–* underwent a change in meaning. In the RV there occur prayers for one to be saved from harm *devānām uta martyānām*. In Avestan there are prayers of the heroes to be saved from harm *daēvanąm uta mašyanąm*. The occurrence of cognate phrases in similar contexts suggests that prayers for deliverance from harm caused by men and devas go back to Indo-Iranian times. Such contexts could easily aid the degradation of the term *daēva–* to the meaning "demon."[87] The Sanskrit word *ásura–* began with the same meaning as Avestan *ahura–*, that is "lord," but it came to be synonymous with "god." *Asuryàm* thus meant "divine sovereignty." It was Varuṇa who was most frequently called asura.[88] *Váruṇa–* was the Indic name for the supreme,

84. Dandekar, *Vedische Mensch*, p. 28. Dandekar, "Asura Varuṇa," p. 179.
85. Dandekar, "Asura Varuṇa," p. 180.
86. *Ibid.*, p. 189.
87. James Darmesteter, *Ormazd et Ahriman, leurs origins et leur histoire*, Bibliotheque de l'école des hautes études, 29th fascicle (Paris: F. Vieweg, 1877), pp. 265-6.
88. *Ibid.*, p. 47.

moral, omniscient, sovereign, creator asura recognized by the Indo-Iranians. In Iran he was called Ahura Mazdā.[89] But *varuṇa–* already existed in Indo-Iranian times as **varana–* meaning "sky." This is proven by Greek *οὐρανός*. It appears in Avestan as *varəna–*.[90] This Varuṇa-Ahura is in fact Indo-European since it compares with Zeus and Jupiter.[91] Folk etymology of *ásura–* into *a-su-ra* probably aided the tendency of this word to be used with a negative connotation in later times. But it should be noted that the change was only in the use of the word and not in the character of some being or beings. No ancient asura god becomes a later asura demon.[92]

Criticism of Darmesteter's Position

Whether or not Darmesteter's theory about the reason for the degradation of the term *daēva–* is accepted, it is very significant that he argues that the change occurred within the Iranian language independently of any development or contact with the Indic language. *Āsura–* and *daēva–* underwent similar changes in meaning, but in different places and for different reasons. I agree with him that Sanskrit *ásura–* began with the basic meaning "lord," but it never became synonymous with "god." It was certainly used more frequently of gods, but continued to be used of men as well. *Váruṇa–* cannot be said to be Indo-Iranian for the reason he gives because it cannot be derived from **varana–*.

R. G. Bhandarkar and K. R. V. Raja

Various scholars have attempted to relate *ásura–* with the Semitic word *aššur*. K. R. V. Raja seems to have been the first to do this when he suggested in a 1908 pamphlet that the Indo-Aryans borrowed *ásura–* from the Assyrians.[93] In 1918 R.G. Bhandarkar argued along similar lines. He pointed out that in the RV *ásura–* is usually an epithet of a god, but a few times denotes beings hostile to the gods and sometimes enemies of man.[94] A passage in

89. *Ibid.*, p. 67.
90. *Ibid.*, p. 69.
91. *Ibid.*, p. 83.
92. *Ibid.*, p. 269.
93. K. R. V. Raja, "Asura Maya," *Journal of the Royal Asiatic Society of Great Britain and Ireland*, January, 1917, pp. 131-2.
94. R. G. Bhandarkar, ""The Aryans in the Land of the Asuras," *The Journal of the Bombay Branch of the Royal Asiatic Society* 25 (1918): 76.

Pantañjali's Mahābhāṣya indicates that asuras were non-Brāhmaṇic foreigners.[95] The Śatapatha Brāhmaṇa also indicates that asuras speak a foreign language.[96] A treaty discovered in Asia Minor lists five Vedic deities as deities of a people called the Mitanni.[97] If these were the same people who later entered India, then the pre-Vedic people were in contact with the Assyrians. who were the northern neighbors of the Mitanni.[98] In later times when these people entered India and had hostile encounters with the indigenous dasyus, they mentioned in their poetry their memories or traditions of similar hostitle encounters they had with the Assyrians, whom they called asuras.[99] Thus *ásura–* was first used as an epithet for gods, then for humans hostile to the wandering Aryans (that is, for Assyrians), then for a mythical race of beings hostile to the gods, then for foreigners without an implication of hostility.[100]

Criticism of Bhandarkar's Position

The main problem with Bhandarkar's theory is the equation of the Mitanni with pre-Vedic Indians. As Keith pointed out, these people could have been only one of many groups of Indo-Iranian speaking people and may well have had no further contact with those who later entered India.[101] A second problem is that his theory requires assuming that there were two different words *ásura–*, one of which was used as an epithet for gods and the other of which had the other three meanings he lists of "enemy," "mythical being," and "foreigner." It is certainly possible that there were two different words *asura–*, but if a theory can be given which explains things as adequately from a single word *ásura–*, this would be preferable because it is more parsimonious. We shall also see later that *dásyu–* and *ásura–* in a hostile sense appear in the texts in a complimentary distribution with *ásura–* occurring in the later texts. This fact does not go well with Bhandarkar's theory either. If he were correct, *ásura–* should appear as a term for enemies in

95. *Ibid.*, p. 77.
96. *Ibid.*, p. 78.
97. *Ibid.*, p. 76.
98. *Ibid.*, p. 78.
99. *Ibid.*, pp. 78-9.
100. *Ibid.*, p. 79.
101. A. Berriedale Keith, "Mitanni, Iran and India," in *Dr. Modi Memorial Volume* (Bombay: Fort Printing Press, 1939), pp. 82-3.

the earliest parts of the RV where encounters with the dasyus are described. His references to foreign languages mentioned in the Mahābhāṣya and ŚB are also erroneous. The phrases in question are different dialects of Sanskrit and not foreign languages.

A. Banerji-Sastri

The most detailed exposition of the theory that *ásura–* derived from the Assyrians was offered by Banerji-Sastri. His book *Asura India*[102] was not available to me, but I did have access to four lengthy articles published by him in the same year that undoubtedly give the main thrust of his theory. He said that Patañjali in the second century B.C.E. remembered asuras as deficient in grammar, but that Patañjali arrived at this conclusion by misunderstanding a passage from the Śatapatha Brāhmaṇa. Thus one must take the second century B.C.E. as the latest period for finding any historical information about asuras.[103] Aššur is the key for understanding early Indian history. The history of this city becomes obscure between the twelfth century B.C.E. and tenth century B.C.E. The RV holds the key to filling in this missing piece of history.[104] During this period the Assyrians invaded India by sea, sailing to the mouth of the Indus and conquering the land from the waterways.[105] The Bhaviṣya Purāṇa reports that the asuras came from across the sea of salt water.[106] These asuras are described in the RV as dark skinned (*hiraṇyahasta asura*).[107] "The sea was the Asura element."[108] Thus we find the name of the great asura god Varuṇa compounded with *mitrá–* to refer to his friendliness to sailors.[109] The Dāsas were the earliest settlers in India, then came the Asuras, and finally the Aryas.[110] The Rāmāyaṇa tells the story of the conquest of the last asura stronghold in Ceylon by the

102. A. Banerji-Sastri, *Asura India* (Patna, 1926).
103. A. Banerji-Sastri, "The Asuras in Indo-Iranian Literature," *The Journal of the Bihar and Orissa Research Society* 12 (1926): 110-1.
104. *Ibid.*, p. 114.
105. *Ibid.*, pp. 117-20.
106. *Ibid.*, p. 118.
107. *Ibid.*, pp. 118 and 124.
108. A. Banerji-Sastri, "Asura Expansion by Sea." *The Journal of the Bihar and Orissa Research Society* 12 (1926): 336.
109. *Ibid.*, p. 341.
110. A. Banerji-Sastri, "Asura Expansion in India." *The Journal of the Bihar and Orissa Research Society* 12(1926): 246.

Aryas.[111] Various "linguistic" evidence is also brought in to support various points in this story. "Bhṛgu is suspiciously akin to Phrigian by a simple application of well known phonetic laws."[112] "*Mleccha–* is allied to *Mlech*, *Malku* an Assyrian form still used as *Mlek* or *Malek* in Baluchistan and as *Malik* in the Indus valley."[113] "Pre-Aryan *Nṛtu* in India seems to have travelled north as Tacitus' *Nerthus* in North Germany and Scandinavia.... Both *Nṛtu* and *Nerthus* are derived from the root *nṛt*."[114] *Uṣas–* is pre-Aryan and probably a borrowing of Egyptian *Isis*.[115]

Criticism of Banerji-Sastri's Position

Barnett in his review of Banerji-Sastri's book suggests:

> that the author's understanding of Avesta and Avestic religion is strikingly faulty and his knowledge of Assyrian apparently second-hand; that his method of comparative philology is prehistoric...; and that generally his combinations and conclusions attest his power of imagination rather than his capacity of judgement.[116]

I shall add a few more specific criticisms. He says that the RV supplies the evidence for the activities of the Assyrians in the period from about 1200-1000 B.C.E. But the section of his paper dealing with Indic records in the subtitle indicates a date of 1500 B.C.E. for these sources.[117] It is strange that the RV should be composed 300 years before the historical events it reports. It is also peculiar that he emphasized the navigating abilities of the asuras, since the Assyrians were certainly not known for their abilities as sailors. Though he ruled out at the beginning of his first article use of any source from later than second century B.C.E., he frequently refers to a statement in the Bhaviṣya Purāṇa that the asuras came from across the salt sea.[118] *Hiraṇyahasta–* does not mean "dark-skin-

111. *Ibid.*, pp. 244-5.
112. Banerji-Sastri, "Asuras in Indo-Iranian Literature," p. 126.
113. Banerji-Sastri, "Asura Expansion by Sea," pp. 354-5.
114. A. Banerji-Sastri, "Asura Institutions," *The Journal of the Bihar and Orissa Research Society* 12 (1926): 519.
115. *Ibid.*, pp. 514-5.
116. L. D. Barnett, "Review of *Asura India* by A. Banerji-Sastri," *Journal of the Royal Asiatic Society of Great Britain and Ireland*, July 1928, p. 670.
117. Banerji-Sastri, "Asuras in Indo-Iranian Literature," p. 123.
118. *Ibid.*, p. 118. Banerji-Sastri, "Asura Expansion by Sea," pp. 358 and 360.

ned." It means "having golden hands" and occurs once in the RV with *ásura–* as an epithet of Savitṛ, the sun (RV 1.35.10). *Mitrā-varuṇā–* does not mean that Varuṇa was a friend of sailors. *Bhṛgu–* is not related to *Phrigian. Mleccha–* is more likely to be explained as onomatopoeic. *Uṣas–* is Indo-European since it is cognate with Greek *ἠώς.*[119] and is not related to *Isis.* And he does not seem to notice that suggesting that *nṛtu–* and *Nerthus* are cognate directly contradicts his suggestion that the goddess is pre-Aryan.

A. Padmanabhayya

Padmanabhayya begins where Banerji-Sastri left off and continues his facile identifications of ancient peoples even farther. He begins by equating Dravida, Asura, and Bhṛgu and attempts to extend this equation in his article to include Pelasgian, Phygian [*sic*], Hittite, Phoenician, Greek, Etruscan, Latin, and Frank.[120] He concludes that Varuṇa was borrowed from the Elamites since the Matsya Purāṇa says Suṣan was Varuṇa's city and Sushan was the capital of Elam.[121] I shall not give any more details or offer any criticism except to say that I find his theory totally unacceptable.

H. Sköld

H. Sköld argued quite effectively against any derivation of *ásura–* from *aššur* in a short article in 1924.[122] First he pointed out that the *š* in *aššur* should appear in Sanskrit as *ś* and in Avestan as *s*, not as the *s* and *h* we have in *ásura–* and *ahura–*.[123] He also pointed out that transliterated forms of Ahura Mazdā and Aššur appear in Persian, Babylonian, and Elamite texts. But in none of these languages do the words show a phonological similarity that would favor the proposed borrowing.[124] I think this final criticism of Sköld's can be accepted as applying to all of the theories summarized above which assume that *ásura–* was borrowed from the Assyrians.

119. Manfred Mayrhofer, *Kurzgefasstes etymologisches Wörterbuch des Altindischen*, 3 vols. (Heidelberg: Carl Winter Universitätsverlag, 1953, 1963, and 1976), vol. 1, p. 113.

120. A Padmanabhayya, "Ancient Bhṛgus," *The Journal of Oriental Research Madras* 5 (1931): 56.

121. *Ibid.*, p. 59.

122. Hannes Sköld, "Were the Asuras Assyrians?" *The Journal of the Royal Asiatic Society of Great Britain and Ireland*, April 1924, pp. 265-7.

123. *Ibid.*, p. 266.

124. *Ibid.*

S. C. Roy

S.C. Roy proposed a theory which did not derive *ásura–* from *aššur*, but is similar to the theories which do in suggesting that the asuras were a group of people who once occupied India. He pointed out that *ásura–* sometimes referred to superhuman enemies, but often to human foes.[125] Other terms such as *daitya–* and *dānava–* are applied to these same tribes of enemies or others like them. The Mūṇḍas and others have a tradition that India was previously occupied by a metal-using people called Asuras.[126] One tribe of the Mūṇḍa group are called Asuras today. These are probably descendents of the ancient Asuras.[127]

Criticism of Roy's Position

This theory rests on the idea that the asuras formed a group of people in India in the period of the earliest texts. This is contradicted by the usage of the word of the RV. In most of its occurrences there it refers to gods. When it is used of people, some are enemies, but others are not.

Ananda K. Coomaraswamy

Coomaraswamy argues that devas and asuras are consubstantial, but of different orientations. Thus *ásura–* and *devá–* can be applied to the same figure, according to his mode of operation.[128] Devas and asuras are Angels and Titans, powers of Light and powers of Darkness in the RV.[129]

Criticism of Coomaraswamy's Position

Coomaraswamy's way of looking at the matter may give his readers some insight into some of the Brāhmaṇical discussions, especially with regard to the relationship of Vṛtra with Soma and the Brāhmaṇical statements that Vṛtra was a Brāhmaṇa. But his categories are not applicable to the early Ṛgvedic usage of *ásura–*.

125. Rai Bahadur S. C. Roy, "The Asuras—Ancient and Modern," *The Journal of the Bihar and Orissa Research Society* 12 (1926): 147.
126. *Ibid.*, pp. 147-8.
127. *Ibid.*, p. 148.
128. Ananda K. Coomaraswamy, "Angel and Titan: An Essay in Vedic Ontology," *Journal of the American Oriental Society* 55 (1935): 373-4.
129. *Ibid.*, p. 373.

His discussion is rather a-chronological and does not help us trace with any precision the development of the word *ásura–* through time.

R. Shamasastry

According to R. Shamasastry, "the Vedic gods are no other than the seven planets, the twenty-seven asterisms, Agastya or Canopus, and Sunasira, the Dog-star Serius and a few other periodical stars. These are the Devas. The Asuras are the imaginary dark spirits of night."[130] Thus "eclipses, occulations of the planets are the most important subject matter of the Vedic hymns necessitating the performance of suitable sacrifices to appease the gods."[131] I find this theory totally unacceptable.

Jean Przyluski

Przyluski has a refreshingly unique theory to explain how *ásura–* came to be used for hostile beings. First he pointed out that positive names are often used as euphemisms for evil beings. One can recall the use of *śiva–* as a name for the ferocious god Rudra.[132] Thus *ásura–* was first used for the great gods, then euphemistically for local genii.[133] The positive title *ásura–* was originally borrowed from the Akkadian title *aššur*.[134]

Criticism of Przyluski's Position

We have already seen arguments against the claim that *ásura–* is borrowed from *aššur*. It is also unlikely that *ásura–* was first used for hostile beings as a euphemism in order to please them. In most of the oldest occurrences of this word as a term for hostile beings, the gods are said to have killed them or are asked to do so. Such contexts do not require pleasing these beings. The analogy with *śiva–* is also unconvincing since it is unlikely that this word began to be used for Rudra in an attempt to make him more favorable to the worshipper.

130. R. Shamasastry, "Vedic Gods," in *B. C. Law Volume*, ed. by D. R. Bhandarkar, K. A. Nilakanta Sastri, B. M. Barua, B. K. Ghosh, and P. K. Gode (Calcutta: The Indian Research Institute, 1945), p. 277.

131. *Ibid.*, p. 281.

132. Jean Przyluski, "Deva et asura," *Rocznik Orjentalistyczny* 8 (1931-2): 26.

133. *Ibid.*, pp. 27-8.

134. *Ibid.*, p. 28.

Leopold von Schroeder

Von Schroeder explains how *ásura–* could be used for gods in the RV and later for demons by assuming that there were originally two words pronounced the same. One word meant "lord" or "highest ruler" and was used for gods. The other meant "spirit" and was used for demons. The first of these words then dropped out of usage in later India.[135] T. Burrow also assumes that there were homonyms *ásura–* meaning "lord" and *ásura–* meaning "demon."[136]

Criticism of von Schroeder's Position

It is virtually impossible to disprove such a theory. But the development of the use of *ásura–* with a pejorative connotation seems to be understandable without making the assumption of homonyms, and a more parsimonious explanation is always preferable if it explains things as adequately. That *ásura–* occurs mainly in the plural in the negative meaning and in the singular in the positive meaning also argues against this theory.

T. Burrows

Burrows argues against the theory of an Indo-Iranian group of gods called asuras who later become demons.

> The Vedic gods who are considered to have belonged to the *asura* class are Varuṇa, Mitra, and the Ādityas, so the theory would imply that the Ādityas become demons, which is contrary to the facts....
> It is also wrong to speak of a class of gods known as Asuras since the term is never so used.[137]

Thus the only change was in the meaning of the word *ásura–*. Such a change became possible because *asura–* "lord" fell into disuse in the ordinary language, though remaining familiar in the sacred

135. Leopold von Schroeder, *Arische Religion*, vol. 1 (Leipzig: H. Haessel Verlag, 1914), p. 318, n.1.

136. T. Burrows, *The Sanskrit Language*, 2nd ed. (London: Faber and Faber, 1965), p. 40.

137. T. Burrows, "The Proto-Indoaryans," *Journal of the Royal Asiatic Society of Great Britain and Ireland* 1973, no. 2, p. 129.

texts."[138] The change in the connotation of *māyā* to mean evil magic and the occurrence of the phrase *asurasya māyā* probably contributed to the developing of a bad connotation for *ásura–*.[139] This suggestion apparently replaces his earlier claim mentioned in the last section that there were two different words spelled *ásura–*.

Criticism of T. Burrows' Position

These remarks by Burrows can be accepted as they are—perhaps with some reservation about the influence of the word *māyā–* on the change in meaning of *ásura–*. But this falls short of explaining how and why the meaning of *ásura–* changed.

Alfred Hillebrandt

Hillebrandt accepts "lord" as the basic meaning of *ásura–*.[140] He adds some useful and interpretative comments to von Bradke's study. For example, he points out that of the twelve occurrences of *ásura–* in the RV in a bad sense only four are in the Family Books.[141] Also, Indra is never called *ásura–* in the Family Books.[142] The relative rarity of *ásura–* in the Family Books indicates a weakening of the asura cult at this time.[143] The extreme rarity of *ásura–* in Book Six of the RV is probably because this book comes from an area closer to Iran than any of the other books.[144] The degradation of the term *ásura–* occurred because of the encounters between Indians and Iranians after their separation, but before Zaraθuštra's reform.[145] The phrase *he 'lavo* attributed to the asuras in the Śatapatha Brāhmaṇa indicates that Indian enemies from the east are also included among the asuras, since this phrase would be a Prakrit form from that area.[146]

138. *Ibid.*
139. *Ibid.*, p. 129.
140. Alfred Hillebrandt, *Vedische Mythologie*, 3 vols. (Breslau: Verlag von M. and H. Marcus, 1902), vol. 3, pp. 431 and 433.
141. *Ibid.*, pp. 438-9.
142. *Ibid.*, p. 439.
143. *Ibid.*
144. *Ibid.*
145. *Ibid.*, pp. 435-8. See especially p. 438, n. 1.
146. Hillebrandt, *Vedische Mythologie*, vol 2., p. 440.

Criticism of Hillebrandt's Position

Hillebrandt's observation that Indra is called an asura only in late Ṛgvedic times is noteworthy and will have to be considered later. But his theory that the degradation of *ásura–* was due to encounters with the Iranians is problematical. Keith points out that he simply does not amass sufficient evidence to prove this.[147]

I. J. S. Taraporewala

Taraporewala noted that *sura–* first occurs in the Maitrāyaṇī Upaniṣad and suggests that it is a late formation made after the initial *a* of *ásura–* was reinterpreted as the privative *a–*.[148] He also pointed out that the word *ahura–* occurs once in Vedic literature in the Mantra Brāhmaṇa (1.6.21).[149] It occurs there in a list of deities invoked beside one named Kṛśana. Taraporewala concludes "that both these deities are Aryan deities, i.e., they belong to a period before the two peoples separated. Ahura needs no comment."[150] *Kṛśana* is linked with Avestan *Kərəsāni.* Thus both of these names are relics of a tradition going back to the Indo-Iranian period.

Criticism of Taraporewala's Position

Taraporewala is surely right in his explanation of the origin of *sura–*. But his explanation of the occurrence of *ahura–* in the Mantra Brāhmaṇa is not sufficient. It does not explain why the word appears with an *h* instead of an *s*, since the Indo-Iranian form would have *s*, and such an *s* would be preserved in Sanskrit.

Herman Lommel

Lommel notes that *ásura–* is often applied to the Vedic gods, especially the Ādityas.[151] If this epithet is especially applied to the

147. Keith, *Religion and Philosophy*, vol. 1, p. 232.

148. I. J. S. Taraporewala, "Some Vedic Words Viewed in the Light of the Gathas and Other Avesta Texts," *Journal of the Bombay Branch of the Royal Asiatic Society* 26 (1951): 123.

149. Irach J. S. Taraporewala, "The Word अहुर (*ahura*) in Sanskrit and the Gobhilas," in *Indo-Iranian Studies* (London: Kegan Paul, Trench, Trübner & Co., 1925) P. 143.

150. *Ibid.*, p. 146.

151. Herman Lommel, *Religion und Kultur der Alten Arier*, vol. 1 (Frankfort am Main: Vittorio Klostermann, 1935), p. 73.

Ādityas, it is because they are rulers in a way that other gods such as Indra and Agni are not.[152] But the main Āditya—Varuṇa—did not derive from the same Indo-Iranian god as Ahura Mazdā.[153] *Daēva–* took on a negative connotation in Iran as a result of Zaraθuštra's reform. Zaraθuštra overthrew the old folk beliefs with such zeal that the old word for god came to mean false god.[154]

Criticism of Lommel's Position

Lommel's idea that the epithet *ásura–* was especially applicable to the Ādityas seems to be rather widespread, but dubious. The word is sometimes used of various Ādityas, and perhaps once of the Ādityas as a group. But it is not used of them with unusual frequency. That it was applied to them because they were rulers may well be true, but Indra and Agni are a poor choice of examples for contrast, since they are also sometimes called asura. I must side with Gonda against Lommel and Hillebrandt on the issue of whether Varuṇa and Ahura Mazdā are derived from the same Indo-Iranian god. It seems most likely that they are.[155] Lommel's explanation of the degradation of *daēva–* is important because it treats the development as purely Iranian, independent of India.

V. Fausböll

Fausböll bases his discussion of *ásura–* mainly on epic texts. He points out that the asuras and devas were half brothers, the asuras being older.[156] The asuras are skilled in magic and can transform their shape or become invisible.[157] Several things indicate that asuras were originally the aborigines of India. (1) They live in mountains, forests, and in the earth. (2) They are older than the suras, and the earth originally belonged to them. (3) They are at enmity with the suras. (4) The gods nonetheless make alliances with them. (5) The asuras are grouped with different Hindu tribes. (6) In the Mahābhārata War some asuras aided the Kurus. (7) The des-

152. *Ibid.*
153. *Ibid.*, pp. 71-2.
154. *Ibid.*, p. 76.
155. Jan Gonda, *The Dual Deities in the Religion of the Veda* (Amsterdam: North-Holland Publishing Co., 1974), pp. 160-2.
156. V. Fausböll, *Indian Mythology according to the Mahābhārata* (London: Luzac & Co., 1902), pp. 2-3.
157. *Ibid.*, pp. 6-7.

cription of them as having many shapes would be well suited to describe people who carry on a guerilla warfare.[158]

Criticism of Fausböll's Position

Fausböll reports many important aspects of the description of asuras in the late literature. The problem is: do these descriptions apply to figures who are called asura in the early RV? Most do not. I agree with some of his reasons for taking *ásura–* to refer to Indian aborigines at some point in history, but I do not accept this as the original meaning of *ásura–*.

T. Segerstedt

In two rather lengthy articles Segerstedt extends Fausböll's idea that *ásura–* referred to the aboriginal Indians.[159] After critically reviewing previous theories, he concludes that none of them adequately explained why asuras and devas exist as two divine groups in the RV.[160] In the Brāhmaṇas devas and asuras appear as two different classes of beings which are in conflict, but with the devas always victorious.[161] Sacrifice often plays the decisive role in these conflicts.[162] Thus the contrast between devas and asuras was cultic. An unacceptable sacrificial practice would be called asuric. This cultic difference rests in turn on a racial difference.[163] Their language is that of *mlecchas*. Indra is said to vanquish the *asurasya varṇa*.[164] In the AV the asuras are much as in the RV.[165] The asuras are depicted as having been defeated, but the struggle is not described.[166] *Ásura–* usually appears in the plural and refers to a divine class.[167] Asuras are occasionally, but significantly linked with dāsas and dasyus.[168] But the asuras are not depicted as powerful

158. *Ibid.*, pp. 41-2.
159. T. Segerstedt, "Les Asuras dans la religion vedique," *Revue de l'histoire des religions* 57 (1908): 157-203. "Les Asuras dans la religion vedique (Suite et fin)," *Revue de l'Histoire des religions* 57 (1908): 293-316.
160. Segerstedt, "Asuras," part 1, p. 160.
161. *Ibid.*, p. 161.
162. *Ibid.*, p. 162.
163. *Ibid.*, p. 163.
164. *Ibid.*, p. 164.
165. *Ibid.*, p. 167.
166. *Ibid.*
167. *Ibid.*, p. 168.
168. *Ibid.*, p. 169.

enemies of the devas.[169] In the RV *ásura–* in the singular usually refers to a god, but in the plural has almost the character of a class of divine beings hostile to the devas. Thus *ásura–* must have had a neutral meaning.[170] Asuras also appear as human adversaries of the Aryans.[171] The conclusion from all this is that *ásura–* in the RV designates a vanquished people and their gods.[172] Conquered people are often thought to possess magic, hence asuras are associated with māyā.[173] *Ásura–* is best translated "lord" or "master" and does not have a connotation of "divine."[174] It follows from all of this that some of the deities in the RV called *ásura–* must have been borrowed from the indigenous people.[175] From these gods the title could be transferred to other gods such as Indra.[176] Four such indigenous gods are Varuṇa, Rudra, Pūṣan, and the Maruts.[177] The remainder of Segerstedt's two articles contains an account of these four deities pointing out the characteristics of them that suggest that they are borrowed into the pantheon.

Criticism of Segerstedt's Position

Such a brief summary does not do justice to these articles. Much of their value is in their reporting several statements made about asuras in the texts and giving references for these. Naturally this summary omits most of these references, but they are quite valuable to a researcher.

Segerstedt considers asuras and devas as two different divine groups in the RV. I have already indicated that the asuras do not seem to form a group in the early parts of the RV, and in the later parts they are anti-godly, not divine. Many of Segerstedt's arguments that *ásura–* referred to the indigenous people in the Brāhmaṇa period might be acceptable. However, he errs in projecting this situation backward into the period of the early RV. There is a radical difference in the way the term is used in these two time periods. Consequently, his contention that Varuṇa, Rudra, Pūṣan,

169. *Ibid.*
170. *Ibid.*, pp. 170-1.
171. *Ibid.*, pp. 171-2.
172. *Ibid.*. p. 175.
173. *Ibid.*, pp. 175-9.
174. *Ibid.*, p. 181.
175. *Ibid.*
176. *Ibid.*, pp. 185-6.
177. *Ibid.*, p. 187.

and the Maruts are borrowed from the indigenous people must be rejected. I cannot agree with him in separating Varuṇa from Ahura Mazdā.[178] *Pūṣan–* is etymologically related to Greek πᾱ́ν[179] and functionally much like *'Ερμης*[180] and is therefore inherited from the Indo-Europeans.

Paul Thieme

Thieme argues against the derivation of Varuṇa and Ahura Mazdā from the same Indo-Iranian deity. He says that *Varuṇa cannot be posited for the Indo-Iranian period without an attestation in Avestan.[181] If Indo-Iranian *Varuṇa existed, why does it not appear in Avestan, since the other three chief Ādityas do? There are also a few verses in the RV that suggest that there was a god named Asura who was distinct from Mitrā-varuṇā.[182] *Mitrā́-váruṇā–* and *Miθra-ahura–* probably reflect an Indo-Iranian compound, but this should be reconstructed with *ásura–* as the second member with the assumption that the Indians substituted *varuṇa–* for *ásura–*.[183]

Criticism of Thieme's Position

I agree with Gonda in his criticisms of these ideas. The absence of *varuṇa–* in Avestan is not sufficient reason for denying the common origin of Varuṇa and Ahura Mazdā.[184] Nor must one necessarily understand the verses quoted by Thieme as containing *ásura–* as a proper name.[185] Opting for the Iranian rather than the Sanskrit form for the second member of the compound is possible, but a bit arbitrary and certainly not necessary.

178. *Ibid.*

179. Mayrhofer, *Wöterbuch*, vol. 2, p. 326.

180. See the article by Calvert Watkins, "Studies in Indo-European Legal Language, Institution, and Mythology," in *Indo-European and Indo-Europeans*, ed. by George Cardona, Henry M. Hoenigswald, and Alfred Senn (Philadelphia: University of Pennsylvania Press, 1970), pp. 321-54.

181. Paul Thieme, "The 'Aryan' Gods of the Mitanni Treaties," *Journal of the American Oriental Society* 80 (1960): 308.

182. *Ibid.*, pp. 308-9.

183. *Ibid.*, p. 309.

184. Gonda, *Dual Deities*, p. 162.

185. *Ibid.*, p. 161, n. 173. Karl Friedrich Geldner, *Der Rig-Veda aus dem Sanskrit ins Deutsche Übersetzt und mit einem Laufenden Kommentar versehen*, 3 vols., Harvard Oriental Series, vols. 33-5 (Cambridge: Harvard University Press, 1951), vol. 2, pp. 71-2.

Ilya Gerschevitch

Gerschevitch also denies the common origin of Varuṇa and Ahura Mazdā.[186] He posits instead an Iranian god *Vouruna who was worshipped in pre-Zaraθuštrian Iran and was derived from the same god as Indian Varuṇa. Zaraθuštra incorporated the worship of this god with the worship of his god to get the Zaraθuštrian god Ahura Mazdā.[187] When Zoroastrianism was made the state religion, worshippers of *Vouruna could easily substitute *ahura–* for **Vouruna–* since *ahura–* was one of his epithets, and this would satisfy those who insisted on worship of Ahura Mazdā.[188]

Criticism of Gerschevitch's Position

This theory fits well with Thieme's and is open to some of the same criticisms. The theory is not impossible, but it requires so much speculative reconstruction that it is difficult to accept without considerably more evidence.

Mary Boyce

Mary Boyce suggests that the Indo-Iranian tradition of high kings seems to be reflected in development of belief in asuras.[189] *Asura–/ahura–* was used for both men and gods in both India and Iran.[190] In Iran only three gods are ever called ahura. These were probably the original Indo-Iranian "Lords," and the title was only gradually extended to other gods in the RV.[191] Of these three asuras Mitra most easily lends himself to study.[192] In India, Varuṇa is closely associated with this god. In fact, he takes over many of the characteristics of Indo-Iranian Mitra and thus appears stern.[193] The Vedic parallel of Ahura Mazdā—the second of these three asuras—was probably the nameless asura who appears a

186. Ilya Gerschevitch, *The Avestan Hymn to Mithra* (Cambridge, University Press, 1967), p. 45.
187. *Ibid.*, p. 47.
188. *Ibid.*, p. 48-9.
189. Mary Boyce, *A History of Zoroastrianism*, vol. 1, Handbuch der Orientalistik, erste Abteilung, 8. Band, 1. Abschnitt, Lieferung 2 (Leiden/Köln: E. J. Brill, 1975), p. 4.
190. *Ibid* , p . 23
191. *Ibid.*
192. *Ibid.*, p. 24.
193. *Ibid.*, p. 36.

few times in the RV.[194] This same asura may have been called Asura *Medhā.[195] The third Indo-Iranian asura was Apām Napāt. This deity is, in fact, the same as Vedic Varuṇa, even though he appears under both names in the RV.[196] This gives a similar triadic structure of "Lords" in both India and Iran.[197] When the pre-Zaraθuštrian Iranians used *ahura–*, they apparently referred to *Vouruna and not Ahura Mazdā. "Mazdā is seldom invoked without the title Ahura, and never, as far as can be established, as 'Ahura' alone; even in Zoroaster's *Gāthās*, where title and name are still separate, the prophet never uses the proper name without the title following, at least within the same hymn."[198] The only god who was addressed by *ahura–* alone was *Vouruna Apąm Napāt, who was regularly called *ahura– bərəzant–*.[199] Thus the dual compound *mitra ahura bərəzanta* must refer to Miθra and Apąm Napāt.[200] In the Yasna Haptaŋhaiti one can see many characteristics of *Vouruna transferred to Ahura Mazdā.[201] "Why it should be that in India Asura *Medhā seems to have lost his proper name, becoming simply 'the Asura,' whereas in Iran this befell *Vouruna instead, remains obscure."[202]

Criticism of Boyce's Position

This theory seems to assume at every point on which India and Iran differ that Iran has preserved the Indo-Iranian situation and India has innovated. This is certainly methodologically erroneous. Thus Ms. Boyce assumes that the three deities who were called ahura in Iran are the only three who were called ahura in the Indo-Iranian period and that the other ten or twelve Vedic gods who are called asura are later innovations. In fact, none of these three explicitly receives the epithet *ásura–* in the RV except the one who has *Asura* as his name, if there was such a god. Ahura Mazdā does not appear in the RV by that name. Mitra does not receive that

194. *Ibid*,. pp. 37-8.
195. *Ibid.*, p. 40.
196. *Ibid.*, pp. 43-8.
197. *Ibid.*, p. 48.
198. *Ibid.*
199. *Ibid.*, p. 49.
200. *Ibid.*
201. *Ibid.*, p. 51.
202. *Ibid.*

epithet by himself, although Mitrāvaruṇā does. Apām Napāt is not called asura, but one poet does speak of his asuric (*asuryà–*) greatness. Ms. Boyce assumes that Varuṇa takes over his stern characteristics from Mitra rather than assuming that Miθra takes over his stern characteristics from Varuṇa. (Or perhaps he takes such characteristics from Indra. Among other possible arguments for this one should note that Miθra is said to carry a *vazra* (= Sanskrit *vajra*), a weapon almost exclusively wielded by Indra in the RV.) She follows Thieme in assuming that there was a god named Asura in the RV. As suggested above this assumption rests on the interpretation of three verses which could easily be interpreted differently. It is totally arbitrary to add that if there were such a deity he could have the epithet *medhā. Her arguments for equating Vedic Varuṇa and Apām Napāt are not very convincing. Thus the similar triadic structure of asuras for both India and Iran is arrived at only by considerable manipulation of the Vedic data to make it conform to the Avestan material. I question her statement that Ahura Mazdā was never invoked by the word *ahura–* alone. There are thirteen verses in the Gāthās in which *ahura–* occurs without *mazdā* and apparently refers to Ahura Mazdā.[203] Thus it is not convincing that *ahura–* must refer to Apām Napāt in the compound *miθra ahura bərəzanta*. In the Yasna Haptaŋhaiti, Ahura Mazdā appears with many characteristics reminiscent of Vedic Varuṇa that are not mentioned in the Gāthās. That these were transferred to Ahura Mazdā is an assumption. (If Ahura Mazdā and Varuṇa derived from the same Indo-Iranian god, they were merely inherited. Zaraθuštra may have chosen for whatever reason not to mention these characteristics in his hymns of praise.) It is indeed unexplained why in India Asura *Medhā should only appear as Asura, and in Iran *Vouruna is known only as Ahura. Perhaps the solution is that the two reconstructions are wrong.

Arthur A. Macdonell

According to Macdonell *ásura–* is the ordinary word for the aerial foe of the gods. In the AV it has only the sense of a demon.[204] But of course in the RV it had a more positive sense. The basic

203. Y 28.8, 31.15, 33.3, 33.13, 44.5, 44.6, 44.12, 44.13, 44.19, 46.6, 46.15, 48.1, 48.7.

204. Arthur A. Macdonell, *A History of Sanskrit Literature* (Delhi: Motilal Banarsidass, second Indian edition, 1971), p. 94.

meaning there seems to have been "possessor of occult power called māyā."[205] Thus *ásura–* is especially applied to Varuṇa and Mitrāvaruṇā, whose māyā is also often mentioned. But māyā is also often associated with evil beings. Hence *ásura–* was also applicable to hostile beings.[206] Toward the end of Ṛgvedic period the application of *ásura–* to gods fell into disuse. "This tendency was in all likelihood accelerated by the need of a word denoting the hostile demonic powers generally, as well as by an incipient popular etymology, which saw a negative (*a-sura–*) in the word and led to the invention of *sura–*, 'god,' a term first found in the Upaniṣads."[207]

Criticism of Macdonell's Position

Macdonell is mistaken about the meaning of *ásura–* in the AV. It usually means demon there, but does occur a few times with the positive meaning, as we shall see when we examine verses from there. The sentence quoted above about factors that accelerated the decline of the word is probably correct. A passage in the *Nirukta* confirms that such an etymology was known at an early period.[208] The suggestion that an asura is one who possesses māyā requires more attention. It is true that an asura is sometimes said to have māyā, but is this a defining characteristic? Grassmann lists the following as being called *māyin*: Varuṇa, Indra, Maruts, Śuṣṇa, Namuci, mṛga, ahi, Vṛtra, Soma, yajata, Dānava, Arbuda, Pipru, martya, Bṛṣaya, Aśvins, devas, rākṣasas, varpanīti, and ṛtāyani. There are twelve proper names in this list. Five of these (Varuṇa, Indra, Maruts, Soma, and Pipru) are called asura in the RV. The other seven (Śuṣṇa, Namuci, Vṛtra, Dānava, Arbuda, Bṛṣaya, and Aśvins) are not. However, Namuci is called Āsura, and Arbuda and Bṛṣaya are sufficiently rare in occurrence that they should be left out of consideration in such statistics. The correlation is certainly high enough to make the suggestion quite plausible, but is not totally convincing. Macdonell's comments on *ásura–* seem generally accurate, but lack detail.

205. Macdonell, *History*, p. 94.

206. Arthur A. Macdonell, *Vedic Mythology* (Delhi: Motilal Banarsidass, 1974, original edition 1898), p. 156.

207. Macdonell, *History*, p. 94.

208. Nirukta 3.8. See Lakshman Sarup, *The Nighaṇṭu and the Nirukta* (Delhi: Motilal Banarsidass, second reprint 1967), pp. ६२-६३, trans. on p. 42.

Hermann Oldenberg

Oldenberg basically agrees with Macdonell. He points out that a few Dāsas conquered by Indra are called asura or son of the asura.[209] But *ásura–* is especially used of gods who have māyā. However, māyā is also characteristic of evil demons.[210] Thus *ásura–* means more than just "lord."[211] The pejorative side of *ásura–* was always there and through time became the only use of the word.[212] The folk etymology which took the *a* of asura as a privative prefix also probably added to the decline of this word.[213] Thus the development of the meaning of *daēva–* in Iran and *ásura–* in later India were independent. The first came through religious reform and the second from limiting a word with both good and bad connotations to only the bad ones.[214] It cannot be maintained with certainty that there was a group of demons called asuras in the beginning.[215] There is also nothing to indicate that asuras formed a group of gods in the Veda.[216] Asura-killer just means one who kills enemies who have supernatural power.[217] In later texts asura enemies and dasyus often fall together.[218] Varuṇa and his circle of gods are often called asura in the RV.[219] Varuṇa and Ahura Mazdā derive from the same Indo-Iranian god—a god who was not the greatest, but had elements which allowed him to develop into the only one.[220] There are several reasons for linking Varuṇa with Ahura Mazdā including their similar relationships with ṛta/Aša and their close connections with Mitra/Miθra.[221] There are similar correlations between the Ādityas and the Aməša Spəntas.[222] Thus there were

209 Hermann Oldenberg, *Die Religion des Veda* (Darmstadt: Wissenschaftliche Buchgesellschaft, 1970, original edition 1917), p. 158.

210. *Ibid.*, p. 159.

211. *Ibid.*, p. 160.

212. *Ibid.*, p. 161.

213. *Ibid.*

214. *Ibid.*, pp. 161-2., n. 2.

215. *Ibid.*, p. 162.

216. Hermann Oldenberg, "Varuṇa und die Ādityas," *Zeitschrift der Deutschen Morgenlandeschen Gesellschaft* 50 (1896): 46, note.

217. Oldenberg, *Religion*, p. 162.

218. *Ibid.*, p. 162, n. 2.

219. Hermann Oldenberg, "Zarathustra," *Deutsche Rundschau* 12 (1898): 429.

220. *Ibid.*, pp. 429-30

221. Oldenberg, "Varuṇa," pp. 47-9.

222. *Ibid.*, p. 49.

seven closely connected lords among the Indo-Iranian gods.[223] These were, in fact, the moon (Varuṇa), the sun (Mitra), and the five planets (other Ādityas).[224] These were probably borrowed from another people, probably Semitic.[225]

Criticism of Oldenberg's Position

I agree with most of Oldenberg's ideas about *ásura–*. Māyā does seem to be a characteristic of an asura, but is perhaps not the defining characteristic. Ahura Mazdā should be linked in his origins with Varuṇa. However, the equation of the Ādityas and the Aməša Spəntas is not convincing. Some figures who are called Āditya in the RV, such as Mitra, Aryaman, and Bhaga, do show up in the Avesta, but not as Aməša Spəntas. It is even less convincing that this group of seven Vedic gods (if seven is indeed the correct number) is borrowed from a non-Indo-European pantheon.

Karl F. Geldner

Geldner agrees with Oldenberg that the use of māyā brought Varuṇa and the asuras in general into discredit.[226] I have already commented on the relation of *māyā–* with *ásura–*. I would also like to point out once again that it is not so much a matter of asuras becoming discredited, but rather a group of already discredited beings coming to be called asuras.

C. S. Venkatesvaran

Venkatesvaran says that *ásura–* is connected with *ásu–* and "originally denoted an incorporeal spiritual being often associated with wisdom."[227] *Ásura–* derives from √as "to be active." It thus refers to a being who is active, superhuman, or divine.[228] It may have gotten its negative connotation by being associated with māyā. Thus, perhaps it originally meant a good spirit with occult power and fell into disuse for gods when māyā became a negative

223. Oldenberg, "Zarathustra," p. 429.
224. *Ibid.*, p. 431.
225. *Ibid.*, p. 432, note.
226. Richard Pischel and Karl F. Geldner, *Vedische Studien*, 2 vols. (Stuttgart: Verlag von W. Kohlhammer, 1889), vol. 1, p. 142.
227. C. S. Venkatesvaran, "The Vedic Conception of 'Asura,' " *The Poona Orientalist* 13(1948): 57.
228. *Ibid.*, p. 58.

entity.[229] The formation of *sura–* firmly fixed *ásura–* with a pejorative connotation.[230]

Criticism of Venkatesvaran's Position

Evidence seems to be lacking that an asura must be incorporeal or spiritual. Also, the word *sura–* first occurs in texts long after *ásura–* is firmly fixed with a pejorative connotation.

Jan Gonda

According to Gonda *ásura–* is applied in the RV to Mitra, Varuṇa, Indra, Agni, Sky, Uṣas, Apām Napāt, Rudra, and the Ādityas.[231] It seems to have been an Aryan term for a powerful lord or god. An asura is usually characterized by creative activity. The word was especially used of beings who possessed māyā. But asura-power and māyā are ethically neutral and can apply to gods or demons.[232] The asuras had to relinquish lordship to Indra after Agni, Soma, and Varuṇa went over to the side of the gods.[233] Varuṇa was the greatest asura.[234] He remained lord of the asuras and of water in the later pantheon.[235]

Criticism of Gonda's Position

Ásura– is applied to Mitra only when the name is compounded with that of Varuṇa. It is never directly applied to Uṣas or Apām Napāt, but derivatives of the word are used in connection with these two deities. The suggestion that the asuras relinquished lordship after Agni, Soma, and Varuṇa defected is based on the interpretation of RV 10.124. This hymn will have to be considered in detail later.

Suggested Etymologies of Ásura–

Von Bradke said that *ásura–* could derive from √as "to be" or

229. *Ibid.*, pp. 59-60.
230. *Ibid.*, p. 60.
231. Jan Gonda, *Die Religionen Indiens*, vol. 1 (Stuttgart: W. Kohlhammer Verlag, 1960), p. 75.
232. *Ibid.*, p. 75.
233. *Ibid.*, p. 76.
234. *Ibid.*, p. 81.
235. *Ibid.*, p. 227.

√ans, "to support," but he preferred a derivation from √ans.[236] Polomé wishes to connect *ásura-* with Germanic **ansuz* and sees the sovereign character of the *áss* Oðinn as supporting this.[237] He also wishes to connect it with Hittite *haššus*, which means king.[238] Vendryes argues for an etymological connection between Sanskrit *ásura–*, Latin *erus*, and Avestan *ahū–* and *ahura–*.[239] Schlerath objects to the derivation of *ásura–* from *ásu–* because *–ra* in proto-Indo-European was a primary suffix and not secondary.[240] It was not until the first book of the RV that *-ra* begins to be used as a suffix on words which already have a suffix.[241] Thus *ásura–* should be analyzed as *as-ura*.[242] Thus he derives Avestan *ahu–* and *ahura–*, Indic *ásura–*, Hittite *haššu*, and Latin *erus* from reconstructed root **axs–* meaning "beget."[243]

Criticism of Suggested Etymologies

Schlerath's refusal to accept *ásura–* as *asu+ra–* is not acceptable, because *–ra–* does seem to function as a secondary suffix before the time of the RV. However, it does seem justifiable to derive *ahu–*, *ahura–*, *ásura–*, and *haššu* from the same root, and Germanic **ansuz* is probably also from this root. There seems to have been an Indo-European word **Hesu–* from which came Avestan *ahu–* "Lord" and Hittite *ḫaššu* "king" and an Indo-Iranian derivative of this word, **asura–*, from which Avestan *ahura–* and Vedic *ásura–* derive.

236. P. von Bradke, "Beitrage zur altindischen Religions- und Sprach-geschichte," *Zeitschrift der Deutschen Morgenlandischen Gesellschaft* 40 (1886): 347-8.

237. E. Polomé, "L'etymologie du terme germanique *ansuz 'dieu soverain,' " *Étude Germanique* 8 (1953): 41.

238. *Ibid.*, p. 42.

239. J. Vendryes, "Les correspondance de vocabulaire entre l'indo-iranien et l'italo-celtique," *Memoires de la Société de Linguistique de Paris* 20 (1918): 269.

240. Bernfried Schlerath, "Altindisch *asu*-, Awestisch *ahu*- und ähnlich klingende Wörter," in *Pratidānam: Indian, Iranian and Indo-European Studies presented to Franciscus Bernardus Jacobus Kuiper on his Sixtieth Birthday*, ed. by J. C. Heesterman, G. H. Schoker, and V. I. Subramoniam (The Hague: Mouton, 1968), p. 144.

241. *Ibid.*, p. 145.

242. *Ibid.*

243. *Ibid.*, p. 146.

Conclusions of Survey

From this survey of suggestions offered by various scholars on the meaning of *ásura–* in the RV, it should be clear that further research on this topic is needed. Some proposed suggestions can be ruled out already. *Ásura–* did not derive from *aššur*. But other suggestions must be dealt with further as the material from the Vedic literature is examined. The relationship between asura and māyā should be examined. Perhaps the most serious question is whether the asuras at some point in history or prehistory of Indic religion formed a defined group of gods. Several scholars have maintained that there was such a group and reconstructed the history of Indo-Iranian and early Indic religion around this theory. However, I maintain that there was never any such group of gods. An examination of the Vedic verses containing *ásura–* will show that there is in fact insufficient evidence for claiming the existence of a defined group of gods called asuras.

CHAPTER II

ÁSURA- IN THE FAMILY BOOKS OF THE RV

The Family Books of the RV (Books 2-7) contain the oldest hymns and are therefore a natural place to begin a study of the development of the word *ásura*-. Each verse in which the word appears will be quoted, translated, and discussed. The verses are grouped together according to who is called asura.

The god most frequently called asura in the Family Books is Agni.

pitā́ yajñā́nām ásuro vipaścítāṃ
  vimā́nam agnír vayúnaṃ ca vāghátām
ā́ viveśa ródasī bhū́rivarpasā
  purupriyó bhandate dhā́mabhiḥ kavíḥ. RV 3.3.4

"Father of the sacrifices, asura of the wise ones, Agni is the standard and reference of the sacrificers. He entered the multiform world-halves. The very dear poet is praised for his displays." (Hymn to Agni Vaiśvānara)

The genitive *vipaścítām* "of the wise ones" may give us some clue to the meaning of *ásura*- here. The genitive must be used either in a partitive meaning or with an implied verbal meaning of *ásura*-. The only possibly appropriate verbal usage would be as a genitive of rulership.[1] Thus the poet suggests either that Agni is an asura among other wise ones or an asura who rules over wise ones.

gómāṁ agné 'vimāṁ aśvī́ yajñó
  nṛvátsakhā sádam íd apramṛṣyáḥ
íḷāvāṁ eṣó asura prajā́vān
  dīrghó rayíḥ pṛthubudhnáḥ sabhā́vān. RV 4.2.5.

"O Agni, this sacrifice, having cows, sheep, horses, manly friends, always not-to-be-neglected, having nourishment, offspring,

1. For uses of the genitive, see Bertold Delbrück, *Altindische Syntax*, 1888, reprint (Darmstadt: Wissenschaftliche Buchgesellschaft, 1976) pp. 151-64.

O asura, is a long-lasting treasure, having wide-spread territory, (and good) company." (Hymn to Agni)[2]

prā́gnáye bṛhaté yajñíyāya
ṛtásya vṛ́ṣṇe ásurāya mánma
ghṛtáṃ ná yajñá āsyè súpūtaṃ
gíraṃ bhare vṛṣabhā́ya pratīcī́ṃ. RV 5.12.1

"(I bring) forth a praise-song for high, offering-worthy Agni, the bull of *ṛta*, the asura: I bear a song for the bull placed before (him) like well purified ghee in (his) mouth at a sacrifice." (Hymn to Agni)

prá vedháse kaváye védyāya
gíraṃ bhare yaśáse pūrvyā́ya
ghṛtáprasatto ásuraḥ suśévo
rāyó dhartā́ dharúṇo vásvo agníḥ. RV. 5.15.1

"I bear forth a song for the wise poet, worthy of recognition, glorious, primordial. The beloved asura seated in ghee, supporter of wealth, bearer of treasure, is Agni." (Hymn to Agni)

īḷényaṃ vo ásuraṃ sudákṣam
antár dūtáṃ ródasī satyavā́caṃ
manuṣvád agníṃ mánunā sámiddhaṃ
sám adhvarā́ya sádam ín mahema. RV 7.2.3

"Let us consecrate always for the sacrifice Agni, kindled by Manu in the manner of Manu, the asura worthy of being praised by us, very powerful, the messenger of true speech between the two world-halves." (Āpram Hymn)

prá samrā́jo ásurasya práśastiṃ
puṃsáḥ kṛṣṭīnā́m anumā́dyasya
índrasyeva prá tavásas kṛtā́ni
vánde dārúṃ vándamāno vivakmi. RV 7.6.1

2. The only information this verse gives about the meaning of *ásura-* is that it can be used as an epithet for Agni. I shall not offer comments on such verses. The little information they give is clear from their translation.

"(I speak) forth the praise of the universal monarch, the asura, the man of the people, who is to be acclaimed. I praise the deeds of the one powerful as Indra. I speak praising the breaker (?).[3] (Hymn to Vaiśvānara)

This verse does not mention Agni by name, but the hymn is addressed to Agni Vaiśvānara, and there is no reason to doubt that this verse is meant to refer to him. *Samrā́j–* could be an adjective in this verse modifying *ásura–* and meaning "all ruling" asura.

áhā yád indra sudínā vyucchā́n
  dádho yát ketúm upamáṃ samátsu
ny àgníḥ sīdad ásuro ná hótā
  huvānó átra subhágāya devā́n.   RV 7.30.3

"O Indra, so that bright days may shine forth, so that you may place the highest banner in the battles, Agni the *hotṛ* sits down like an asura calling here the gods for the one who has a good share." (Hymn to Indra)

Agni is not actually called an asura in this verse, but is said to behave like one. He sits down like an asura. This will make sense when we have established the meaning of *ásura–*.[4]

Savitṛ is twice called asura in the Family Books.

tád devásya savitúr vā́ryaṃ mahád
  vṛṇīmáhe ásurasya prácetasaḥ
chardír yéna dāśúṣe yácchati tmánā
  tán no mahā́m̐ úd ayān devó aktúbhiḥ.   RV 4.53.1

"We wish this desirable (thing) of the god Savitṛ, of the wise asura, by which he personally grants protection to the pious one. The great god has raised this up for us with his rays (?)." (Hymn to Savitṛ)

práti prayā́ṇam ásurasya vidvā́n
  sūktáir deváṃ savitā́raṃ duvasya

3. *Dārú-* is *hapax*.

4. To anticipate later conclusions, this means that Agni behaves like a lord in sitting down at the sacrifice. Perhaps this means that his place on the altar is one of honor as is the seat of an asura.

úpa bruvīta námasā vijānáñ
  jyéṣṭhaṃ ca rátnaṃ vibhájantam āyóḥ. RV 5.49.2

"Aware of the going forth of the asura, favor the god Savitṛ with songs. The knowing one should encourage (him) with prostration and (also encourage) the one distributing the great treasure of Āyu." (Hymn to Viśve Devāḥ)

I think that *ásurasya* can be taken to refer to Savitṛ here.

Varuṇa is twice called asura in the Family Books, and Mitrāvaruṇā get that epithet two times as well.

tváṃ víśveṣāṃ varuṇāsi rā́jā
  yé ca devā́ asura yé ca mártāḥ
śatáṃ no rāsva śarádo vicákṣe
  'śyā́māyūṃṣi súdhitāni pū́rvā. RV 2.27.10

"You, O Varuṇa, are king of all, both who are gods and who are mortals, O asura. Grant to us to see a hundred autumns. May we attain ancient, well-established life-spans." (Hymn to Ādityas)

mā́ no vadháir varuṇa yé ta iṣṭā́v
  énaḥ kṛṇvántam asura bhrīṇánti
mā́ jyótiṣaḥ pravasathā́ni ganma
  ví ṣū́ mṛ́dhaḥ śiśratho jīváse naḥ. RV 2.28.7

"(Strike) us not, O Varuṇa, in your search with the weapons which strike the one committing sin, O asura. May we not go to privations of light. Keep injuries well away that we may live." (Hymn to Varuṇa)

imā́ṃ vāṃ mitrāvaruṇā suvṛktím
  íṣaṃ ná kṛṇve asurā návīyaḥ
inó vām anyáḥ padavír ádabdho
  jánaṃ ca mitró yatati bruvāṇáḥ. RV 7.36.2

"I make anew this song like nourishment for you two, O Mitrāvaruṇā, O asuras. One powerful one of you is an undeceivable path-finder (?), and the one called Mitra unites the people."[5] (Hymn to Viśve Devāḥ)

In classical Sanskrit *ina-* means "Lord master," but at this stage of the language it is more likely just an adjective meaning "powerful."

tā́ hí devā́nām ásurā tā́v aryā́
  tā́ naḥ kṣitī́ḥ karatam ūrjáyantīḥ
aśyā́ma mitrāvaruṇā vayáṃ vāṃ
  dyā́vā ca yátra pīpáyann áhā ca. RV 7.65.2

"Since these two are asuras of the gods, these noble ones, may they make our abodes swelling. May we reach you, O Mitrāvaruṇā, where heaven and earth and the days swell." (Hymn to Mitrāvaruṇā)

This verse contains a bit more information about asuras than most so far. Mitrāvaruṇā are called "asuras of the gods." The genitive *devā́nām* depends on *ásura-* and can therefore give us some valuable information about the meaning of the word. Of the possible functions of the genitive, the genitive of possession can be ruled out—it is unlikely that Mitrāvaruṇā are considered to be "asuras possessed by the gods." This genitive may be used partitively. Thus the poet may mean that Mitrāvaruṇā are asuras among the gods. But the genitive could also be used because of an implied verbal function of *ásura-*. Of the possibilities here the usage of the genitive to indicate that over which one rules is the only reasonable possibility.[6] Although the partitive function of the genitive is equally likely in this context, I shall argue below that a genitive used with *ásura-* in RV 2.1.6 must be a genitive of rulership.

Rudra is referred to as asura two or three times in the Family Books.

tám u ṣṭuhi yáḥ sviṣúḥ sudhánvā
  yó víśvasya kṣáyati bheṣajásya
yákṣvā mahé saumanasā́ya rudráṃ
  námobhir devám ásuram duvasya. RV 5.42.11

5. The meaning of *padavī́-* is uncertain.
6. See Delbrück, *Syntax*, pp. 151-64 for uses of the genitive.

"Praise him who has good arrows and a good bow, who rules over all medicine. Sacrifice for great well-being to Rudra; favor the god, the asura with prostrations." (Hymn to various deities)

Here Rudra is called asura, but he is also called deva in the same verse. In fact, the two words are adjacent in the text and in the same case. All of the beings who have been called asura in the verses we have examined so far are called deva elsewhere, but this is the first example we have seen where the same being is called deva and asura at the same time. This verse should make one very suspicious of any theory that maintains that devas and asuras were two different divine groups in early Vedic religion.[7] It should also make one suspicious of a theory which says that a being can be either a deva or an asura at different times depending on his actions at the time.[8] Rudra is referred to here at one and the same time as both an asura and a deva.

tvám agne rudró ásuro mahó divás
  tváṃ śárdho mā́rutaṃ pṛkṣá īśiṣe
tváṃ vā́tair aruṇáir yāsi śaṅgayás
  tváṃ pūṣā́ vidhatáḥ pāsi nú tmánā. RV 2.1.6

"You, O Agni, (as) Rudra, (are) the asura of great heaven; you (as) the Marut troop rule over strength; you go with the reddish winds bringing health to the households; you (as) Pūṣan in person indeed protect the worshippers." (Hymn to Agni)

Here Agni can be called the asura of great heaven because he is identified with Rudra. This verse is typical of many verses in the RV which identify Agni with various gods. Geldner raises the question of whether *ásura–* here should be translated "Gebieter" and construed with *mahò divás* or whether *putráḥ* should be added to go with these words and the phrase translated "Rudra, the asura, (the son) of great heaven."[9] However, the parallelism favors the way I have translated the verse. This verse also has a genitive (*mahò divás*) dependent on *ásura–*. In this case the parti-

7. See, for example, the views of Norman Brown and F. B. J. Kuiper summarized in chapter 1.

8. See the summary of Ananda Coomaraswamy's views in chapter 1.

9. Geldner, *Der Rig-Veda*, vol. 1, p. 276, note on 5a.

tive genitive is impossible, and the genitive of possession makes no sense. Thus the genitive must be dependent on an implied verbal aspect of *ásura–*. Of the possibilities here the most common verbal usage of the genitive—the genitive of rulership—is the most reasonable. Thus Rudra is described as the asura who rules over great heaven.[10]

ā́ vāṃ yéṣṭhāśvinā huvádhyai
vā́tasya pátman ráthyasya puṣṭáu
utá vā divó ásurāya mánma
prā́ndhāṃsīva yájyave bharadhvam. RV 5.41.3

"O Aśvins, I shall call you who go most quickly in the flight of the wind in the prosperity of chariot-possession. Indeed bring for the asura of the sky a prayer like somas for the worshipper." (Hymn to Viśve Devāḥ)

This verse does not mention the name of the asura, but if the "asura of the great sky" was Rudra in the last verse, then "asura of the sky" is likely to refer to Rudra here, too. Both Geldner and Sāyaṇa agree that that phrase refers to Rudra.[11] This is probable, if not certain.

Dyaus seems to be called asura once and perhaps three times in the Family Books.

imé bhojā́ áṅgiraso vírūpā
divás putrā́so ásurasya vīrā́ḥ
viśvā́mitrāya dádato maghā́ni
sahasrasāvé prá tiranta ā́yuḥ. RV 3.53.7

"These generous Aṅgirases in another form, sons of the sky, heroes of the asura, giving gifts to Viśvāmitra in the thousand-fold soma pressing cross forth to long life." (Hymn to various deities)

The asura is again not named. The proximity of the phrases "sons of the sky" and "heroes of the asura" suggests that the asura here is the sky. Comparison with RV 10.10.2 and 10.67.2, which

10. See Delbrück, *Syntax*, pp. 151-64 for functions of the genitive.
11. Geldner, *Der Rig-Veda*, vol. 2, p. 40, note on 3c.

contain similar phrases, confirm this view.[12] It is noteworthy that an asura can have heroes (*vīrá*–).

trír uttamā́ dūṇā́śā rocanā́ni
  tráyo rājanty ásurasya vīrā́ḥ
ṛtā́vāna iṣirā́ dūḷábhāsas
  trír ā́ divó vidáthe santu devā́ḥ. RV 3.56.8

"Threefold are the highest difficult-to-reach light-realms. Three heroes of the asura rule. May the *ṛta*-possessing, vigorous (?), difficult-to-deceive gods be at the sacrifice three times a day." (Hymn to Viśve Devāḥ)

Again the asura is not named. According to Geldner, "Asura ist der Himmel als Urgott, seine drei Mannen die obersten Āditya's."[13] This explanation is quite plausible, but not compelling. It remains uncertain who the asura is here. But one should note that an asura can have heroes who rule "under" him.

prá saptáhotā sanakā́d arocata
  mātúr upásthe yád áśocad ū́dhani
ná ní miṣati surā́ṇo divédive
  yád ásurasya jaṭhárād ájāyata. RV 3.29.14

"The one with seven priests shone forth from antiquity when he glowed in the lap of his mother, in her udder. The pleasing one did not close his eyes day after day since he was born from the belly of the asura." (Hymn to various deities)

This verse is problematical. According to Geldner the asura here is Vṛtra.[14] He bases this conclusion on an analysis of RV 10.124. 3-4. But we shall see later when we examine this hymn that it is not clear that Vṛtra is the asura of the hymn. Vṛtra is, in fact, never explicitly called asura before the brāhmaṇa portion of the MS. Lüders says that the asura here is Dyaus and interprets the verse as referring to the heavenly origin of the earthly fire—a con-

12. These verses are quoted and discussed in chapter 4.

13. Geldner, *Der Rig-Veda*, vol. 1, p. 404, note on 8b.

14. *Ibid.*, p. 363, note on 14d.

cept well known in the RV.[15] I prefer Lüders' interpretation to Geldner's, but cannot exclude Geldner's as impossible.

Aryaman, Pūṣan, and Parjanya are each called asura once in the Family Books.

prá śántamā váruṇaṃ dī́dhitī gī́r
  mitráṃ bhágam áditiṃ nūnám aśyāḥ
pṛ́ṣadyoniḥ páñcahotā śṛṇotv
  átūrtapanthā ásuro mayobhúḥ. RV 5.42.1

"Now may the most welcome song with devotion reach Varuṇa, Mitra, Bhaga, Aditi. May the asura who dwells in the sacrificial butter (?), who has five priests, whose path is not crossed, who is pleasing, hear." (Hymn to various deities)

The word *átūrtapantha–* seems to be the key to figuring out who the asura is in this verse. It occurs only one other time in the Saṃhitās (RV 10.64.5), and there it is an epithet of Aryaman. Thus it is likely that *ásura–* refers to Aryaman in this verse. This is made even more likely by the occurrence of Varuṇa, Mitra, and Bhaga in the verse since these three as well as Aryaman are all *Ādityas* and are often mentioned together. Nevertheless, the verse gives very little indication of the real meaning of *ásura–*.

svastí no mimītām aśvínā bhágaḥ
  svastí devy áditir anarváṇaḥ
svastí pūṣā́ ásuro dadhātu naḥ
  svastí dyā́vāpṛthivī́ sucetúnā. RV 5.51.11

"May the Aśvins (and) Bhaga measure out well-being to us. (May) the goddess Aditi (and) the unapproachable ones (do so). (May) the asura Pūṣan place well-being on us. (May) Heaven and Earth beneficently (give us) well-being." (Hymn to Viśve Devāḥ)

divó no vṛṣṭím maruto rarīdhvaṃ
  prá pinvata vṛ́ṣṇo áśvasya dhā́rāḥ
arvā́ṅ eténa stanayitnúnéhy
  apó niṣiñcánn ásuraḥ pitā́ naḥ. RV 5.83.6

15. Heinrich Lüders, *Varuṇa*, edited by Ludwig Alsdorf, 2 vols. (Göttingen: Vandenhoeck & Ruprecht, 1951 and 1959), vol. 2, p. 390.

"O Maruts, give to us the rain of the sky, cause to swell the rivers of the male horse. Come toward us with this thunder sprinkling water (as) our father asura." (Hymn to Parjanya)

Although the asura is not explicitly named in this verse, it is from a hymn to Parjanya, and *ásura–* no doubt refers to him here. Parjanya even seems to be called the father asura here.

Ásura– seems to be used for humans four times in the Family Books—twice of foes and twice of friends.

bŕ̥haspate tápuṣā́śneva vidhya
  vŕ̥kadvaraso ásurasya vīrā́n
yáthā jaghántha dhr̥ṣatā́ purā́ cid
  evā́ jahi śátrum asmā́kam indra. RV 2.30.4

"O Br̥haspati, slay as if with a burning sling-stone the heroes of the asura Vr̥kadvaras. Just as you killed courageously previously, even so kill our enemy, O Indra." (Hymn to various deities)

Vŕ̥kadvaras– occurs nowhere else in Vedic literature, so one cannot be certain that it does not refer to some seldom-mentioned, super-human, demonic being. But the most natural way to take it is as the proper name of an enemy whose troops are opposed to those of the poet's patron. The verse also tells us an important fact about asuras. An asura can have fighting men. It is significant that *ásura–* occurs here as a term for an ememy.

índrāviṣṇū dr̥ṃhitā́ḥ śámbarasya
  náva púro navatíṃ ca śnathiṣṭaṃ
śatáṃ varcíṇaḥ sahásraṃ ca sākáṃ
  hathó apraty ásurasya vīrā́n. RV 7.99.5

"O Indrāviṣṇū, you destroyed the ninety-nine firm castles of Śambara. You slew without contest the one thousand one hundred heroes of the asura Varcin at the same time." (Hymn to various deities)

Varcín– occurs one other time in the RV (2.14.6), but all that is said of him there is that Indra scattered one thousand of his (men). Thus again we cannot be absolutely certain that this asura is human, but that certainly seems to be the most natural way to understand the verse. The rest of the information confirms that of the previous verse. An asura can be one who has a force of fighting men and can be an enemy.

ánasvantā sátpatir māmahe me
gā́vā cétiṣṭho ásuro maghónaḥ
traivṛṣṇó agne daśábhiḥ sahásrair
váiśvānara tryàruṇaś ciketa. RV 5.27.1

"The leader of the raid, the asura who is more excellent than (any other) patron, has given me two cows together with a wagon. Tryaruṇa, son of Trivṛṣṇa, has distinguished himself with ten thousand, O Agni Vaiśvānara." (Hymn to various deities)

The meaning of *sátpati–* is crucial here. In my translation I have followed a suggestion by I. Kuhn.[16] The translation "leader of the raid" for *sátpati–* is consistent with the verses we have just seen that speak of asuras who have fighting men (*vīrá–*). We can be quite certain that the asura in this verse is human, since he is a patron of the poet. If the second half of this verse refers to the same person as the first half—and there is no reason to doubt that it does—this asura is named Tryaruṇa. The name occurs one other time in the RV in a verse in which his generosity is again praised and Agni Vaiśvānara is asked to protect him. (RV 5.27.2)

asmé vīró marutaḥ śuṣmy àstu
jánānāṃ yó ásuro vidhartā́
apó yéna sukṣitáye tárema–
ádha svám óko abhí vaḥ syāma. RV 7.56.24

"O Maruts, may there be for us a powerful hero who is an asura of the people (and) a distributer, by whom we may cross the waters for a safe dwelling. Now may we be more esteemed for you than your own dwelling." (Hymn to Maruts)

16. I. Kuhn (aput H. J. Schindler, *Das Wurzelnomen im Arischen und Griechischen*, unpublished dissertation, Würzburg, 1972) sees in *sát*- of *sátpati*- a noun **sát*- "raid" and compares *sátvan*- "who makes a raid." Wackernagel suggests instead that *sátpati*- be translated "Gildemeister." (Wackernagel, *Altindische Grammatik*, Band 2, 1, p. 55.)

Geldner translates b. "der der Gebieter und Bestimmer der Völker ist,"[17] and Renou translates it "l 'Asura des peuples, le distributeur."[18] In his notes Renou comments "*asura* au sens de 'chef'."[19] The genitive *jánānām* is either a partitive genitive ("asura among the people") or a genitive of ruling ("asura over the people"). From the verses we have seen so far the second alternative seems more likely. The asura here is a human leader of the people.

These last four verses which speak of human asuras are very instructive. They make it virtually impossible for anyone to maintain that *ásura–* in the RV originally referred to a member of a certain class of divine beings. To argue that the word properly referred to some divine beings and was only used of humans metaphorically is unconvincing.[20] To say that *ásura–* was used of people only in later times is arbitrary since these four verses come from the Family Books, the oldest section of the RV.[21] These human asuras seem to be leaders of groups of people—especially groups of fighting men. But since the last verse spoke of an asura who would lead the people to a safe dwelling, it is perhaps better not to take the word as a technical term for some purely military leader. The word can also be used for an enemy leader. The translation "lord" fits all these usages quite well.

There are a few verses in the Family Books in which it is unclear to whom the word *ásura–* refers.

ātíṣṭhantaṃ pári víśve abhūṣañ
  chríyo vásānaś carati svárociḥ
mahát tā́d vŕ̥ṣṇo ásurasya nā́ma–
  ā́ viśvárūpo amŕ̥tāni tasthau. RV 3.38.4

"All surround the one mounting (the chariot). The self-luminous one putting on splendors wanders. This is the great name of the virile [or: of the bull] asura: Viśvarūpa mounts to immortal (deeds?)." (Hymn to Indra)

17. Geldner, *Der Rig-Veda*, vol. 2, p. 232.

18. Louis Renou, *Études Vedique et Pāṇinéennes*, 17 vols., Publications de l'institute de civilisation indienne (Paris: E. de Boccard, 1955-1969), vol. 10, p. 43.

19. Renou, *Études*, vol. 10, p. 102.

20. See Otto, *Gefühl*, p. 187.

21. We shall also see in the appendix that *ahura-* occurs in the Avesta referring to people. Thus there is good reason to believe that *ásura-* could refer to people in Indo-Iranian times.

This verse is obscure, and so is the hymn in which it is contained. The asura is called Viśvarūpa. *Viśvárūpa–* appears as an epithet of various gods, most frequently Tvaṣṭṛ,[22] but it is unclear that he is referred to here. This seems to be a creation hymn,[23] but it is put in the series of hymns to Indra and is labeled as a hymn to Indra in the Anukramaṇī. So *ásura–* here could refer to Indra. Both Whitney and Bloomfield take it as referring to Indra when they discuss the verse where it appears in the AV.[24] In the AV this verse appears in a hymn used at the consecration of a king. (AV 4.8.) In that context *ásura–* is used to refer to the king regardless of who the original referent may have been. This gives some confirmation of the recognition of a relationship between *ásura–* and kingship by the later Vedic tradition. But the verse is sufficiently obscure that one should not depend very heavily on it in trying to determine the meaning of *ásura–*. If *ásura–* does refer to Indra here, it is the only place in the Family Books where it does, and that should make one cautious in so interpreting it.

samrā́jā ugrā́ vṛṣabhā́ divás pátī
  pṛthivyā́ mitrā́váruṇā vícarṣaṇī
citrébhir abhráir úpa tiṣṭhath rávaṃ
  dyā́ṃ vṛṣayatho ásurasya māyáyā. RV 5.63.3

"Universal monarchs, powerful bulls, lords of heaven (and) of earth (are) excellent Mitrāvaruṇā. With multicolored clouds you mount the roar. You cause the sky to rain by the magic of an asura." (Hymn to Mitrāvaruṇā)

The crucial problem with this verse is whether one supplies *an* or *the* before *asura* in the translation, or whether one translates without an article. Thieme opts for the last of these three possibilities and sees this verse as indicating that there was a god named Asura in the RV.[25] But it is not necessary to interpret the verse that

22. See Hermann Grassmann, *Wörterbuch zum Rigveda*, reprint (Wiesbaden: Otto Harrassowitz, 1964) under *viśvárūpa*-.
23. Geldner, *Der Rig-Veda*, vol. 1, p. 379.
24. William Dwight Whitney, *Atharva-Veda-Saṁhitā*, 2 vols., Harvard Oriental Series, vols. 7-8, reprint (Delhi: Motilal Banarsidass, 1971), vol. 1, p. 157. Maurice Bloomfield, *Hymns of the Atharva-Veda*, Sacred Books of the East Series, vol. 42, 1897, reprint (Delhi: Motilal Banarsidass, 1973), p. 380.
25. Paul Thieme, "Mitanni Treaties," pp. 308-9. He supports this idea of a god named Asura by understanding RV 5. 83.6d—which was interpreted above as referring to Parjanya —as also referring to this god Asura.

way, and it would be better to explain it without assuming the existence of another god if such an explanation is as satisfying. Sāyaṇa takes *ásura–* as referring to Parjanya.[26] This is quite reasonable if the above interpretation of RV 5.83.6 is correct. Geldner prefers to take *ásura–* to refer to Varuṇa, or perhaps to take the phrase *ásurasya māyā́–* more generally to mean "the magical power which an asura possesses."[27] I prefer this last suggestion. Thus the verse would mean that Mitrāvaruṇā cause the sky to rain by exercising the *māyā–* power which they as asuras possess. But regardless of who the asura is, this verse does tell us that an asura can have *māyā.*

dhármaṇā mitrāvaruṇā vipaścitā
  vratā́ rakṣethe ásurasya māyáyā
ṛténa víśvaṃ bhúvanaṃ ví rājathaḥ
  sū́ryam ā́ dhattho diví cíttryaṃ ráthaṃ.   RV 5.63.7

"O Mitrāvaruṇā who know the inspiration, you protect the vows with *dharma*, with the magic of an asura. You rule the whole world with *ṛta*. You place in the sky the sun, the gleaming chariot." (Hymn to Mitrāvaruṇā)

This verse is in the same hymn as the last one and presents the same difficulty, so I need not repeat that discussion. These are the only two verses we have encountered so far that mention *māyā*, but they do seem to indicate that *māyā* is characteristic of an asura. The phrase *ásurasya māyā́–* occurs again in RV 10.177.1, but that verse sheds little light on its meaning.[28]

Summary and Conclusions

These are all of the twenty-nine occurrences of *ásura–* in the Family Books of the RV. It occurs six times as an epithet of Agni (3.3.4, 4.2.5, 5.12.1, 5.15.1, 7.2.3, and 7.6.1) and once more in connection with Agni when he is compared with an asura (7.30.3). It occurs twice with Savitṛ (4.53.1 and 5.49.2), twice with Varuṇa (2.27.10 and 2.28.7), and twice with Mitrāvaruṇā (7.36.2 and 7.65.2). Rudra is called asura in at least two and probably three

26. Geldner, *Der Rig-Veda*, vol. 2, pp. 71-2, note on 3d.
27. *Ibid.*
28. This verse is quoted and discussed in chapter IV.

verses (2.1.6, 5.42.11, and 5.41.3). Dyaus is the asura in one verse (3.53.7) and could be the asura in two others (3.56.8 and 3.29.10). Aryaman (5.42.1), Pūṣan (5.51.11), and Parjanya (5. 83.6) are called asura once each. Humans appear as asuras in four verses. Two of these human asuras are friends of the poet (5.27.1 and 7.56.24), and two are foes (2.30.4 and 7.99.5). For the other three occurrences of *ásura–* it is uncertain to whom the word refers (3.38.4, 5.63.3, and 5.63.7).

Some characteristics of asuras begin to emerge from these verses. The occurrences of genitives of rulership are especially instructive. Thus there is mention of an asura of the gods (7.65.2), an asura of the people (7.56.24), an asura of wise ones (3.3.4), and an asura of heaven (2.1.6 and 5.41.3). "Asura of heaven" in fact seems to be a characteristic term for Rudra. Parjanya is referred to as the "father asura" (5.83.6). Other occurrences of *ásura–* in the genitive case are also instructive. There are two mentions of the māyā of the asura (5.63.3 and 5.63.7). Four verses speak of the heroes of the asura (2.30.4, 3.53.7, 3.56.8, and 7.99.5). The occurrence of *ásura–* and *devá–* in apposition in one verse makes it appear impossible that these two terms could refer to two different groups of deities (5.42.11). The occurrrence of *ásura–* as an epithet for seven other beings who are elsewhere called devas confirms this.

All this seems to confirm the often suggested translation "lord" for *ásura–*. I am quite in agreement with that translation. An asura seems to be some sort of leader who is respected and has at his command some fighting force. In addition, he may wield a sort of magical power called māyā. Such a lord can be either a god or a human, but since the RV is a collection of hymns to gods, *ásura–* occurs much more often of gods in that text.

If *ásura–* does mean lord in the sense I have outlined above, then it is not surprising to see it used of virtually any god. It is not surprising to see it used so often of Agni if one bears in mind that Agni is very frequently mentioned,[29] that he is often called on for aid, and that he is frequently called lord or king. Varuṇa and Mitrāvaruṇā receive this epithet rather often considering how infrequently they are mentioned. But this epithet is quite appropriate for deities such as these who represent sovereignty. However, it

29. About twenty per cent of the hymns in the RV are addressed to him.

does seem peculiar that Indra is so rarely (if ever) called asura in the Family Books. Finding the reason for this would probably require a careful study of the development of the figure Indra from the early RV to the late RV. Perhaps the answer lies in his representing more of a lone warrior figure in the early RV and acquiring characteristics of a leader/sovereign later. But this is pure speculation, and the problem is beyond the scope of this study.

It is worth noting that *ásura–* has not yet appeared in the plural. It has appeared only in the singular (and dual with Mitrāvaruṇā) as an epithet for particular beings. Those who maintain theories that there was some sort of organized group called Asuras in this early period owe their readers an explanation for the total lack of mention of any group of asuras in the Family Books.

CHAPTER III

DERIVATIVES AND COMPOUNDS OF *ÁSURA*– IN THE FAMILY BOOKS OF THE RV

Von Bradke thought that the fundamental meaning of *ásura*– could best be seen in the uses of its derivative *asuryà*–.[1] I cannot completely agree with him here. Nonetheless, the occurrences of the derivatives of *ásura*– should at least be examined to see if they are compatible with the results of our study of *ásura*– and if they add any details to our understanding of the concept. In this chapter I shall examine the occurrences of the derivatives of *ásura*– in the Family Books. I shall first examine the occurrences of *asuryàm* (the noun) and *asuratvá*–, then *asuryà*– (the adjective), then *āsurá*– and *asurahán*–. The occurrences of the first three will be grouped according to the deity to whom the term applies. In my translations I shall render *asuryàm* and *asuratvá*–by "asuraship," *asuryà*– and *āsurá*– by "asuric," and *asurahán*– by "asura-killer." The reader however should note in each case how appropriate "lordship, right to rule, authority" and "lordly" would be for translations.

Asuryàm is ascribed to Agni twice in the Family Books.

tvám̥ no agne adbhuta
  krátvā dákṣasya maṃhánā
tvé asuryàm ā́ruhat
  krāṇā́ mitró ná yajñíyaḥ. RV 5.10.2

"You, O wonderful Agni, by insight, by generosity of will—the asuraship ascended to you—by cooperation are like Mitra worthy of worship for us." (Hymn to Agni)

The parenthetical clause referring to asuraship tells us little more than that it is an attribute of Agni, and the occurrences of *ásura*– as an epithet for him have already indicated that. However, the form of the word deserves some comment. Even though the

1. von Bradke, *Dyâus Asura*, p. 29.

final syllable is marked with an independent *svarita* in the text, the meter demands that they be read as a glide and not a vowel. Thus *asuryàm* is three syllables and not four as one would expect from this accentuation. The same is true for every occurrence of this word in the RV, even in the Family Books, although the adjective *asuryà–* has the expected extra syllable twelve out of thirteen times. Thus Grassmann and Oldenberg suggest that the noun should actually be accented *asuryám.*[2] This word has a metrical shape of short-long-short and thus can be used easily in an *anuṣṭubh* verse. This is, in fact, the first *anuṣṭubh* verse we have seen so far. *Ásura–* in all of its inflectional forms has two short syllables in a row. This does not fit well into an *anuṣṭubh* or *gāyatrī* meter, but can easily be used in *triṣṭubh* or *jagatī* if it is placed in the break in the middle of the *pāda*. Thus all of the verses in the preceding chapter were in *triṣṭubh* or *jagatī*, and the word *ásura–* began on the fifth or sixth syllable of the *pāda* with only one exception.[3]

tvé asuryàṃ vásavo ny ṝṇvan
  krátuṃ hí te mitramaho juṣánta
tváṃ dásyūm̐r ókaso agna āja
  urú jyótir janáyann ā́ryāya. RV 7.5.6

"The Vasus placed asuraship in you, for they enjoyed your insight, O one great as Mitra. You drove the dasyus from (their) dwelling, O Agni, giving birth to broad light for the Aryan." (Hymn to Vaiśvānara)

Here we are told that asuraship was placed in Agni by the Vasus because of his *krátu–*. Geldner translates *krátu–* here by *Rat*. Renou translates it as *pouvoir-spirituel.* Grassmann prefers *Geisteskraft* or *geistigen Einfluss.* Gonda prefers to translate *krátu–* by "mental power and resourcefulness."[4] The Śatapatha Brāhmaṇa

2. Grassmann, *Wörterbuch*, under *asurýa*. Hermann Oldenberg, "Ṛgveda VI, 1-20," *Zeitschrift der Deutschen Morgenlandischen Gesellschaft* 55 (1901): 325-6. For the latest discussion of this see Elmar Seebold, *Das System der indogermanischen Halbvokale* (Heidelberg: Carl Winter, Universitätsverlag, 1972), pp. 243ff.

3. In RV 3.29.14 *ásurasya* began on the third syllable of a *jagatī pāda* and thus produced a metrical irregularity.

4. Jan Gonda, *Epithets in the Ṛgveda* ('S-Gravenhage: Mouton & Co., 1959), p. 91. Jan Gonda, *The Vedic God Mitra* (Leiden: E. J. Brill, 1972), p. 27.

defines it thus: "whenever he desires anything in his mind, as 'Would that this were mine! I might do this!' that is intelligence [*krátu*–]." (sá yád evá mánasā kāmáyata 'idáṃ me syād idáṃ kurvīyéti sá evá krátuḥ. ŚB 4.1.4.1).[5] Thus this verse from the RV says that the Vasus made Agni an asura because of his ability to think creatively and plan. Such "resourcefulness" is certainly desirable in a lord or leader. This same *krátu*– was mentioned in the last verse, too, but was not so definitely linked with *asuryàm* there.

Asuryàm is once ascribed to Varuṇa and three times to Mitrāvaruṇā in the Family Books.

ahám rā́jā váruṇo máhyaṃ tā́ny
  asuryā̀ṇi prathamā́ dhārayanta
krátuṃ sacante váruṇasya devā́
  rā́jāmi kṛṣṭér upamásya vavréḥ. RV 4.42.2.

"I am king Varuṇa. To me in the beginning they assigned the asuraships. The gods follow the insights of Varuṇa. I rule the people of the highest bodily-form." (Hymn to various deities)

Varuṇa was established as an asura from the first. Once again *krátu*– is mentioned in a context that suggests that it is an important quality for an asura. But this verse and the last one suggest another important aspect of asuraness. It seems to be bestowed on one and not an inherent quality.

The verb which I have translated "assign" here is √dhṛ–. It might be instructive to look at some other objects with which this verb occurs. The basic meaning of the word is "to make firm, establish, determine." It occurs with objects such as "heaven and earth" (pṛthivī́m utá dyā́m. RV 1.154.4, 3.59.1, 6.51.8, 5.62.3 dyā́m pṛthivī́m. RV 3.44.3 pṛthivī́m dyā́m utémā́m. RV 3.32.8, 10.121.1), "earth" (pṛthivī́m. RV 7.99.3, 1.67.3, 1.103.2, 2.17.5), "the world halves" (ródasī RV 8.15.2, 4.42.3, 6.17.7, 1.62.7), "the sun in the sky" (sū́ryaṃ diví. RV 8.12.30 diví sū́ryam. RV 1.52.8), "the atmosphere" (antárikṣam. RV 6.47.4), "secure dwelling" (kṣémam. RV 1.66.2), "races of people" (kṛṣṭī́s. RV 7.85.3), "wealth" (rayím. RV 8.13.12, 10.19.1, 9.12.9, 1.30.22, 10.24.1,

5. Translation quoted from Julius Eggeling, *The Śatapatha-Brāhmaṇa*, 5 vols., Sacred Books of the East, vols. 12, 26, 41, 43, 44; 1882, 1885, 1894, 1897, 1900. Reprint (Delhi: Motilal Banarsidass, 1972), vol. 2, p. 269.

8.95.8 rátnam. RV 4.1.18), and "cooked (milk) in cows" (góṣu pakvám. RV 6.44.24, 8.32.25 āmā́su pakvám. RV 6.17.6 páyas kṛṣṇā́su. RV 8.93.13). But the verb also appears with more abstract objects such as "mind" (mánas. RV 10.60.8, 10.60.9, 10.59.5), "spiritual power" (dákṣam. RV 1.156.4 krátum. RV 10.25.4), "Indra-power" (indriyám. RV 1.103.1), and "rulership" (kṣatrám. RV 6.67.6, 5.27.6 kṣatrā́ṇi. RV 4.4.8 kṣatrā́ RV 10.60.5 kṣatríyam. RV 7.104.13 rāṣṭrám. RV 10.173.2, 10.173.5).[6] Thus this verb √dhṛ– seems to be used to speak of establishing order (with "earth," "sky," "sun," etc.) or to bestow some good (with "wealth"). The use of this verb with *asuryám* seems to have both these connotations since establishing a leader bestows good on the community by establishing order within the community.

tā́ hí kṣatrám ávihrutaṃ
  samyág asuryàm ā́śāte
ádha vratéva mā́nuṣaṃ
  svàr ṇá dhāyi darśatáṃ. RV 5.66.2

"Since these two have attained dominion which cannot be overthrown (and) asuraship together, therefore the human (vow) is established like the (divine) vows, visible like the sun." (Hymn to Mitrāvaruṇā)

Here dominion and asuraship are linked as two things simultaneously attained by Mitrāvaruṇā. Again asuraship is attained and not an inherent quality.

práti vāṃ sū́ra údite sūktáir
  mitráṃ huve váruṇaṃ pūtádakṣaṃ
yáyor asuryàm ákṣitaṃ jyéṣṭhaṃ
  víśvasya yā́mann ācítā jigatnú. RV 7.65.1

"I call to you two with songs when the sun has risen, Mitra (and) pure-minded Varuṇa, whose asuraship is everlasting (and) excellent, hastening (and) attentive to each on your rounds." (Hymn to Mitrāvaruṇā)

6. This list is not exhaustive. See Grassmann, *Wörterbuch*, under *dhṛ* for a complete listing.

yā́ dhārā́yanta devā́ḥ
  sudákṣā dákṣapitarā
asuryā̀ya prámahasā. RV 7.66.2

"...the splendid ones of good understanding whose father is Understanding whom the gods support for asuraship." (Hymn to various deities)

This is only a sentence fragment. The first half of the sentence is in the preceding verse. It tells us that this verse refers to Mitrāvaruṇā, but gives no further information about asuraship. This verse says again that asuraship is bestowed and not inherent, and the verb is again √dhṛ, but the expression is changed so that the one on whom it is bestowed is the object and *asuryàm* appears in the dative case.

Asuraship is once ascribed to Rudra and once to Somārudrā in the Family Books.

sthirébhir áṅgaiḥ pururū́pa ugró
  babhrúḥ śukrébhiḥ pipiśe híraṇyaiḥ
ī́śānād asyá bhúvanasya bhū́rer
  ná vā́ u yoṣad rudrā́d asuryàm. RV 2.33.9

"The multiformed, powerful, brown one with powerful limbs is adorned with gleaming gold. Indeed asuraship should not go far from Rudra, who rules this great world." (Hymn to Indra)

sómārudrā dhārā́yethām asuryàm
  prá vām iṣṭáyó 'ram aśnuvantu
dámedame saptá rátnā dádhānā
  śám no bhūtam dvipáde śám cátuṣpade. RV 6.74.1

"O Somārudrā, maintain (your) asuraship. May (our) wishes reach you appropriately. Placing the seven treasures in each house, be beneficial to our biped (group), beneficial to (our) quadruped (group)." (Hymn to Somārudrā)

Here Somārudrā are asked to maintain asuraship—presumably their own since their is no mention of another to whom they would assign it, although the same verb √dhṛ is used that was previously used when the gods assigned asuraship to another. But the verse gives no further information about the nature of asuraship.

The Ādityas are involved with asuraship once in the Family Books.

dhāráyanta ādityā́so jágat sthā́
devā́ víśvasya bhúvanasya gopā́ḥ
dīrghā́dhiyo rákṣamāṇā asuryàm
ṛtā́vānaś cáyamānā ṛṇā́ni. RV 2.27.4

"The Ādityas maintain what moves (and) what stands still, the gods, the protectors of the whole world, having long-lasting visions, protecting asuraship, possessing ṛta, avenging sins." (Hymn to Ādityas)

The Ādityas protect asuraship. What does this mean? If *ásura–* does in fact mean "lord" or "one with some type of authority," then perhaps the Ādityas protect asuraship as a normal part of their maintaining *ṛta*. Maintaining *ṛta* involves maintaining order of all types, and protecting asuraship would mean preserving the ordered hierarchy implied when one has the position of asura with whatever authority that gives him over others. The verb √dhṛ appears here again, but with "what moves and what stands still" as its object.

Three verses in the Family Books ascribe asuraship to Indra.

divó ná túbhyam ánv indra satrā́–
asuryàṃ devébhir dhāyi víśvam
áhiṃ yád vṛtrám apó vavrivā́ṃsaṃ
hánn ṛjīṣin víṣṇunā sacānáḥ. RV 6.20.2

"O Indra, the whole asuraship like (that) of the Sky was granted to you altogether by the gods when you, O drinker of Soma dregs, accompanied by Viṣṇu slew the serpent Vṛtra who was covering the waters." (Hymn to Indra)

Apparently the gods made Indra an asura in recognition of his prowess in killing Vṛtra. His asuraship is compared with that of Dyaus. This is the first clear reference we have seen that Indra is an asura. It is worth noting that this reference occurs in Book Six—a book in which the word *ásura–* never appears. It is also noteworthy that asuraship was bestowed on Indra in recognition of his heroism.

ádhā manye bṛhád asuryàm asya
  yā́ni dādhā́ra nákir ā́ mināti
divédive sū́ryo darśató bhūd
  ví sádmāny urviyā́ sukrátur dhāt. RV 6.30.2

"Thus I think his asuraship is great. What he supports, none disturbs. Each day the sun becomes visible. The one with good power distributes dwellings far and wide." (Hymn to Indra)

Indra is not explicitly named in this verse, but the hymn is to Indra, and he is named in the preceding verse, so *asya* surely refers to him here. Asuraship is again ascribed to Indra, and again the verse is from Book Six. The verb √dhṛ- occurs again, but not with *asuryàm* as object.

satrā́ mádāsas táva viśvájanyāḥ
  satrā́ rā́yó 'dha yé pā́rthivāsaḥ
satrā́ vā́jānām abhavo vibhaktā́
  yád devéṣu dhāráyathā asuryàm. RV 6.36.1

"Fully yours are the intoxications known to all, fully the riches which are earthly. Fully you became the distributor of booty when you assumed the asuraship among the gods." (Hymn to Indra)

Although Indra is not named in this verse, the hymn is addressed to him, and he is certainly the one referred to by "you." He is said to distribute booty when assuming (√dhṛ- again) asuraship among the gods. Distribution of booty was the task of a tribal leader or one who led raids on enemies. Thus the asura here appears to behave as would a tribal leader.

These are all the verses in the Family Books which contain the noun *asuryàm*. But the word *asuratvá* —an abstract derivative of *ásura-* and more or less synonymous with *asuryàm*—occurs in one hymn in the fourth pāda of every verse, which is repeated as a refrain. I shall quote only the first verse.

uṣásaḥ pū́rvā ádha yád vyūṣúr
  mahád ví jajñe akṣáraṃ padé góḥ
vratā́ devā́nām úpa nú prabhū́ṣan
  mahád devā́nām asuratvám ékam. RV 3.55.1

"When the previous dawns shone forth, the great word was born in the place of the cow. Supporting indeed the vows of the gods (I proclaim): great is the unique asuraship of the gods." (Hymn to Viśve Devāḥ)

This refrain definitely presents problems to those who try to maintain that devas and asuras were two different groups of divine beings in the early Vedic period. It seems to mean that the lordship of all the gods is great and special (*éka–*).

The adjective *asuryà–* occurs three or four times in the Family Books in reference to Indra.

áva sya śūrā́dhvano nā́nte
'smín no adyá sávane mandádhyai
śáṃsāty ukthám uśáneva vedhā́ś
cikitúṣe asuryā̀ya mánma. RV 4.16.2

"O hero, unyoke as at the end of the way in order to get drunk today in this pressing of ours. (He) should sing a song as wise Uśana, a devotional song for the wise asuric one." (Hymn to Indra)

The hymn is addressed to Indra, so "the asuric one" presumably refers to him. Little indication of the meaning of *asuryà–* is given.

devā́ś cit te asuryā̀ya pū́rvé
'nu kṣatrā́ya mamire sáhāṃsi
índro maghā́ni dayate viṣáhya–
índraṃ vā́jasya johuvanta sātaú. RV 7.21.7

"Even the ancient gods credit to you powers for asuric rulership. Indra having conquered distributes gifts. They call on Indra in the attainment of booty." (Hymn to Indra)

Once again distribution of booty appears in close connection with an asura. The use of *asuryà–* to modify *kṣatrá–* reinforces the relationship between *ásura–* and ruling or temporal authority.

ná te gíro ápi mṛṣye turásya
ná suṣṭutím asuryàsya vidvā́n
sádā te nā́ma svayaśo vivakmi. RV 7.22.5

"I do not neglect the praises of strong you, not the good praise of the asuric one, wise (I). Always I proclaim your name, O self-glorious one." (Hymn to Indra)

Pāda b should perhaps instead be translated "not the praise, knowing (your) asuric (nature)." But neither translation tells us anything substantial about *asuryà*–. The hymn is addressed to Indra, so this verse presumably refers to him.

tád ín nv asya vṛṣabhásya dhenór
  ā́ nā́mabhir mamire sákmyaṃ góḥ
anyádanyad asuryàṃ vásānā
  ní māyíno mamire rūpám asmin. RV 3.38.7

"This is indeed of the one (who is) a bull (and) a cow. They have measured out with names the essence of the cow. Putting on this after that asuric power, the māyā-possessors fitted the form on this one." (Hymn to Indra)

The meaning of this verse remains obscure as does the hymn from which it comes.[7] The hymn is attributed to Indra, but it is uncertain that he is really the one referred to in this verse. Nor is it clear who the *māyā*– possessors are. It is best not to base any important conclusions on such an obscure verse.

Asuryà– occurs once each in connection with Bṛhaspati, Apām Napāt, and Sarasvatī.

devā́ś cit te asurya prácetaso
  bṛ́haspate yajñíyaṃ bhāgám ānaśuḥ
usrā́ iva sū́ryo jyótiṣā mahó
  víśveṣām íj janitā́ bráhmaṇām asi. RV 2.23.2

"O asuric Bṛhaspati, the wise gods obtained a sacrifice-worthy share from you. As the great sun (begets) the dawns with light, you are the begetter of all chants." (Hymn to various deities)

This verse tells us little about the meaning of *asuryà*–, but it is the first verse we have seen that mentions Bṛhaspati in any connection with asura. Apparently he, too, is lordly.

7. We encountered this same hymn earlier when we discussed the occurrence of *ásura*- in verse four.

imáṃ sv asmai hṛdá ā́ sútaṣṭaṃ
mántraṃ vocema kuvíd asya védat
apā́ṃ nápād asuryàsya mahnā́
víśvāny aryó bhúvanā jajāna. RV 2.35.2

"May we speak from our heart for this one a well-made formula—I trust, he will understand it. Noble Apām Napāt by the greatness of his asuric power engendered all the worlds." (Hymn to Apām Napāt)

Geldner translates with *Asuramacht* and Renou with *pouvoir-asuryen*. The meter indicates that *asuryàsya* should be five syllables and not four—that is, the adjective and not the noun. The neuter of the adjective can be used to mean "asuric power" just as the neuter of *indriyá–* can be used to mean "Indraic power." This is the first verse we have seen that explicitly connects Apām Napāt with *ásura–*, and in fact the only such verse extant.

bṛhád u gāyiṣe váco
'suryā̀ nadī́nāṃ
sárasvatīm ín mahayā suvṛktíbhiḥ
stómair vasiṣṭha ródasī. RV 7.96.1

"I wish to sing a high word: (she is) the asuric one among rivers. Magnify indeed Sarasvatī with songs, with praises, O Vasiṣṭha, and the world-halves." (Hymn to various deities)

I have followed Geldner in translating ab. Sarasvatī is identified here as the lordly one among rivers. This is the first verse we have encountered relating Sarasvatī with *ásura–*. In fact, it is the first verse relating any female being with *ásura–*.

The word *āsurá–* occurs four times in the Family Books—once of Agni, once of Varuṇa, and twice of Svarbhānu.

tánūnápād ucyate gárbha āsuró
nárāśáṃso bhavati yád vijā́yate
mātaríśvā yád ámimīta mātári
vā́tasya sárgo abhavat sárīmaṇi. RV 3.29.11

"The āsuric embryo is called Tanūnapāt; he becomes Narāśaṃsa when he is born; Mātariśvan when he forms himself in his mother; he becomes the gust of wind in his course." (Hymn to various deities)

This is one of the many verses in the RV that identifies Agni with several different deities or gives him several names. It should not be surprising to see him called āsuric since he is often called an asura. The verse gives little clue as to the nuances of *āsurá–*.

imā́m ū ṣv ā̀surásya śrutásya
mahī́ṃ māyā́ṃ váruṇasya prá vocam
mā́neneva tasthivā́m̐ antárikṣe
ví yó mamé pṛthivī́ṃ sū́ryeṇa. RV 5.85.5

"I shall proclaim well this great māyā of famous āsuric Varuṇa, who stood in the atmosphere and measured out the earth with the sun as if with a measuring cord." (Hymn to Varuṇa)

Here we find Varuṇa called āsuric and explicitly linked to *māyā*. Neither statement should be surprising. In addition, this *māyā* seems to be thought of as creative activity.

yát tvā sūrya svàrbhānus
támasā́vidhyad āsuráḥ
ákṣetravid yáthā mugdhó
bhúvanāny adīdhayuḥ. RV 5.40.5

yáṃ vái sū́ryaṃ svàrbhānus
támasā́vidhyad āsuráḥ
átrayas tám ánv avindan
nahy ànyé áśaknuvan. RV 5.40.9

"When āsuric Svarbhānu pierced you with darkness, O Sūrya, (then) the worlds appeared like one lost not knowing the area."

"Sūrya, whom indeed āsuric Svarbhānu pierced with darkness, him the Atris found again; no others were able to." (Hymn to various deities)

These two verses are from the same hymn and practically identical in the clauses relevant to this study and are therefore treated together. For the first time in this study a derivative of *ásura–* appears in relation to a demonic being. But this passage may not be as old as most in the Family Books. The hymn itself is too long. It is the last one in the series of Indra hymns in the Fifth Book. It is nine verses long, but the hymn before it is only five. The fact that the hymns to each deity are arranged in order of decreasing size makes the antiquity of this hymn in the collection questionable. The hymn breaks down into two distinct parts—verses 1-4 and verses 5-9—which bear no recognizable relation to each other.[8] Verses 1-4 form a normal hymn to Indra and are in the proper place in the collection for a hymn of this length. Verses 5-9 tell the story of Svarbhānu darkening the sun and the Atris repairing the damage. The name *svàrbhānu–* occurs four times in this passage and nowhere else in RV, although it does turn up later in the Paippalāda Saṃhitā, the prose portions of the Black Yajur Veda, and the Brāhmaṇas. Thus it appears that verses 5-9 were originally a separate hymn. The use of *āsurá–* to refer to individual demons becomes regular by the time of the Brāhmaṇas. However, there is nothing else to indicate that the hymn in 5-9 is late.

There are two occurrences of *asurahán–* in the Family Books.

tán no ví voco yádi te purā́ cij
  jaritā́ra ānaśúḥ sumnám indra
kás te bhāgáḥ kíṃ váyo dudhra khidvaḥ
  púruhūta purūvaso 'suraghnáḥ. RV 6.22.4

"Tell us this: whether of old the singers obtained your grace, O Indra? What is your share? What is the strength-food of (you) the asura-killer, O undaunted destroyer (?), much called on, with many riches." (Hymn to Indra)

Indra is a killer of asuras. But since *ásura–* has not yet occurred with any meaning related to demons (although the last two verses contained *āsurá–* in this meaning), it is not necessary to think it means demon here. The epithet is simply used to express how powerful Indra is. He is a killer of lords or conquerer of kings. He can kill even a powerful asura who has host of fighting men (*vīrá–*). We have in fact seen *ásura–* used twice before to refer to enemy leaders whose men the gods slew (RV 2.30.4 and 7.99.5). A similar expression occurs in early Irish literature. "Moen the only one, since he was a child, he slew kings, a splendid throw, Labraid grandson of Lorc." (Moen oen ó ba noed níba nós ardríg, oirt rígu, rout án, uaë Luirc Labraid.)[9]

8. See Geldner, *Der Rig-Veda*, vol. 2, p. 38.

9. Text and translation quoted from Myles Dillon, "Celt and Hindu," The Osborn Bergin Memorial Lecture III (Dublin: University College, 1973), p. 11.

prágnáye viśvaśúce dhiyandhè
'suraghné nánma dhītíṃ bharadhvaṃ
bháre havír ná barhíṣi prīṇānó
vaiśvānarā́ya yátaye matīnā́ṃ. RV 7.13.1

"Bring forth a song, a hymn, for Agni, who is all flames, the giver of visions, the asura-killer. I bear (it) like an oblation on the sacrificial straw pleasing (him) for Vaiśvānara the driver of thoughts." (Hymn to Vaiśvānara)

Asurahán– here means the same as in the previous verse.

Summary and Conclusions

This is all twenty-six of the verses in which a derivative or compound of *ásura–* occurs in the Family Books. The noun *asuryàm* occurs twelve times—three times in relation with Mitrāvaruṇā, three times with Indra, twice with Agni, and once each with Varuṇa, Rudra, Somārudrā, and the Ādityas. The adjective *asuryà–* occurs three (or perhaps four) times with Indra and once each with Bṛhaspati, Apām Napāt, and Sarasvatī. *Ā́surá–* occurs once with Agni, once with Varuṇa, and twice with Svarbhānu. *Asurahán–* occurs once with Indra and once of Agni. *Asuratvá–* occurs once with the devas. The beings who are new in this list are Indra, the Ādityas, Somārudrā, Bṛhaspati, Apām Napāt, Sarasvatī, Svarbhānu, and the devas as a whole. Of these only Indra is mentioned more than once, and this is a bit of a surprise since he never clearly gets the epithet *ásura–* in the Family Books. The only occurrences of *asuryàm* in relation with Indra are in the Sixth Book, where the word *ásura–* does not appear. But *asuryà–* does occur related with Indra in the Fourth and Seventh (and perhaps Third) Books. Thus it appears that Indra was considered by these poets to have the qualities of an asura even if they were reluctant to use this epithet for him.

Perhaps the most significant new thing that appears about *ásura–* from a look at its derivatives and compounds is the frequent mention of the gods supporting or maintaining ($\sqrt{}$dhṛ–) *asuryàm* for a particular god or supporting that god for *asuryàm*. This indicates that one was not an asura from birth or by his nature, but was made an asura by the consent and support of those who followed him. Although all of the passages dealt with here are concerned with gods and not humans, there is no reason to doubt that the same was true for human asuras. An asura seems to have been a lord or leader chosen by his people who maintains his authority by their continuing to support and follow him. Thus his insight or planning ability (*krátu–*) was an important quality.

CHAPTER IV

ÁSURA– IN BOOKS ONE, EIGHT, NINE AND TEN OF THE RV

I shall turn now to the occurrences of *ásura*– in the remainder of the RV (Books One, Eight, Nine, and Ten). I shall examine first the singular occurrences, then the dual, then the plural, but saving all the occurrences in hymn 10.124 for a more thorough consideration at the end of the chapter.

Asura– occurs at least twice and perhaps three times with Agni.

úd īraya pitárā jārá ā́ bhágam
  íyakṣati haryató hṛttá iṣyati
vívakti váhniḥ svapasyáte makhás
  taviṣyáte ásuro vépate matī́. RV 10.11.6

"Stir up the two parents (i.e., the two kindling sticks) as a lover (stirs) the vulva. The desired one (i.e., fire) desires; he comes forth from the heart. The carrier (of the offering) speaks; the happy one (?) works well. The asura grows strong; he is excited with (our) poem." (Hymn to Agni)

The translation of this verse is rather uncertain because the exact meaning of several words is uncertain. But the hymn is addressed to Agni, and the general description of the one called asura here seems to fit Agni.

yádī ghṛtébhir ā́huto
  vā́śīm agnír bhárata úc cā́va ca
ásura iva nirṇíjam. RV 8.19.23

"When Agni oblated with ghee bears the axe up and down, like an asura an ornamental garment..." (Hymn to various deities)

Agni is not called an asura here, but is said to behave like an asura with an ornamental garment. It is tempting to think here of some special costume that sets the asura apart from his followers, but it is unsafe to posit such a mark of distinction for an asura on the basis of this one verse. Perhaps it just means that a powerful asura is also likely to be wealthy enough to have fine clothing.

háva eṣām ásuro nakṣata dyā́ṃ
  śravasyatā́ mánasā niṃsata kṣā́ṃ
cákṣāṇā yátra suvitā́ya devā́
  dyáur ná vā́rebhiḥ kṛṇávanta sváiḥ. RV 10.74.2

"When these were invoked the asura attained the sky. He kissed the earth with a glory-seeking mind, while the gods appearing for a good journey will act by their own desires like the sky." (Hymn to Indra)

Geldner is probably correct in identifying the asura in this verse as Agni.[1]

Ásura– is used three times of Varuṇa.

áva te hé̩lo varuṇa námobhir
  áva yajñébhir īmahe havírbhiḥ
kṣáyann asmábhyam asura pracetā
  rā́jann énāṃsi śiśrathaḥ kṛtā́ni. RV 1.24.14

"O Varuṇa, we turn aside your anger with prostrations, with sacrifices, with oblations. O ruling wise asura king, release us from sins committed." (Hymn to various deities)

Here occur the already familiar connections of the asura with kingship and wisdom.

ástabhnād dyā́m ásuro viśvávedā
  ámimīta varimā́ṇaṃ pṛthivyā́ḥ
ā́sīdad víśvā bhúvanāni samrā́ḍ
  víśvét tā́ni váruṇasya vratā́ni. RV 8.42.1

"The all-knowing asura made firm the sky; he measured out the extent of the earth. The overlord settled over all worlds. All these are Varuṇa's ordinances." (Hymn to various deities)

asā́v anyó asura sūyata dyáus
  tváṃ víśveṣāṃ varuṇāsi rā́jā
mūrdhā́ ráthasya cākan
  náitā́vatáinasāntakadhrúk. RV 10.132.4

1. Geldner, *Der Rig-Veda*, vol. 3, p. 254, note on 2a.

"That other one, the sky, was consecrated (as king), O asura. O Varuṇa, you are king of all. The master enjoys the chariot, not threatened by death by so great a sin." (Hymn to various deities)

The translation of this verse is very uncertain. It tells us little about the meaning of *ásura*–, but kingship is once again mentioned in connection with it.

Ásura– appears four times referring to Indra.

tvám̥ rā́jendra yé ca devā́
  rákṣā nṝ́n pāhy àsura tvám asmā́n
tvám̥ sátpatir maghávā nas tárutras
  tvám̥ satyó vásavānaḥ sahodā́ḥ. RV 1.174.1

"You are king, O Indra, even (over those) who are gods. Protect the men, O asura; may you protect us. You are the leader of the raid, O generous one, our savior. You are the true possessor of wealth (and) giver of power." (Hymn to Indra)

tám u tvā nūnám asura prácetasam̥
  rādho bhāgám ivemahe
mahī́va kṝ́ttiḥ śaraṇā́ ta indra
  prá te sumnā́ no aśnavan. RV 8.90.6

"O asura, we go now to you the wise one for a gift as for a share. O Indra, may your protections, your graces, reach forth to us like a great leather cover." (Hymn to Indra)

ā́ ródasī háryamāṇo mahitvā́
  návyam̥navyam̥ haryasi mánma nú priyám̥
prá pastyàm asura haryatám̥ gór
  āvíṣ kṛdhi háraye sū́ryāya. RV 10.96.11

"(You) the desired one, (fill) up the two world-halves with your greatness; you always desire a dear new song. O asura, make the desired abode of the cow visible for the golden sun." (Haristutiḥ hymn)

The content makes it fairly certain that Indra is the asura here. Little new information appears.

evā́ mahó asura vakṣáthāya
  vamrakáḥ paḍbhír úpa sarpad índraṃ
sá iyānáḥ karati svastím asmā
  íṣam ū́rjaṃ sukṣitíṃ víśvam ā́bhāḥ. RV 10.99.12

"Thus, O asura, Vamraka crept up on Indra by foot in order to increase his greatness. He being supplicated should make prosperity for this one. He brought refreshment, nourishment, a good dwelling place, everything." (Hymn to Indra)

In this verse the poet Vamra seems to make a pun on his name, which means "ant," to compare his approaching Indra with a hymn to the approach of a little ant (*vamraká–*). Thus the asura here is again Indra. It tells us nothing new about *ásura–*.

Soma is twice called an asura.

śvetáṃ rūpáṃ kṛṇute yát síṣāsati
  sómo mīḍhvā́m̐ ásuro veda bhū́manaḥ
dhiyā́ śámī sacate sém abhí pravád
  divás kábandham áva darṣad udríṇam. RV 9.74.7

"He makes (for himself) the white color when he wants to succeed. Soma, the gracious asura, knows the world. He is accompanied by vision and (sacrificial) action. The path (leads) him. May he rip open from below the water-skin of the sky." (Hymn to Soma)

This translation of pāda c is highly doubtful. It is unclear how *pravát* fits syntactically. Nevertheless, in this verse Soma is called a generous asura.

ā́ haryatā́ya dhṛṣṇáve
  dhánus tanvanti páuṃsyaṃ
śukrā́ṃ vayanty ásurāya nirṇíjaṃ
  vipā́m ágre mahīyúvaḥ. RV 9.99.1

"They stretch the bow, the strength, for the honorable, courageous one. The great-feeling ones weave a brilliant ornamental garment for the asura at the beginning of the speeches." (Hymn to Soma)

Presumably the ornamental garment is the filter of sheep's wool woven for the asura Soma.[2] We have seen *nirṇíj*– associated with *ásura*– before in RV 8.19.23.

Ásura– occurs at least twice with Dyaus and probably three more times as well.

índrāya hí dyáur ásuro ánamnata–
  índrāya mahī́ pṛthivī́ várīmabhir
  dyumnásātā várīmabhiḥ
índraṃ víśve sajóṣaso
  devā́so dadhire puráḥ
índrāya víśvā sávanāni mā́nuṣā
  rātā́ni santu mā́nuṣā. RV 1.131.1

"Since the asura Heaven bowed to Indra, the great Earth with its wide extensions, in the battle for heavenly splendor with its wide extensions, all the gods united placed Indra in front. May all which is pressed by man (and) offered by man be for Indra." (Hymn to Indra)

It would not be safe to interpret this verse as referring to a struggle between Dyaus and Indra for actual leadership.

ṛtáṃ śáṃsanta ṛjú dī́dhyānā
  divás putrā́so ásurasya vīrā́ḥ
vípraṃ padám áṅgiraso dádhānā
  yajñásya dhā́ma prathamáṃ mananta. RV 10.67.2

"Speaking *ṛta*, thinking correctly, the sons of the sky, the heroes of the asura, the Aṅgirases, making the inspired speaker (i.e. Bṛhaspati) their trail (i.e. marker), think on the first form of the sacrifice." (Hymn to Bṛhaspati)

The entire second line of this verse also occurs as the second line of RV 3.53.7.[3] Dyaus appears to be the asura. This verse also reminds us that an asura can have a fighting force.

2. Macdonell notes that this filter is sometimes called *nirṇíj*- (Macdonell, *Vedic Mythology*, p. 107). Geldner interprets the ornamental garment instead as the milk that is mixed with the soma (Geldner, *Der Rig-Veda*, vol. 3, p. 103, note on 1c).

3. This verse was quoted and discussed in chapter 2.

ná te sákhā sakhyáṃ vaṣṭy etát
  sálakṣmā yád víṣurūpā bhávāti
mahás putrā́so ásurasya vīrā́
  divó dhartā́ra urviyā́ pári khyan. RV 10.10.2

(Yama rejects the advances of his sister with these words:) "Your friend does not wish this friendship wherein she who has the same mark (i.e. who is closely related) becomes one of a different form. The sons of the great one, heroes of the asura, sustainers of the sky look around far and wide." (Hymn is a dialogue of Yama and Yamī)

It is uncertain who the asura is here. Geldner is probably right in suggesting that it is Dyaus.[4] Whitney translates "the sons of the great asura, heroes" and interprets this to mean Varuṇa's spies, but this is unlikely.[5]

asyéd eṣā́ sumatíḥ paprathānā́–
  ábhavat pūrvyā́ bhū́manā gáuḥ
asyá sánīḷā ásurasya yónau
  samāná ā́ bháraṇe bíbhramāṇāḥ. RV 10.31.6

"This grace of this one spreading out became the primordial cow on the earth. In the lap of this one the asura are the siblings being carried in the same load." (Hymn to Viśve Devāḥ)

The siblings are perhaps the Maruts, but more likely the whole race of gods. Dyaus is probably the asura. *Asyá* seems to be used in this verse to mean "heaven" as *iyám* is often used to mean "earth."

árcā divé bṛhaté śūṣyàṃ vácaḥ
  svákṣatraṃ yásya dhṛṣató dhṛṣán mánaḥ
bṛháccravā ásuro barhánā kṛtáḥ
  puró háribhyāṃ vṛṣabhó rátho hí ṣáḥ. RV 1.54.3

"Sing a loudly resounding word for the exalted Sky, of which bold one the bold mind is self-ruling. The asura who has exalted glory, made energetic, (is yoked) with two fallow steeds in front, for the bull is the chariot." (Hymn to Indra)

4. Geldner, *Der Rig-Veda*, vol. 3, p. 413, note on 2c.
5. Whitney, *Atharva-Veda*, vol. 2, p. 816.

This verse is obscure, and the translation of the last pāda is uncertain. Geldner thinks the asura is Dyaus,[6] but Renou thinks he is Indra.[7] Geldner seems right here, since the bull should be Indra.

One hymn apparently speaks of Tvaṣṭṛ as an asura.

tát savitā́ vo 'mṛtatvám ā́suvad
  ágohyaṃ yác chraváyanta aítana
tyám cic camasám ásurasya bhákṣaṇam
  ékaṃ sántam akṛṇutā cáturvayaṃ. RV 1.110.3

"Then Savitṛ provided for you immortality when you came invoking Agohya. You even made this cup, the drinking-dish (?gift) of the asura, which was one, (to be) four." (Hymn to Ṛbhus)

This hymn is dedicated to the Ṛbhus. The cup which they made into four was made by Tvaṣṭṛ, so he is probably the one referred to as asura here.[8]

Twice in the same hymn Savitṛ is called *ásuraḥ sunīthā́ḥ*.

híraṇyahasto ásuraḥ sunīthā́ḥ
  sumṛḷīkā́ḥ svávā̃ṅ yātv arvā́ṅ
apasédhan rakṣáso yātudhā́nān
  ásthād deváḥ pratidoṣáṃ gṛṇānā́ḥ. RV 1.35.10

"May the golden-handed, good-leading, merciful, helpful asura come this way. Driving away demons and sorcerers, the god has stood being praised each night." (Hymn to various deities)

This verse is addressed to Savitṛ, and he is the one referred to as asura. The epithet "good-leading" (*sunīthá–*) occurs with *ásura–* here. This epithet seems quite appropriate for a lord.

ví suparṇó antárikṣāṇy akhyad
  gabhīrávepā ásuraḥ sunīthā́ḥ
kvèdā́nīṃ sū́ryaḥ káś ciketa
  katamā́ṃ dyā́ṃ raśmír asyā́ tatāna. RV 1.35.7

6. Geldner, *Der Rig-Veda*, vol. 1, p. 70, note 1.
7. Renou, *Étude*, vol. 17, p. 20.
8. See Macdonell, *Vedic Mythology*, p. 133.

"The fair-winged one has looked across the atmosphere, the deep-speaking (?), good-leading asura. Where is Sūrya now? Who knows? To which heaven does the ray of this (*Savitṛ*) reach?" (Hymn to various deities)

This hymn contrasts Sūrya and Savitṛ throughout, so *asya* here refers to Savitṛ.

Rudra is referred to as an asura in two verses found in these books.

yáthā rudrásya sūnávo
divó váśanty ásurasya vedhásaḥ
yúvānas táthéd asat. RV 8.20.17

"In which way the sons of Rudra, masters of the asura of the Sky, will wish, the young ones, in that way it will be." (Hymn to Maruts)[9]

There is an ambiguity in this verse caused by *divó* and *ásurasya* both being in the genitive case. If these words are meant to be in apposition, then the translation should be "strong one (?) of the asura Sky." In my translation I have instead taken the genitive *divó* to depend on *ásurasya*. The occurrences of the phrase "asura of the sky" in RV 2.1.6 and 5.41.3 referring to Rudra as the asura make this translation look best here.[10] Thus Rudra is the asura here.

prá vaḥ pā́ntaṃ raghumanyavó 'ndho
yajñáṃ rudrā́ya mīḷhúṣe bharadhvaṃ
divó astoṣy ásurasya vīráir
iṣudhyéva marúto ródasyoḥ. RV 1.122.1

"Bring forth your Soma drink as a sacrifice for generous Rudra, O zealous ones. I praised (him) together with the heroes of the asura of the Sky, as if (I praised) the Maruts with strength-bringing in heaven and earth." (Hymn to Viśve Devāḥ)

9. The exact meaning of *vedhás*- is disputed. For references see Mayrhofer, *Wörterbuch*, under *vedhás*-.
10. These verses are quoted and discussed in chapter 2.

This translation of pāda d is uncertain. *Divó* and *ásurasya* are both in the genitive case and create the same ambiguity as in the last verse. But the other occurrences of "asura of heaven" referring to Rudra that have already been cited make it safe to assume that *ásura–* refers to Rudra here, too.

Ásura– in the singular is used three times of humans in these parts of the RV.

śatáṃ rā́jño nā́dhamānasya niṣkā́ñ
chatám áśvān práyatān sadyá ā́daṃ
śatáṃ kakṣī́vām̐ ásurasya gónāṃ
diví śrávo 'járam ā́ tatāna. RV 1.126.2

"I Kakṣīvān immediately received 100 gold pieces from the king who stood in need, 100 horses which were given, 100 cattle from the asura. (His) unending glory stretches to the sky." (Hymn to various deities)

The asura is here a king who, being in difficulties, had need of and rewarded highly the religious services of the poet Kakṣīvān.

prá tád duḥśī́me pṛ́thavāne vené
prá rāmé vocam ásure maghávatsu
yé yuktvā́ya páñca śatā́–
asmayú pathā́ viśrā́vy eṣāṃ. RV 10.93.14

"I proclaim this before Duḥśīma, Pṛthavāna, Vena, and Rāma the asura, (all these) generous ones, who having yoked 500, made known what is favorable to us on their path." (Hymn to Viśve Devāḥ)

The shift in construction between c and d cannot be rendered literally in English. The asura here is Rāma, a human, one of a number of generous patrons of the poet.

ví sū́ryo mádhye amucad rátham̐ divó
vidád dāsā́ya pratimā́nam ā́ryaḥ
dṛḷhā́ni pípror ásurasya māyína
índro vy ā̀syac cakṛvā́m̐ ṛjíśvanā. RV 10.138.3

"Sūrya unharnessed the chariot in the middle of the sky. The Aryan found a counterweight for the dāsa. Indra working with

Ṛjiśvan shattered the fortresses of the māyā-possessing asura Pipru." (Hymn to Indra)

In this verse the asura is named Pipru, possesses māyā, and is an enemy of Ṛjiśvan. The context indicates that Pipru was a dāsa and Ṛjiśvan an Aryan. Pipru is also mentioned in nine other verses in the RV. In five of these it is stated again that Pipru was defeated for Ṛjiśvan (RV 1.51.5, 4.16.13, 5.29.11, 6.20.7, 10.99.11). Pipru is not *explicitly* called a dāsa or dasyu, but does seem to be one of those people of the indigenous race against whom the invading Aryans fought. Thus Indra is said to have destroyed the fortresses of Pipru and aided Ṛjiśvan in the dasyu-killing (RV 1.51.5). He is said to have delivered powerful Pipru Mṛgaya to Ṛjiśvan and to have thrown down the 50,000 black ones (RV 4.16.13). Pipru is vowless (*avratá–*, RV 1.101.2). Perhaps this indicates that he was of a different religion than Ṛjiśvan. He also has fortresses (*púr–*, RV 1.51.5, 4.16.13, 6.18.8, 6.20.7). Thus he appears to be a leader of a group of indigenous people. Pipru's māyā is mentioned again in RV 6.20.7, where he is said to have serpent-māyā (*áhimāya–*). Perhaps the attribution of māyā to the indigenous leaders was due at least in part to a misunderstanding and mistrust of their culture and religious practices. This is suggested by RV 1.51.5ab: "You blew away by means of māyā the māyā-possessing ones who offered in their own way on a shoulder bone." (tváṃ māyā́bhir ápa māyíno 'dhamaḥ/svadhā́bhir yé ádhi śúptāv ájuhvata.)

This verse is important because it offers a clue to how *ásura–* could develop the meaning "demon" in the later language. The word appears here in a perfectly acceptable old usage—it refers to an enemy lord. But the character to whom it refers need only be considered in a mythological instead of a historical setting in order to be seen as a demon. He is an enemy to the gods (being *avratá–* and being defeated by Indra) and possesses that mysterious power of māyā that demons are later said to possess. He is also named in lists which contain other demonic figures such as Vṛtra (RV 1.103.8), Namuci (RV 2.14.5), and Śuṣṇa (RV 2.14.5, 6.18.8).

There are four more occurrences of *ásura–* in the singular in these sections of the RV in which the referent is unclear.

krāṇā́ rudrā́ marúto viśvákṛṣṭayo
divā́ḥ śyenā́so ásurasya nīḷáyaḥ
tébhiś caṣṭe váruṇo mitró aryamā́–
índro devébhir arvaśébhir árvaśaḥ. RV 10.92.6

"Active are the Maruts, the Rudra-sons, who rule all people, the eagles of the sky, the co-dwellers of the asura. With these is seen Varuṇa, Mitra, Aryaman, rapid Indra with the rapid gods." (Hymn to Viśve Devāḥ)

Geldner claims the asura is Dyaus.[11] But Rudra would be as reasonable a guess.

pataṅgám aktám ásurasya māyáyā
hṛdā́ paśyanti mánasā vipaścítaḥ
samudré antáḥ kaváyo ví cakṣate
márīcīnām padám icchanti vedhásaḥ. RV 10.177.1

"The inspired ones see with the heart, with the mind, the bird annointed by the māyā of the asura. The seers see inside the ocean; the wise ones seek the track of the rays." (Hymn to Māyābheda)

This verse could refer to the myth of the Svarbhānu hiding the sun with darkness until it was found by the Atris. If so, this is the only occurrence of *ásura–* in the singular referring to a mythological evil or demonic being.

dvídhā sūnávó 'suraṃ svarvídam
ā́sthāpayanta tṛtī́yena kármaṇā
svā́ṃ prajā́ṃ pitáraḥ pítryaṃ sáha
ā́vareṣv adadhus tántum ā́tatam. RV 10.56.6

"The sons have erected the sun-winning asura in two ways with the third action. The fathers placed in the later ones their own offspring, the fatherly power, the drawn-out thread." (Hymn to Viśve Devāḥ)

Geldner suggests that the asura here is Dyaus.[12] The verse says little to clarify the meaning of *ásura–*.

11. Geldner, *Der Rig-Veda*, vol. 3, p. 291, note on 6b.
12. *Ibid.*, p. 221, note on 6ab.

srákve drapsásya dhámataḥ sám asvarann
  ṛtásya yónā sámaranta nā́bhayaḥ
trī́nt sá mūrdhnó ásuraś cakra ārábhe
  satyásya nā́vaḥ sukṛ́tam apīparan. RV 9.73.1

"In the teeth (of the pressing stones) sound together (the sounds) of the roaring drop. The relatives assemble in the womb of *ṛta.* The asura made for himself three heads in order to grasp (the soma). The ships of truth carry the well prepared one across." (Hymn to Soma)

This verse is obscure. It is unclear who the asura is.

Ásura– occurs twice in the dual in these sections of the RV, both times referring to Mitrāvaruṇā.

mahā́ntā mitrā́váruṇā
  samrā́jā devā́v ásurā
ṛtā́vānāv ṛtám ā́ ghoṣato bṛhát. RV 8.25.4

"The great overlords Mitrāvaruṇā, gods, asuras, possessors of *ṛta,* proclaim exalted *ṛta.*" (Hymn to various deities)

Here occurs again the simultaneous usage of *devá–* and *ásura–* for the same gods. These two asuras are also called overlords (*samrā́j–*).

prá sā́ kṣitír asura yā́ máhi priyá
  ṛ́tāvānāv ṛtám ā́ ghoṣatho bṛhát
yuvám̐ divó bṛhotó dákṣam ābhúvam̐
  gā́m̐ ná dhury úpa yuñjāthe apáḥ. RV 1.151.4

"May the tribe which is very dear excel, O Asuras! O possessors of *ṛta,* you proclaim exalted *ṛta.* You (harness) the helpful power of the exalted sky; you harness the waters as a cow to a yoke." (Hymn to various deities)

The word *asura* here is a rare occurrence of a vocative dual ending in a short *a.*[13] The verse contains little new information about *ásura–*. In fact, the second line is identical with the last line of the preceding verse except for the number of the verb.

13. Wackernagel, *Altindische Grammatik,* vol. 3, p. 53.

Summary of Singular Occurrences and Conclusions

These are all the occurrences of *ásura–* in the singular and dual in Books One, Eight, Nine, and Ten of the RV (except for an occurrence in the singular in RV 10.124.3, which will be considered later in this chapter). They generally confirm what we have already seen about *ásura–*. This epithet occurs with Agni two or three times (10.11.6, 8.19.23, 10.74.2), with Varuṇa three times (1.24.14, 8.42.1, 10.132.4), with Indra four times (1.174.1, 8.90.6, 10.96.11, 10.99.12), with Soma twice (9.74.7, 9.99.1), with Dyaus at least twice and probably three more times (1.131.1, 10.67.2, 10.10.2, 10.31.6, 1.54.3), with Tvaṣṭṛ once (1.110.3), with Savitṛ twice (1.35.10, 1.35.7), with Rudra twice (8.20.17, 1.22.1), with humans three times (1.126.2, 10.93.14, 10.138.3) with Mitrāvaruṇā twice (8.25.4, 1.151.4), and in verses where the referent is uncertain four times (10.92.6, 10.177.1, 10.56.6, 9.73.1). It is not surprising that Soma is first called an asura only in Book Nine, since nearly all the hymns to Soma in the RV are in Book Nine. Indra was not called an asura in the Family Books, but *asuryà–* was used of him there. Tvaṣṭṛ is new to our list of gods called asura. Of the three uses of *ásura–* for humans, the use for an enemy is significant because it suggests a way in which the connotation of the word can shift from good to bad. The occurrence of *ásura–* in RV 10.177.1 remains rather puzzling. If the asura in this verse really is Svarbhānu as he appears to be, then this is the only verse in the RV in which the word appears in the singular referring to a mythical, demonic being. As we shall see later *āsurá–* rather than *ásura–* is normally used for mythical evil beings referred to in the singular in later texts. However, there is no reason why *ásura–* could not be so used in this verse, and such a usage does not contradict what we have seen so far. In fact it would be very much like the usage of *ásura–* for Pipru in RV 10.138.3. There is no reason why a mythological figure cannot be a lord. Nonetheless, this usage of *ásura–* in the singular is quite rare.

Occurrences in the Plural

However, *ásura–* also occurs in the plural in Books One, Eight, and Ten. The plural does not occur in the Family Books or in Book Nine. It is well known that Books One and Ten contain the latest hymns in the RV, but the antiquity of Book Eight is much debated. Thus it is not surprising to find *ásura*– used with different connotations in the First and Tenth Books, but when it is so used in Book Eight, it will be helpful to try to get some idea of the chronological position of the hymns in which the word occurs. Therefore, I shall discuss indications of the antiquity of each of these hymns when I discuss the relevant verses.

Wüst's theory of the chronological position of the Eighth Book fits well with the theory developed in this thesis. He places Book Eight later than Book Nine and the Family Books, but before Books One and Ten.[14]

We shall turn now to the plural occurrences of *ásura*–in Books One, Eight, and Ten.

té jajñire divá ṛṣvā́sa ukṣáṇo
  rudrásya máryā ásurā arepásaḥ
pāvakā́saḥ śúcayaḥ sū́ryā iva
  sátvāno ná drapsíno ghorávarpasaḥ. RV 1.64.2

"They were born the exalted bulls of the sky, the young men of Rudra, asuras, spotless, purifying, pure, like suns, like warriors, banner-bearing, of awesome appearance."[15] (Hymn to Maruts)

Although we have not seen *ásura*– in the plural before, this application of the term to the Maruts seems quite appropriate. They are apparently called asuras in the same way that they are elsewhere called Rudras. That is, they are sons of the asura (Rudra).

yád vābhipitvé asurā ṛtáṃ yaté
  chardír yemá ví dāśúṣe
vayáṃ tád vo vasavo viśvavedasa
  úpa stheyāma mádhya ā́. RV 8.27.20

"...or when in the evening, O asuras, you spread protection for the pious one going to *ṛta*, then may we be within (that protection) of yours, O all-knowing Vasus." (Hymn to Viśve Devāḥ)

14. Walter Wüst, "Über das Alter des Ṛgveda und die Hauptfragen der indo-iranischen Frühgeschichte," *Wiener Zeitschrift für die Kunde des Morgenlandes* 34:214. His relative chronology looks good, but his absolute chronology is more questionable.

15. *Drapsín*- is a pun here. It can mean "banner-bearing or "rain-bearing."

This verse is addressed to all the gods who are here given the epithets *vásu–* and *ásura–*. In the index to Geldner's translation of the RV *ásura–* is interpreted as referring to the Ādityas in this verse, but there is nothing to support this.[16] A search for indications that the hymn containing this verse is late reveals some evidence. The only occurrence of *bhaktí–* "distribution" in the RV is in verse eleven of this hymn, but it does not have its later meaning of "devotion." The only Ṛgvedic occurrence of *nyáñcana–* "hole" is in verse 18, but it occurs four times in the Paippalāda Saṃhitā and once in the Jaiminīya Brāhmaṇa. *Nimrúc–* "setting (of the sun)", which occurs in verse 19, occurs only three other times in the RV, all in Books One and Ten. It occurs six times in the other Saṃhitās and three times in the Brāhmaṇas. *Prabúdh–* "awakening," which also occurs in verse 19, occurs only one other time in the RV in Book Ten, but nine times in the later Saṃhitās and once in the Brāhmaṇas. These statistics suggest that the vocabulary is relatively late. The resolutions of the semivowels required by the meter show nothing to indicate the age of the hymn.

paró divā́ pará enā́ pṛthivyā́
  paró devébhir ásurair yád ásti
káṃ svid gárbhaṃ prathamáṃ dadhra ā́po
  yátra devā́ḥ samápaśyanta víśve.   RV 10.82.5

"Which is beyond the sky, beyond this earth, beyond the gods (and) the asuras, indeed what embryo did the waters receive at first, where all the gods together looked on?" (Hymn to Viśvakarman)

The asuras here seem to be human lords. The first pāda sets up an opposition between heaven and earth and the second pāda gives a parallel opposition between the gods who rule heaven and the asuras who rule earth.

yáthā devā́ ásureṣu
  śraddhā́m ugréṣu cakriré
eváṃ bhojéṣu yájvasv
  asmā́kam uditáṃ kṛdhi.   RV 10.151.3

16. Johannes Nobel, *Der Rig-Veda*, vieter Teil, *Namen- und Sachregister zur Überstezung*, Harvard Oriental Series, vol. 36 (Cambridge: Harvard University Press, 1957), p. 2, "Asuras" entry under *Āditya*.

"Just as the gods created for themselves trust among the powerful asuras, so make what is spoken by us (to be trustworthy) among the generous offerers." (Hymn to Śraddhā)

The asuras again are human lords.

tigmám ā́yudhaṃ marútām ánīkaṃ
  kás ta indra práti vájraṃ dadharṣa
anāyudhā́so ásurā adevā́ś
  cakréṇa tā́m̐ ápa vapa ṛjīṣin. RV 8.96.9

"The vanguard of Maruts is a sharp weapon. Who withstands your vajra, O Indra? The godless asuras are weaponless. Destroy them with the wheel, O drinker of Soma dregs." (Hymn to various deities)

This is the only place in the RV where *adevá–* occurs with the accent on the final syllable instead of the initial. An initial accent is normal for *karmadhārayas*, but a final accent is normal for *bahuvrīhis*.[17] Thus *ádeva–* should mean "ungodly," and *adevá–* should mean "without gods." Perhaps the *bahuvrīhi* accent is used here to make it clear that the word is a *bahuvrīhi*. If so, then it should definitely be translated "godless asuras" and not "asuras who are not gods." This translation fits perfectly with the uses of *ásura–* we have already seen. In RV 10.138.3, 2.30.4, and 7.99.5 *ásura–* was used to refer to human enemies. That meaning fits this verse, too. Indra is invoked to destroy the godless enemies who stand helpless before him as if they were weaponless. It is only a very short step from here to the concept of asuras as mythological demons. Indications of lateness for this hymn are few. The word *nímiśla–* "attached" occurs in verse 3. The presence of an *l* in this word suggests lateness, but one of its three other occurrences in the RV is in the Family Books. *Śvasátha–* "snort" in verse 7 is *hapax* in the RV, but occurs a few times in the Brāhmaṇas. And in verse 20 the initial *a* of *'dhivaktā́* is not to be restored in reading the verse. This is rare in the RV, but it is unclear that it indicates lateness.[18] There are two injunctives in the hymn (*iṣanta* in verse

17. Wackernagel. *Altindische Grammatik*, vol. 2, part 1, p. 293.

18. For a list of occurrences of *a*- not restored in this context see Christian-Bartholamae, "Der Abhinihitasandhi in Ṛgveda," (*Studien zur indogermanische Sprachgeschichte* 1 (1890): 81-116.

3 and *dhā̆ḥ* in verse 16), so it is probably not among the very latest hymns in the RV.

yā́ indra bhúja ā́bharaḥ
svàrvām̐ ásurebhyaḥ
stotā́ram ín maghavann asya vardhaya
yé ca tvé vṛktábarhiṣaḥ. RV 8.97.1

"O Indra, the pleasures which brilliant you took from the asuras, (with these) enrich the praiser of this (deed), O generous one, and those who have offering straw prepared for you." (Hymn to Indra)

This verse should probably be interpreted along the same lines as the preceding verse. Thus the singer asks that he receive a share of the booty which Indra has helped his patron to obtain from the enemy leaders, the asuras. A parallel theme occurs in RV 8.5.31 where the Aśvins are asked to take away the nourishment of the dāsas and eat them.[19] It is not necessary to interpret *ásura–* in this verse as having the later meaning of "anti-god," although such an interpretation would also make sense.

There is very little to indicate that this hymn is late. The word *keśin–*, which occurs in verse 4, occurs seventeen times in the RV, and all but two are in Books One, Eight, and Ten, The word *meṣá–*, which occurs in verse 12, occurs eleven times in the RV, all in Books One, Eight, and Ten. But since this word occurs in Avestan (*maēša–*), it is certainly old. The distribution of these two lexical items suggests some common tradition connecting this hymn with Books One and Ten, but hardly proves anything about its age. The resolution of semivowels shows no indication of lateness, and at least one injunctive occurs (*vṛṇak* in verse 7).

yád ábravaṃ prathamáṃ vāṃ vṛṇānò
'yáṃ sómo ásurair no vihávyaḥ
tā́ṃ satyā́ṃ śraddhā́m abhy ā́ hí yātám
áthā sómasya pibataṃ sutásya. RV 1.108.6

"Since choosing you at first I said, 'We must compete with the asuras for this soma,' come indeed to this real trust and drink the pressed soma." (Hymn to Indra-Agni)

19. This verse is quoted and discussed in chapter 12.

The speaker is the poet, so the context is clearly human. Thus the asuras against whom the poet wishes to contend for the soma must be the human asuras, the enemies of him and his patron.

tád adyá vācáḥ prathamáṃ masīya
  yénā́surā̃́ abhí devā́ ásāma
ū́rjāda utá yajñiyāsaḥ
  páñca janā máma hotráṃ juṣadhvaṃ. RV 10.53.4

(Agni says:) "I will think now on that first (part) of (my) speech by which we gods may overcome the asuras. May you nourishment-eating ones and ones worthy of worship (and) five peoples enjoy my hotṛship." (Hymn to various deities)

The asuras here could be human enemies, but it is equally possible that they are the mythological opponents of the gods.

hatvā́ya devā́ ásurān yád ā́yan
  devā́ devatvám abhirákṣamāṇāḥ. RV 10.157.4

"The gods having slain the asuras when coming, the gods protecting their godliness (then led back the sun through their art and immediately active life-power appeared all around)." (Hymn to Viśve Devāḥ)

(I have supplied the next verse from Geldner's translation to complete the sentence.) The asuras could be human enemies here, but it seems much more likely that the word refers to mythological opponents of the gods.

Summary of Plural Occurrences and Conclusions

We have now seen all the occurrences of *ásura–* in the RV (except those in RV 10.124, to be dealt with shortly). The plural occurs only in Books One, Eight, and Ten. Thus the hymns in which the plural occurs are all likely to be late, although one or two hymns in Book Eight which contain *ásura–* offer no clear evidence that they are late. The plural occurs ten times. It is used twice with deities—once with the Maruts (1.64.2) and once with the gods in general (8.27.20). It is used twice to refer to human lords without any indication of their being hostile (10.82.5, 10.

151.3). In three other verses asuras appear as human enemies (8. 96.9, 8.97.1, 10.108.6). These verses are important because they show how close the description of human asuras can come to being a description of mythological asuras in the later sense of enemies of the gods. In one verse it is unclear whether human enemy asuras or asuras who are mythological enemies of the gods are intended (10.53.4). Only one verse seems to use *ásura–* to refer to mythological enemies of the gods, and this usage is not certain there (10. 157.4).[20] Thus it appears that *ásura–* begins to have its later meaning only at the very end of the period of the composition of the RV, if indeed this meaning occurs at all in that time period.

Appendix on RV 10.124

There are two more occurrences of *ásura–* in RV 10.124. This hymn has been interpreted as referring to a primordial struggle between devas and asuras in which some deities defected from the camp of the asuras to the camp of the devas. Since this entire hymn is relevant to this study I shall quote and translate it in its entirety and summarize the various interpretations that have been offered.

imáṃ no agna úpa yajñám éhi
pā́ñcayāmaṃ trivṛ́taṃ saptátantuṃ
áso havyavā́ḷ utá naḥ purogā́
jyóg evá dīrgháṃ táma ā́śayiṣṭhāḥ. RV 10.124.1

"(Indra:) 'O Agni, approach this our sacrifice which has five paths, three layers, and seven threads. May you be our oblation-bearer and leader. For a long time you have lain in the long darkness.'" (Hymn to various deities)

ádevād deváḥ pracátā gúhā yán
prapáśyamāno amṛtatvám emi
śiváṃ yát sántam áśivo jáhāmi
svā́t sakhyā́d áraṇīṃ nā́bhim emi. RV 10.124.2

("Agni:) 'I the god go from the ungodly one, going secretly (and) in hiding, seeing immortality. When unfriendly I abandon the friendly being, I go from my own friendship to the strange clan.'"

20. A plural occurrence in RV 10.124.5 may be another such usage. See below.

páśyann anyásyā átithiṃ vayā́yā
ṛtásya dhā́ma ví mime purū́ṇi
śáṃsāmi pitré ásurāya śévam
ayajñiyā́d yajñíyaṃ bhāgám emi. RV 10.124.3

"(Agni:) 'Seeing the guest of the other branch, I measure widely the many forms of *ṛta*. I say a kind word to the father asura. I go from exclusion from the sacrifice to a share in the sacrifice.'"

bahvī́ḥ sámā akaram antár asminn
índraṃ vṛṇānáḥ pitáraṃ jahāmi
agníḥ sómo váruṇas té cyavante
paryā́vard rāṣṭráṃ tád avāmy āyán. RV 10.124.4

"(Agni:) 'Many years I worked in this one. Choosing Indra I abandon the father. Agni, Soma, Varuṇa—they go (forth). The rulership has changed. Coming, I aid this (rulership).'"

nírmāyā u tyé ásurā abhūvan
tváṃ ca mā varuṇa kāmáyāse
ṛténa rājann ánṛtaṃ viviñcán
máma rāṣṭrásyā́dhipatyam éhi. RV 10.124.5

"(Indra:) 'Even these asuras have become without magic. If you love me, O Varuṇa, O king, separating *anṛta* from *ṛta*, come to rulership of my kingdom.'"

idáṃ svàr idám íd āsa vāmám
ayáṃ prakāśá urvàntárikṣaṃ
hánāva vṛtráṃ niréhi soma
havíṣ ṭvā sántaṃ havíṣā yajāma. RV 10.124.6

"(Indra;) 'Here is the sun, here indeed is the good, here is the light, the wide atmosphere. Let us two kill Vṛtra. Come forth, O Soma. We offer with an oblation to you who are the oblation.'"

kavíḥ kavitvā́ diví rūpám ā́sajad
áprabhūtī váruṇo nír apáḥ sṛjat
kṣémaṃ kṛṇvānā́ jánayo ná síndhavas
tā́ asya várṇaṃ śúcayo bharibhrati. RV 10.124.7

"The seer with his seer's ability gives shape to heaven. Because of lack of power Varuṇa sends the water forth. Making comfort like wives, the rivers the shining ones carry around his color."

tā́ asya jyéṣṭham indriyáṃ sacante
  tā́ īmā́ kṣeti svadháyā mádantīḥ
tā́ īṃ víśo ná rā́jānaṃ vṛṇānā́
  bībhatsúvo ápa vṛtrā́d atiṣṭhan. RV 10.124.8

"They follow his greatest Indraic power. He lives with those very ones who are delighting according to their nature. These choosing him as clans their king went away from Vṛtra feeling revulsion."

bībhatsū́nāṃ sayújaṃ haṃsám āhur
  apā́ṃ divyā́nāṃ sakhyé cárantaṃ
anuṣṭúbham ánu carcūryámāṇam
  índraṃ ní cikyuḥ kaváyo manīṣā́. RV 10.124.9

"They call the companion of those who feel revulsion a wild goose wandering in the friendship of the divine waters. The poets with their wisdom perceive Indra ever wandering about according to the *anuṣṭubh*."

There are several indications that this hymn is late. There are several words with semivowels that are often resolved in the older texts but must remain consonants here to fit the meter: *jyòk* in verse 1, *sakhyā́t* in verse 2, *paryā́vart* in verse 4, *tvā* in verse 6, *jyéṣṭham* in verse 8 (which would have the diphthong *e* resolved into two vowels in older texts), and *divyā́nām* in verse 9. Against this are only a few words that show the resolution of semivowels expected in an older text: *svā́t* in verse 2, *tvam* in verse 5, and *sakhyé* in verse 9. There are also two lexical items that are typically late: *prakāśá-* "light" in verse 6 and *anuṣṭúbh-* (name of a meter) in verse 9. These indications are sufficient to show that this hymn is as late as any in the RV.

There has been much written about this hymn, and several interpretations have been offered. Segerstedt says that the hymn recounts how Agni after serving the enemies of the gods for a long time finally comes over to the gods.[21] He says that *ásura–* in the RV and in later Vedic literature designates the conquered indigenous people of India and their gods.[22] But this explanation is not adequate since Agni, Varuṇa, and Soma can hardly have been indigenous gods taken over by the invading Aryans.

Bergaigne practically equates Varuṇa with Vṛtra.[23] He interprets the hymn as saying that Indra has replaced Agni, Varuṇa, and Soma as the highest ruler of the gods.[24] The Father Asura referred to in verse 3 is Varuṇa with whom Agni and Soma have dwelt.[25] "Thus it is incontestable that X. 124 contains a second mention and a perfectly clear mention of the victory of Indra over Varuṇa."[26] The hymn may in fact deal with a victory of Indra over Varuṇa, but this is neither incontestable nor perfectly clear, as we shall see from the variety of interpretations offered.

Hillebrandt also takes the Father Asuras in verse 3 to be Varuṇa.[27] The hymn refers to an old belief in Agni-Varuṇa which is abandoned in favor of a deva religion.[28] He sees verses 6-9 as unconnected with verses 1-5.[29] In a subsequent work he modified this interpretation somewhat. There he said that the Father Asura in verse 3 is not Varuṇa, but the old Indo-Iranian Asura who became Ahura Mazdā in Iran.[30] Thus Agni calls him his Father Asura as fire is called the son of Ahura Mazdā in Iran.[31] Varuṇa stands next to this Asura because he has been an asura since Indo-Iranian times.[32]

Von Schroeder differs from the preceding scholars in taking

21. Segerstedt, "Asuras," part 1, pp. 174ff.
22. *Ibid.*, p. 175.
23. Abel Bergaigne, *Vedic Religion according to the Hymns of the Ṛgveda*, 3 vols., trans. V. G. Paranjpe (Poona: Ārya-saṁskṛti-Prakāśana, 1969, 1971, 1973), vol. 3, pp. 150-1.
24. *Ibid.*, p. 152.
25. *Ibid.*
26. *Ibid.*, p. 153.
27. Alfred Hillebrandt, *Varuṇa und Mitra: ein Beitrag zur Exegese des Veda* (Breslau: G. P. Anderholz' Buchhandlung, 1877), p. 108.
28. *Ibid.*, pp. 108-9.
29. *Ibid.*, pp. 110-11.
30. Hillebrandt, *Vedische Mythologie*, vol. 3, p. 69.
31. *Ibid.*, p. 70.
32. *Ibid.*

the Father Asura of verse 3 to be Rudra.[33] Thus he says that *ásura–* is used in this verse in the same demonic sense in which the plural is used in verse 5 to refer to the dark side of this deity.[34] The hymn has to do with the drama of the great victory of the gods in the spring.[35] (If *ásura–* is used in a pejorative sense for a god here, it is the only such usage of the word in the RV.)

Von Bradke recognized that this hymn is not very old.[36] He considered verses 6-9 to be a later addition.[37] He denies that the Father Asura of verse 3 is Varuṇa, and refuses to come to a firm decision on who he is, though he seems to favor Dyaus.[38] He interprets the hymn as an attempt by a late poet to explain how a formerly highly praised Father Asura could have sunk so low as to be considered a demon. The poet concludes that this happened because Agni left him, and he was thus unable to sacrifice.[39]

Geldner's interpretation is somewhat different. He sees the major theme as a concern for the absence of Agni and relates it to a Brāhmaṇa story of the killing of Vṛtra found in TS 2.5. 1 & 2.[40] This story tells how Tvaṣṭṛ created Vṛtra by throwing soma into the fire. Thus when Indra went to kill Vṛtra, Soma and Agni called out to him from within Vṛtra, and he let them come out before the slaying. Geldner thus takes the Father Asura of verse 3 to be Vṛtra.[41] Varuṇa becomes involved only because he is lord of waters and thus involved in the Vṛtra myth.[42] Hillebrandt objects to this theory that Vṛtra is never an asura in RV and that Geldner really fails to explain Varuṇa's presence in the hymn since he does not appear in the Brāhmaṇa story and is never said to be either in Vṛtra's power or Vṛtra's friend.[43] There is a further problem with taking Vṛtra to be the Father Asura here. The

33. Leopold von Schroeder, *Mysterium und Mimus im Rigveda* (Leipzig: H. Haessel Verlag, 1908), p. 199.
34. *Ibid.*
35. *Ibid.*, p. 200.
36. von Bradke, *Dyâus Asura*, p. 99.
37. *Ibid.*, p. 97.
38. *Ibid.*, p. 99.
39. *Ibid.*, pp. 100-1.
40. Pischel and Geldner, *Vedische Studien*, vol. 2, pp. 293-4.
41. *Ibid.*, p. 301.
42. *Ibid.*, p. 297.
43. Hillebrandt, *Vedische Mythologie*, vol. 3., p. 68, n. 1.

Father Asura is referred to in too positive a manner for him to sound like Vṛtra.

Oldenberg sees in this hymn the story of Agni's running away and hiding.[44] He denies that the hymn reflects any historical encounter between a Varuṇa-cult and an Indra-cult—it concerns purely mythological matters.[45] While Agni has been for a long time in hiding, Indra's strength has grown to surpass that of Varuṇa, Soma, Agni, and the Asuras.[46] This hymn seems to mix the older concept of godly asuras with the younger concept of ungodly asuras.[47]

Brown says of this hymn, "There seems to be unanimous assent to the theory that it is a dialogue containing an invitation from Indra to Agni to leave the Asuras and serve at the sacrifice of the Devas, and an acceptance in reply by Agni. Beyond this point interpretations disagree."[48] The hymn comes from a time when the conflict between asuras and devas is fully recognized and deals with this general conflict.[49] However, the other theories summarized here do not suggest even the "unanimous assent" that he says exists on one point.

There is another interpretation possible if one accepts Lüders' theories on the Indra-Vṛtra myth. He says that Vṛtra had wrapped himself around a stone enclosure in heaven which contained the cosmic ocean, which was the domain of Varuṇa, and held within it Soma and Agni.[50] Thus the dialogue could be Indra's attempt to persuade these three to come to his aid in the struggle against Vṛtra. The Father Asura would then perhaps be Dyaus whom they are reluctant to leave. But this interpretation has as many problems as the others. The going from one's own clan to a strange one is still not fully explained.[51]

I confess that I do not understand this hymn. None of the inter-

44. Hermann Oldenberg, "Ākhyāna-Hymnen in Ṛigveda," *Zeitschrift der Deutschen Morgenländischen Gesellschaft* 39 (1885): 68.

45. *Ibid.*, p. 70.

46. *Ibid.*

47. *Ibid.*, n. 2.

48. W. Norman Brown, "Proselyting the Asuras," *Journal of the American Oriental Society* 39 (1919): 100.

49. *Ibid.*, p. 101.

50. Lüders, *Varuṇa*, vol. 1, especially chapter 5.

51. Lüders himself does not suggest this interpretation as far as I know.

pretations I have summarized seems adequate, but I have no better alternative to offer. It poses some threat to the interpretation of *ásura–* that I am suggesting in that it seems to speak of Agni, Varuṇa, and Soma defecting from the camp of the asuras to that of Indra. If the hymn indeed says that, the statement is unique in the RV. No other verse we have examined (and we have seen all the verses in the RV containing *ásura–*) supports this idea of a hostile group of asuras which includes these three gods. I suggest that one should be very cautious of accepting any theory about the meaning of *ásura–* which rests mainly on the interpretation of such an obscure hymn.

CHAPTER V

DERIVATIVES AND COMPOUNDS OF *ÁSURA–* IN BOOKS ONE, EIGHT, NINE, AND TEN OF THE RV

I turn now to the occurrences of derivatives and compounds of *ásura–* in Books One, Eight, Nine, and Ten of the RV.

The adjective *asuryà–* occurs three times in connection with Indra.

ké té nára indra yé ta iṣé
  yé te sumnáṃ sadhanyàṃ íyakṣān
ké te vā́jāyāsuryā̀ya hinvire
  ké apsú svā́sūrvárāsu páuṃsye. RV 10.50.3

"Who are these men, O Indra, who (act) according to your wish, who beg for your booty-apportioning grace? Which (men) hasten for your asuric strength [or: reward]? Which (men turn to you) in concern for water, their own fields, (and) manly power?" (Hymn to Indra Vaikuṇṭha)

catvā́ri te asuryā̀ṇi nā́ma–
  ádābhyāni mahiṣásya santi
tvám aṅgá tā́ni víśvāni vitse
  yébhiḥ kármāṇi maghavañ cakártha. RV 10.54.5

"Four are the undeceivable asuric names of you the buffalo. You alone know all these by which you did (your) deeds, O generous one." (Hymn to Indra)

Here Indra's secret names are praised as asuric. The verse is addressed to Indra, so there is no doubt that *te* refers to him.

śatáṃ vā vád asurya práti tvā
  sumitrá itthā́staud durmitrá itthā́staut
ā́vo yád dasyuhátye kutsaputrám
  prā́vo yád dasyuhátye kutsavatsám. RV 10.105.11

"Or when one hundred (stood (?)) against you, O asuric one, Good-Friend praised you here, and Bad-Friend praised you there, when you helped the son of Kutsa in the dasyu-slaying, when you helped the dear one of Kutsa in the dasyu-slaying."[1] (Hymn to Indra)

The vocative *asurya* surely refers to Indra since the hymn is addressed to him. It is interesting to note that he can be called asuric when he is opposed to the dasyus even though a dasyu can also be called asura, as we have seen.

Asuryà– appears once in connection with Sūrya.

báṭ sūrya śrávasā mahā́m̐ asi
satrā́ deva mahā́m̐ asi
mahnā́ devā́nām asuryàḥ puróhito
vibhú jyótir ádābhyam. RV 8.101.12

"Truly, O Sūrya, you are great because of (your) glory. O god, you are great everywhere. The asuric one is *purohita* of the gods because of (his) greatness, the undeceivable, powerful light." (Hymn to various deities)

The *purohita* here is apparently Sūrya, but since Agni is usually the *purohita* of the gods, there may be some identification of Agni and Sūrya implied. *Asuryà–* is used together with *devá–* here in such a way that the two words could hardly refer to any mutually exclusive groups.

Asuryà– is used once or twice in connection with Rodasī and once modifying "color."

jóṣad yád īm asuryā̀ sacádhyai
víṣitastukā rodasī́ nṛmáṇāḥ
ā́ sūryéva vidható rátham gāt
tveṣápratīkā nábhaso nétyā́. RV 1.167.5.

"When it pleases the asuric, manly-minded Rodasī with loosened braids to accompany him, she comes like Sūryā to the chariot of her worshipper with shimmering appearance like the approach of a storm-cloud." (Hymn to various deities)

1. It is unclear whether or not *sumitrá*- and *durmitrá*- are proper names. The verb which needs to be supplied in *a* to go with *práti* is also guesswork.

sātír ná vó 'mavatī svàrvatī
  tveṣā́ vípākā marutaḥ pípiṣvatī
bhadrā́ vo rātíḥ pṛṇató ná dákṣiṇā
  pṛthujráyī asuryèva jáñjatī. RV 1.168.7

"O Maruts, just as your conquest—powerful, sun-possessing, strong, ripening (?)—is your gracious gift, like the fee of the generous one—wide-stretching, glittering—like the asuric one." (Hymn to Maruts)

The sense of this verse is far from certain. The asuric one is not named, but Geldner, Renou, and Max Müller all agree that it refers to Rodasī.[2]

prá kṛṣṭihéva śūṣá eti róruvad
  asuryàṃ várṇaṃ ní riṇīte asya táṃ
jáhāti vavríṃ pitúr eti niṣkṛtám
  upaprútaṃ kṛṇute nirṇíjaṃ tánā. RV 9.71.2

"Like a people-killer the courageous one goes forth roaring. He takes off that asuric color. He abandons the covering; he goes as food to the meeting-place. He continually makes the one swimming above into a festive garment." (Hymn to Soma)

This verse addressed to Soma is obscure in meaning, and the translation is uncertain. The verb in *b* could mean that he reveals rather than takes off the asuric color. If Geldner is correct in suggesting that the one swimming above in *d* is the milk with which the soma is mixed, then perhaps the asuric color which Soma takes off in *b* is the tawny or golden color of the plant extract which would be lost when it is mixed with milk.

The noun *asuryàm* is used once in connection with Mitrā–varuṇā and once in a less clear context.

tā́ mātā́ viśvávedasā-
  asuryā̀ya prámahasā
mahī́ jajānā́ditir ṛtā́varī. RV 8.25.3

2. Geldner, *Der Rig-Veda*, vol. 1, p. 246, note on 7d. Renou, *Études*, vol. 10, p. 25. Max Müller, trans., *Vedic Hymns*, part 1, Sacred Books of the East, vol. 32, 1891, reprint (Delhi: Motilal Banarsidass, 1973), p. 284.

"The great mother Aditi who possesses *ṛta* gave birth to these two all-knowing, majestic ones for asuraship." (Hymn to various deities)

This hymn is addressed to Mitrāvaruṇā, and they are the ones who are destined for asuraship according to this verse.

túbhyaṃ śukrā́saḥ śúcayas turaṇyávo
  mádeṣūgrā́ iṣaṇanta bhurváṇy
  apā́m iṣanta bhurváṇi
tvā́ṃ tsārī́ dásamāno
  bhágam īṭṭe takvavī́ye
tváṃ víśvasmād bhúvanāt pāsi dhármaṇā–
  asuryā̀t pāsi dhármaṇā. RV 1.134.5

"The clear, pure, hastening, powerful ones (i.e., the soma juices) move for you in the intoxications, in a swirl. They move in a swirl of water. The tired hunter implores you for luck in the hunt. You protect from the whole world according to (your) natural disposition. You protect from asuraship according to (your) natural disposition." (Hymn to Vāyu)

It is unclear what the asuraship is from which the poet seeks protection. Perhaps he seeks protection from a bad ruler or from domination. Or perhaps this verse is from a hymn that is late enough for *ásura–* and its derivatives to have begun to connote lords of the indigenous people and therefore enemies. The real meaning of this verse remains obscure.

Asuratvá– appears twice in these books.

sá hí dyutā́ vidyútā véti sā́ma
  pṛthúṃ yónim asuratvā́ sasāda
sá sánīḷebhiḥ prasahānó asya
  bhrā́tur ná ṛté saptáthasya māyā́ḥ. RV 10.99.2

"Since he desires the song with light and with lightning, he sat on the broad seat because of his asuraship, overcoming, with his co-nesters and not without his brother, the magic tricks of the seventh one." (Hymn to Indra)

This verse is from a hymn to Indra, and he is surely the one spoken of here. Pādas *c* and *d* seem to refer to his fighting Vṛtra with the aid of Viṣṇu and the Maruts, while *a* and *b* seem to refer to his coming to the sacrifice. I have taken *asuratvā́* to be a causal instrumental meaning that Indra was able or worthy to take his seat at the sacrifice because of his asuraship.

yád uṣa aúcchaḥ prathamā́ vibhā́nām
  ájanayo yéna puṣṭásya puṣṭā́m
yát te jāmitvám ávaraṃ párasyā
  mahán mahatyā́ asuratvám ékaṃ.   RV 10.55.4

"O Uṣas, that you shone forth the first of lights whereby you created the prosperity of prosperity, (and) that (there is) a later kinship (viz. to the days of present time) of you who are the farthest (in the past), (that) is the great, unique asuraness of (you) the great (one)." (Hymn to Indra)

The translation of this verse is not quite certain, but it certainly assigns asuraness to Uṣas.

Āsurá– and *asurahán–* occur once each in these books.

yuváṃ surā́mam aśvinā
  námucāv āsuré sácā
vipipānā́ śubhas patī
  índraṃ kármasv āvataṃ.   RV 10.131.4

"You two, O Aśvins, pressed the *surāma* at the (place of) *āsuric* Namuci, O lords of beauty, (and) helped Indra in (his) deeds." (Hymn to various deities)

The meaning of *surā́ma–* in this verse is unclear. It may be from *su+rāma–* "well pleasing" and thus refer to soma. The verse seems to refer to the myth of Indra's fight with the demon Namuci. (He was aided in this struggle by the Aśvins.) Thus *āsurá–* seems to be used with the same pejorative connotation it has throughout the Brāhmaṇas. This suggests that the hymn from which the verse comes is likely to be late.

vibhrā́ḍ bṛhát súbhṛtaṃ vājasā́tamaṃ
  dhárman divó dharúṇe satyám ā́rpitam
amitrahā́ vṛtrahā́ dasyuhántamaṃ
  jyótir jajñe asurahā́ sapatnahā́.   RV 10.170.2

"The high, shining, well taken care of, most vigor winning, set as true in the base in the foundation of the sky, enemy-killing, Vṛtra-killing, most dasyu-killing, asura-killing, rival-killing light was born." (Hymn to Sūrya)

There is no reason why *asurahán–* here should not mean the same thing it does elsewhere in the RV—"a killer of lords."

Conclusions

These are all the occurrences of derivatives and compounds of *ásura–* in Books One, Eight, Nine, and Ten of the RV. The occurrences of these in connection with Indra and Mitrāvaruṇā confirm our earlier findings. The connections of *ásura–* with Sūrya, Rodasī, and Uṣas are new. The use of *āsurá–* for an individual demon (Svarbhānu) occurred already in the Family Books (RV 5.40.5 and 9). The request for protection from asuraship in RV. 1.134.5 remains puzzling. Perhaps the most surprising thing is the rarity with which these compounds and derivatives appear. In the Family Books *ásura–* occurs 29 times, and derivatives and compounds of it occur 26 times. In the other books *ásura–* occurs 41 times while derivatives and compounds occur only 13 times. This decrease in the use of compounds and derivatives seems to have occurred shortly before the connotation of the word *ásura–* shifted from good to bad.

We have now examined every occurrence of *ásura–*, its compounds, and its derivatives in the RV.

CHAPTER VI

ÁSURA– IN THE ATHARVA VEDA

I turn now to the occurrences of *ásura–* in the Atharva Veda. I shall examine first those occurrences in the Śaunaka recension of this text (which I shall abbreviate AV) and then turn to the occurrences in the Paippalāda Saṃhitā (AVP) which do not occur in the Śaunaka text. I shall begin with the occurrences in the singular.[1]

Agni is called asura once in the AV.

ūrdhvā́ asya samídho bhavanty
  ūrdhvā́ śukrā́ socíṃṣi agnéḥ
dyumáttamā suprátīkaḥ sásūnus
  tánūnápād ásuro bhū́ripāṇiḥ. AV 5.27.1

"Upward goes his fuel; upward the bright, most brilliant flames of Agni. Beautiful, with his son, grandson of himself, asura, many-handed...."[2]

This verse fits well with what we have already seen of Agni as an asura in the RV.

Varuṇa is called an asura once.

ayáṃ devā́nām ásuro ví rājati
  váśā hí satyā́ váruṇasya rā́jñaḥ
tátas pári bráhmaṇā śā́śadāna
  ugrásya manyór úd imáṃ nayāmi. AV 1.10.1

"This asura rules the gods, for the wishes of king Varuṇa (come) true. Distinguishing myself with a chant, I lead this (man) out of this from the anger of the fearsome one."[3]

In this charm against dropsy occurs this clear example of Varuṇa, a ruler of the devas, who is himself a deva, being called an asura.

Prajāpati is called an asura once.

1. Quotes are from the edition of Viśva Bandhu. *Atharva-veda (Śaunaka)*, ed. by Viśva Bandhu, 4 vols. (Hoshiarpur: Vishveshvaranand Vedic Research Institute, 1960-1964). My translations usually follow Whitney's rather closely.

2. This corresponds to AVP 9.1.1 and 2a. The last sentence continues in verse 2.

3. This corresponds to AVP 1.9.1.

prajā́patiḥ salilā́d ā́ samudrā́d
  ā́pa īráyann udadhím ardayāti
prá pyāyatām vṛ́ṣṇo áśvasya réto
  'rvā́ṅ eténa stanayitnúnéhi/
apó niṣiñcánn ásuraḥ pitā́ naḥ. AV 4.15.11 and 12a

"May Prajāpati agitate the cloud sending water from the surging ocean; let the seed of the male horse overflow; come this way with that thunder, sprinkling water, our father asura."[4]

The third, fourth, and fifth lines of this quote appear, with some variations, in RV 5.83.6. But that hymn is addressed to Parjanya, and he appears to be the father asura there.

katháṃ mahé ásurāyābravīr ihá
  katháṃ pitré háraye tveṣánṛmṇaḥ
pṛ́śniṃ varuṇa dákṣiṇāṃ dadāvā́n
  púnarmagha tváṃ mánasācikitsīḥ. AV 5.11.1

"How did you speak here to the great asura, how having brilliant power (did you say) to the tawny father: 'Having given a spotted (cow?) as a sacrificial fee, O Varuṇa, you desired to think with the mind, O one with repeated gifts'."

This verse is from a dialogue between Varuṇa and Atharvan. Most say the speaker is Varuṇa,[5] and thus he is the asura here. The corresponding Paippalāda passage (AVP 8.1.1) has *diva asurāya* in *a*, which Barret emends to *divyāyāsurāya*.

yamásya lokā́d ádhy ā́ babhūvitha
  prámadā mártyān prá yunakṣi dhíraḥ
ekākínā sarátham yāsi vidvā́nt
  svápnaṃ mímāno ásurasya yónau. AV 19.56.1

"You have arisen from the world of Yama. Wise you join mortals with pleasure. Knowing, you go with the solitary one, fashioning sleep (or: a dream) in the place of the asura."[6]

4. This corresponds to AVP 5.7.10.
5. Whitney, *Atharva-Veda*, vol. 1, p. 237.
6. This corresponds to AVP 3.8.1.

This hymn is addressed to Sleep. It is not certain who the asura is, but it is most likely Yama, and the verse means that sleep (or a dream) was created in the world ruled by Yama before coming to the world of men. The phrase *ásurasya yónau* occurred in RV 10.31.6.[7] *Ásura-* occurs again in the plural in verse three of this hymn. There it clearly has the later meaning of "anti-gods."[8]

yáthāsitáḥ pratháyate váśām̐ ánu
  vápūṃṣi kṛṇvánn ásurasya māyáyā
evā́ te śépaḥ sáhasāyám arkó
  'ṅgenā́ṅgaṃ sáṃsamakaṃ kṛṇotu. AV 6.72.1

"As the black snake extends itself at will, making wonderous forms by the magic of the asura, so may this *arka* plant by its power make your penis a limb that fits the limb."[9]

This verse is from a charm for virility. The *arka* is a plant used in the accompanying rite. My translation of *c* and *d* is extremely uncertain, but this half of the verse seems to be of no help in figuring out who the asura is anyway. The identity of the asura remains a mystery.

yáḥ kṛṣṇáḥ keśy ásura
  stambajá utá túṇḍikaḥ
arā́yān asyā muṣkā́bhyāṃ
  bháṃsasópa hanmasi. AV 8.6.5

"The asura who is black, hairy, tufted, and has a snout—we strike the bad ones away from her labia, from her private parts (?)."[10]

This obscure verse is from a charm "to guard a pregnant woman from demons."[11] The relative clause in *ab* is meant to be taken with the object of the main clause. Thus the asura here is some evil being—perhaps a demon or perhaps some sort of vermin.

7. This was quoted and discussed in the last chapter.
8. This verse is quoted and discussed later in this chapter.
9. This corresponds to AVP 19.27.14.
10. This corresponds to AVP 16.79.5.
11. Whitney, *Atharva-Veda*, vol. 2, p. 493.

sá stanayati sá ví dyotate
  sá u áśmānam asyati//
pāpā́ya vā bhadrā́ya vā
  púruṣāyā́surāya vā. AV 13.7.13 and 14 (13.4.41 and 42)[12]

"He thunders; he lightnings; indeed he throws the stone, either for the evil one or for the auspicious one, for the man or for the asura."

The asura here appears to be some type of being distinct from man, but exactly who the asura represents in contrast to man is not clear. It could be men contrasted with their leaders the asuras, or men contrasted with their enemies the asuras, or men contrasted with gods the asuras. The parallelism of the verse favors the last possibility.

Summary of Singular Occurrences and Conclusions

These are all the occurrences of *ásura–* in the singular in the Śaunaka recension of the Atharva Veda. Although most of the verses are obscure, a few things can be noted about them. We find *ásura–* again in familiar usages as an epithet of Agni and of Varuṇa. Varuṇa is even said to be an asura who rules the devas. Prajāpati is called an asura for the first time. He is in fact called the father asura. Only Parjanya was called father asura in the RV, but the verses in which both of these deities received this epithet are almost identical. Four more of the occurrences of *ásura–* also use the word with a good connotation. But in the last two verses *ásura–* could be used in its later meaning of demon or anti-god. It does at least have a bad connotation in these two verses.

Plural Occurrences

There are no dual occurrences of *ásura–* in the AV. The plural occurrences exemplify the entire spectrum of meanings of the word.

samrā́ḍ asy ásurāṇāṃ
  kakún manuṣyā̀ṇām
devā́nām ardhabhā́g asi
  tvám ekavṛṣó bhava. AV 6.86.3

12. The number in parentheses is that of Whitney and Roth's edition of the text.

"You are the overlord of asuras, the chief of men. You are a companion of the gods. May you become the one bull (i.e., leader of the herd)."[13]

This verse is from a charm for supremacy. *Ásura–* here could mean demon or a certain class of beings or it could be used in its archaic meaning of "lord."

ásurāṇāṃ duhitā́si
  sā́ devā́nām asi svásā
divás pṛthivyā́ḥ sáṃbhūtā
  sā́ cakarthārasáṃ viṣáṃ. AV 6.100.3

"You are the daughter of the asuras; you are the sister of the gods. Arisen from the sky, from the earth, you have made the poison ineffective."[14]

The asuras here are contrasted with the gods. This is typical for the later meaning of *ásura–*. However, there is no mention of any hostility on the part of the asuras in this verse. Both devas and asuras are probably mentioned in order to relate the power of the charm to the entire world of non-human beings. Thus the terms "sister" and "daughter" are not to be taken literally to imply a particular relationship between gods and asuras.

There are many passages in the AV in which *ásura–* occurs in the plural referring to enemies of the gods. However, in most cases the precise nature of these enemies is not spelled out. Their foe is usually Indra, but sometimes the gods as a whole. Since the historical enemies of the Aryans (the dasyus) are usually referred to as enemies of Indra, many of these verses could be transitional between the old and new meanings of *ásura–*. It is still used in its old sense of "lord," but in a particular application to enemy lords and thus has the pejorative connotation which becomes standard later. Of course, there is also no way to say that in these verses *ásura–* cannot simply have its later meaning of "enemy of the gods," and *ásura–* must be understood this way in a few of its occurrences.

13. This corresponds to AVP 19.6.12.
14. This corresponds to AVP 19.13.6.

índro ha cakre tvā bāhā́v
ásurebhya stárītave
prā́śaṃ prátiprāśo jahy
arasā́n kṛṇv oṣadhe. AV 2.27.3

"Indra indeed put you on (his) arm for overcoming the asuras. Smite the arguments of my counter-debator; make (them) ineffective, O plant."[15]

This verse is from a charm for victory in a public debate. The asuras appear as enemies overcome by Indra.

pāṭā́m índro vy ā̀śnād
ásurebhya stárītave
prā́śaṃ prátiprāśo jahy
arasā́n kṛṇv oṣadhe. AV 2.27.4

"Indra consumed the *pāṭā* for overcoming the asuras. Smite the arguments of my counter-debator; make (them) ineffective, O plant."[16]

This verse is from the same hymn as the last one and uses *ásura–* in the same way.

yéna devā ásurāṇām
ójāṃsy ávṛṇīdhvam
ténā naḥ śárma yacchata. AV 6.7.3

"O gods, grant us protection by means of that with which you repelled (or: chose (?)) the strengths of the asuras."

There is a problem with this verse. The verb *avṛṇīdhvam* should be from √vṛ "to choose" rather than √vṛ "to repel" since the latter makes no other *nā–* formations. The AVP text (AVP 19.3.12) avoids this problem by having *yāni* in place of *yéna* and *tebhin* (for *tebhis* ?) in place of *ténā*. This allows one to translate: "O gods, grant us those protections, the strengths of the asuras which you chose." But *ásura–* still must not be used here in its old meaning

15. The first half of this verse appears as the last half of AVP 2.16.2, but with *bāhvor* instead of *bāhāv*.

16. The first half of this verse corresponds to the first half of AVP 2.16.3 and 7.12.8.

"lord," since the preceding verse in the text uses *ásura–* with a pejorative connotation.

índraś cakāra prathamáṃ
  nairhastám ásurebhyaḥ
jáyantu sátvāno máma
  sthiréṇéndreṇa medínā. AV 6.65.3

"Indra made the unhanding one first for the asuras. Let my warriors conquer with strong Indra as ally."[17]

This verse is from a charm for success against enemies. The preceding verse of the charm indicates that the *nairhasta* is a weapon that deprives the enemy of his hands. Thus the asuras appear as enemies opposed by Indra.

anénéndro maṇínā vṛtrám ahann
  anénā́surān párābhāvayan manīṣí
anénājayad dyā́vāpṛthiví ubhé
  imé anénājayat pradíśaś cátasraḥ. AV 8.5.3

"With this amulet Indra killed Vṛtra; with this the wise one overthrew the asuras; with this he conquered both heaven and earth; with this he conquered these four directions."[18]

Once again in this verse the asuras are enemies killed by Indra.

brahmacārí janáyan bráhmāpó lokáṃ
  prajā́patiṃ parameṣṭhínaṃ virā́jam
gárbho bhūtvā́ 'mṛ́tasya yónāv
  índro ha bhūtvā́ 'surāṃs tatarha. AV 11.7.7 (11.5.7)

"The student generating the chant, the water, the world, Prajāpati, the most exalted *virāj*; having become an embryo in the womb of *amṛta*, indeed having become Indra, destroyed the asuras."[19]

This verse from a hymn praising the student (*brahmacārin*) equates the student with Indra, who destroys the asuras.

17. The first half of this verse corresponds to the first half of AVP 19.11.9.
18. This corresponds to AVP 16.27.3.
19. This corresponds to AVP 16.153.7, which has however *amṛtan* instead of *asurān*.

yásyāṃ pū́rve pūrvajanā́ vicakriré
  yásyāṃ devā́ ásurān abhyávartayan
gávām áśvānāṃ váyasaś ca viṣṭhā́
  bhágaṃ várcaḥ pṛthiví no dadhātu. AV 12.1.5

"On whom (the earth) of old the ancient people spread themselves, on whom the gods overcame the asuras; the place (?) of cattle, horses, and birds—may the earth grant us fortune and splendor."[20]

The verse locates the battle between gods and asuras on earth.

índrasya bāhū́ stávirau vṛ́ṣāṇau
  citrā́ imā́ vṛṣabháu pārayiṣṇū́
táu yokṣe prathamó yóga ā́gate
  yā́bhyāṃ jitám ásurāṇām svàr yát. AV 19.13.1

"The arms of Indra are strong bulls, these wonderful, successful bulls. When it is time to harness, I first shall yoke them, by which was conquered the sun which belonged to the asuras."[21]

Here the sun is named as part of the booty won by Indra's defeat of the asuras. Thus the asuras here must be mythological enemies as in later texts, but note that they are enemies of Indra as in the RV and not enemies of all the gods as in later texts. We also saw the motif of winning the sun after conquering the asuras in the RV.[22]

práinān chṛṇīhi prá mṛṇā́ rabhasva
  maṇís te astu puraetā́ purástāt
ávārayanta varaṇéna devā́
  abhyācārám ásurāṇāṃ śváḥśvaḥ. AV 10.3.2

"Shatter them, crush (them), take hold (of them); may the amulet in front be your vanguard. The gods warded off the assaults of the asuras day by day with the *varaṇa*."[23]

20. The first half of this verse corresponds to the first half of AVP 17.1.4.
21. This corresponds to AVP 7.4.1. In my translation I have followed Whitney and Roth in taking the AVP reading of *yokṣye* for *yokṣe*.
22. See RV 10.157.4. quoted and discussed in chapter 4.
23. This corresponds to AVP 16.63.2.

This hymn is from a charm involving the use of a *varaṇa* amulet. *Ásura-* occurs here with its late meaning of mythological enemies of the gods.

In some other verses of the AV the fight against the asuras is mentioned in connection with the fight against the dasyus.

yéna devā́ ásurān prā́ṇudanta
  yéndro dásyūn adhamáṃ támo ninā́ya
téna tváṃ kāma máma yé sapátnās
  tā́n asmā́l lokā́t prá ṇudasva dūrám. AV 9.2.17

"With which the gods drove away the asuras, with which Indra led the dasyus to the lowest darkness, with that, O Kāma, may you drive those who are my rivals far from this world."[24]

Here the fight between the gods and the asuras is treated in a fashion parallel to the treatment of the fight between Indra and the dasyus. Throughout the RV references to the Aryans' conquest of the land which they were entering were put in terms of Indra's defeating the dasyus. So this verse may point to some connection between the struggle between gods and asuras and the struggle between Aryans and dasyus. However, it is unlikely that the Indra-dasyu struggle was thought of as purely historical at this time—it was probably already greatly mythologized. (This distinction between historical and mythological is, of course, entirely imposed by us as outside observers. The poets would certainly have made no such distinction.)

yáthā devā́ ásurān prā́ṇudanta
  yáthéndro dásyūn adhamáṃ támo babādhé
táthā tváṃ kāma máma yé sapátnās
  tā́n asmā́l lokā́t prá ṇudasva dūrám. AV 9.2.18

"In which way the gods drove away the asuras, in which way Indra drove the dasyus away to the lowest darkness, in that way, O Kāma, may you drive those who are my rivals far away from this world."[25]

24. This corresponds to AVP 16.77.6.
25. This corresponds to AVP 16.77.7.

This verse is from the same hymn as the preceding one and is almost identical with it.

ayáṃ me varaṇá úrasi
  rā́jā devó vánaspatiḥ
sá me śátrūn ví bādhatām
  índro dásyūn ivā́surān. AV 10.3.11

"May this *varaṇa* on my breast—the tree (that is) king (and) god—drive away my enemies as Indra (drove away) the dasyus, the asuras."[26]

This is from a charm which involves the use of an amulet made from a *varaṇa* tree. It would be difficult to insist that *ásura–* and *dásyu–* are meant to be synonyms here, but it is clear that they are at least considered to be similar groups. Both are enemies defeated by Indra.

yám ábadhnād bṛ́haspátir
  maṇíṃ phā́laṃ ghṛtaścútam
  ugráṃ khadirám ójase
táṃ bíbhrac candrámā maṇíṃ
  ásurāṇāṃ púro 'jayad
  dānavā́nāṃ hiraṇyáyīḥ
só asmai śríyam íd duhe
  bhū́yobhūyeḥ śváḥśvas téna
  tváṃ dviṣató jahi. AV 10.6.10

"The amulet, the plowshare, the ghee-dripping, fearsome, *khadira*, which Bṛhaspati bound on for strength, bearing that amulet the moon conquered the fortresses of the asuras, the golden (fortresses) of the dānavas. It milks forth fortune for him more and more day by day. With that may you kill (our) enemies."[27]

This is from a charm to be used with a plow-shaped amulet made of *khadira* wood. The asuras here are said to have fortresses (*púr–*). This is suggestive of the dasyus, since such fortresses are characteristic of them. This passage is highly mythologized in

26. The second half of this verse corresponds to the second half of AVP 16.64.12.

27. This corresponds to AVP 16.77.7.

speaking of golden fortresses of the dānavas and in calling the moon their enemy. But it still seems to be older than the Brāhmaṇical passages which speak of an opposition between devas as a whole and asuras as a whole. Syntactically *dānavā́nām* could either be in apposition to *ásurāṇām* or be in a second clause. Thus it is unclear whether asuras and dānavas are the same group or two different, but similar groups.

There are also a couple of verses which say that the asuras were defeated at some ancient time—"in the beginning" (*ágre*).

sárve devā́ atyā́yantu
  tríṣandher ā́hutiḥ priyā
sandhā́ṃ mahatī́ṃ rakṣata
  yáyā́gre ásurā jitāḥ. AV 11.12.15 (11.10.15)

"Let all the gods come over here. The offering is dear to Triṣandhi. Protect the great alliance by which the asuras were conquered in the beginning."

This verse is from a prayer to Triṣandhi for help in battle. I have no idea what the alliance (*sandhā́–*) was by which the asuras were conquered, but this apparently took place at the beginning of time (unless *ágre* has some more mundane reference point connected with a ritual). Thus, the verse seems to treat the defeat of the asuras as a primordial mythological event.

yád adó devā́ ásurāṃs
  tváyā́gre nirákurvata
tátas tvám ádhy oṣadhe
  'pāmārgó ajāyathāḥ. AV 4.19.4

"When there in the beginning the gods drove away the asuras by means of you, then, O plant, you were born as *apāmārga*."[28]

This verse is from a charm which involves the *apāmārga* plant. In some other verses of the AV the hostile side of the asuras is hardly mentioned, but they are clearly referred to as a distinct class of beings.

28. This corresponds to AVP 2.25.4.

kévalīndrāya duduhé hí gṛṣṭír
vásaṃ pīyū́ṣaṃ prathamáṃ dúhānā
áthātarpayac catúraś caturdhā́
devā́n manuṣyā̀m̐ ásurān utá ṛ́ṣīn. RV 8.9.24

"Since the young cow alone gave forth milk for Indra at his will the first beestings, being milked, thus she gratified in four ways the four —gods, men, asuras, and seers."[29]

The asuras are named here as one of four distinct classes of beings. The young cow is probably Virāj as in 8.13.1-4 below.

vaśā́m evā́mṛ́tam āhur
vaśā́ṃ mṛtyúm úpāsate
vaśédáṃ sárvam abhavad
devā́ manuṣyā̀ ásurāḥ pitára ṛ́ṣayaḥ. AV 10.10.26

"They call the cow immortality; they worship the cow as death. The cow became this world—gods, men, asuras, *pitṛs*, seers."[30]

This verse is from a hymn praising the cow. Again we find asuras in a list of types of beings. The list is the same as in the previous verse except for the insertion of *pitáraḥ*.

sód akrāmat sā́ 'surān ā́gacchat tā́m ásurā úpāhvayanta mā́ya éhī́ti. tásyā virócanaḥ prā́hrādir vatsá ā́sīd ayaspātráṃ pā́tram. tā́ṃ dvímūrdhā 'rtvyò 'dhok tā́ṃ māyā́m evā́dhok. tā́ṃ māyā́m ásurā úpa jīvanty upajīvanī́yo bhavati yá eváṃ véda. AV 8.13. 1-4 (8.10.22)

"She ascended; she came to the asuras. The asuras called to her, 'O Māyā, come.' Virocana the son of Prahrāda was her calf. The metal vessel was the vessel. Dvimūrdhan the son of Ṛtu milked her. Thus he milked Māyā. The asuras subsist upon that Māyā. He who knows this becomes one to be subsisted upon."[31]

This is a prose passage from a very late section of the AV. It is typical of many Brāhmaṇa passages. The subject here is Virāj. In the portion of the text following this the same story is repeated

29. This corresponds to AVP 16.20.1.
30. This corresponds to AVP 16.109.6.
31. This corresponds to AVP 16.135.1.

several times with slight changes. She appears to men, who milk cultivation and grain from her, and the story is repeated for various other classes of beings with different products. Thus in this passage asuras again appear as a distinct class of beings. Asuras also appear here as the proper possessors of māyā. Dvimūrdhan, the particular asura named in the passage, does not appear often anywhere else. His name literally means "having two heads."

bṛhadgávā́surebhyó 'dhi devā́n
úpāvartata mahimā́nam icchán
tásmai svápnāya dadhur ā́dhipatyaṃ
trayastriṃśā́saḥ svàr ānaśānā́ḥ. AV 19.56.3

"The one with great cattle, desiring greatness turned from the asuras to the gods. The thirty-three, reaching heaven, granted overlordship to that sleep."[32]

This verse is from the same hymn to sleep from which we took a previous verse.[33] The asuras appear here as a class of beings distinct from the gods whom Sleep rejects in favor of the gods. This is a familiar type of story in the Brāhmaṇas. These texts contain several stories in which some being stands between the gods and the asuras and is lured to the side of the gods in one way or another or in which the gods lure some being away from the asuras and with this new being as ally defeat the asuras.

yā́ṃ medhā́m ṛbhávo vidúr
yā́ṃ medhā́m ásurā vidúḥ
ṛ́ṣayo bhadrā́m medhā́ṃ yā́ṃ vidús
tā́ṃ máyy ā́ veśayāmasi. AV 6.108.3

"The wisdom which the Ṛbhus know, the wisdom which the asuras know, the auspicious wisdom which the seers know, that we cause to enter me."

This verse is from a charm for wisdom. The asuras appear again as a distinct class of beings.

The asuras appear in a few verses clearly as enemies of men or seers rather than of the gods.

32. This corresponds to AVP 3.8.3.
33. See AV 19.56.1 discussed above.

yéna soma sāhantya–
  ásurān randháyāsi naḥ
téna no ádhi vocata. AV 6.7.2

"By what, O conquering Soma, you will make the asuras subject to us, by that bless us."[34]

The asuras appear here as enemies of the people rather than the gods. The verb √*radh*, which appears here in the present causative with *asurān* as its object, appears in the present causative eighteen times in the RV, always with human enemies as its object. Thus it seems most likely that *ásurān* in this verse refers to human enemies. Consequently the verse is probably rather old.

yéna ṛ́ṣayo balám ádyotayan yujā́
  yénā́surāṇām áyuvanta māyā́ḥ
yénāgnínā paṇín índro jigā́ya
  sá no muñcatv áṃhasaḥ. AV 4.23.5

"With whom as ally the seers manifested (their) strength, with whom they warded off the māyās of the asuras, with which Agni Indra conquered the Paṇis, may that one release us from distress."[35]

Since the asuras here are pitted against human ṛṣis, they, too, are likely to be human. Thus *ásura–* again seems to be used in an old meaning referring to human enemies.

áyojālā ásurā māyíno
  'yasmáyaiḥ pā́śair aṅkíno yé cáranti
tā́ṃs te randhayāmi hárasā jātavedaḥ
  sahásrarṣṭiḥ sapátnān pramṛṇán pāhi vájraḥ. AV 19.66.1.

"The māyā-possessing asuras who have metal nets, who wander about having hooks with nooses made of metal, these I make subject to you with the flame, O Jātavedas. May you, the vajra having one thousand spears, protect (us) crushing our rivals."[36]

34. This corresponds to AVP 19.3.11.
35. This corresponds to AVP 4.33.5.
36. This corresponds to AVP 16.150.5. I was unable to recognize any meter, so I divided the pādas following Bloomfield's *Concordance*. Maurice Bloomfield, *A Vedic Concordance*, Harvard Oriental Series, vol. 10, 1906, reprint (Delhi: Motilal Banarsidass, 1964).

This is a one-verse hymn to Agni, so there is no context to help explain it. The asuras with their metal implements could be historical human enemies against whom the people fought with fire. But the description could also fit mythological demons against whom incantations accompanied by the ritual use of fire are directed. I see no basis for a certain decision here. The second alternative sounds *a priori* more plausible, but the scarcity of clear references to asuraṣ as demonic beings rather than rivals of the gods weakens its acceptability. The occurrence of the verb √*radh* in the present causative also suggests that the context of this verse is human.

In some verses the asuras appear as some type of malevolent beings.

nīcáiḥ khananty ásurā
  arusrā́ṇam idám̐ mahát
tád āsrāvásya bheṣajám̐
  tád u rógam anīnaśat. AV 2.3.3

"The asuras dig down this great wound-healer; that is the remedy of discharge; that destroyed the disease."

This verse is from a charm to prevent excessive discharges from the body. The asuras here are apparently credited with having buried the means of cure. The following verse makes it clear that this was a malevolent act.

ásurās tvā ny àkhanan
  devā́s tvód avapan púnaḥ
vātī́kṛtasya bheṣajī́m
  átho kṣiptásya bheṣajī́m. AV 6.109.3

"The asuras dug you in; the gods dug you up again, a cure for *vātīkṛta*, likewise a cure for a missile wound."[37]

This verse is from a charm dealing with the curative property of a certain herb. *Vātīkṛta* is the name of some disease it cures. The asuras are credited with having buried this herb, but it is the gods, their usual rivals, who dig it up again.

37. This corresponds to AVP 19.27.10.

Summary of Plural Occurrences and Conclusions

We have now seen all the occurrences of *ásura-* in the AV. The plural ranges through a wide spectrum of meanings. In a few verses asuras appear as human enemies (AV 6.7.2, 4.23.5, 19.66.1). In several other verses they are enemies —whether human or supernatural is often unclear—who are opposed by Indra (AV 2. 27.3, 2.27.4, 6.65.3, 8.5.3, 11.7.7, 19.13.1, 10.3.11). These verses are especially interesting because they seem to be transitional between the earlier and later meanings of *ásura-*. The earlier meaning is evidenced in the fact that in many of these verses *ásura-* could still refer to human enemies. That these asuras are opposed by Indra and not all the gods together also reflects the older meaning of *ásura-*. (When we examine the dasyus and dāsas later we shall see that they are human enemies of the Aryans who are characteristically opposed by Indra.) In fact in several of these verses in which the asuras are opposed by Indra, the word *dásyu-* or *dāsá-* could be substituted for *ásura-* without substantially changing the meaning of the verse. Yet in many of these verses the asuras could also be understood as supernatural enemies of the gods. Of course the poet used the word with a definite meaning in mind, probably the older one in most cases, but the fact that it is difficult for us to decide which meaning was intended shows just how close this older meaning was to the newer one in certain contexts. In several other verses of the AV *ásura-* appears in the meaning it has later throughout the Brāhmaṇas—a group of supernatural being opposed to the gods. Thus in some cases the asuras appear as enemies who oppose all the gods (AV 12.1.5, 10.3.2, 9.2.17, 9.2.18, 8.13.1-4, 19.56.3). And in some verses the asuras seem to be a clearly defined group of beings distinct from other such well defined groups (AV 6.100.3, 8.9.24, 10.10.26, 8.13.1-4, 19.56.3, 6.108.3).

Appendix on Ásura- in the AVP

The verses containing *ásura-* which are in the AVP but not in the AV are problematical due to the terrible condition of the manuscript on which one must depend for most of the text. Two of the verses which the *VVRI Index* lists as containing *ásura-* do not in fact contain this word when the text is more carefully examined.[38]

38. AVP 1.98.1 and 4.70.2.

Ten more of them are impossible to translate due to the corrupt state of the text.[39] Some sense can be made of the remaining nine if we accept Barret's emendations of the manuscript readings. I shall quote these texts with his emendations, except for texts from Books One– Four which I shall quote from Bhattacharyya's edition of the Orissan manuscripts.

Only one verse in this group seems to use *ásura–* with a good connotation. This is also the only verse in this group in which *ásura–* appears in the singular.

asuro 'sīndrāṇām
  āyuṣmān śataśāradaḥ
sa indra iva deveṣu
  tviṣīmān viśa ā vada. AVP 10.3.6[40]

"You are the asura of Indras, life-possessing for one hundred years. May you, like Indra among the gods, energetic, speak to the clans."

Here the "asura of Indras" seems to refer to a great leader of clans, a lord of lords, who is compared with Indra.

In at least four of these verses asuras appear as enemies of some sort.

ayam agan phalgumaṇir
  balena baladāḥ saha
yenendro dasyūnāṃ vīrān
  asurāṇām avāsṛjat. AVP 19.31.8[41]

"Here has come a reddish jewel which gives power together with power, with which Indra scattered the heroes of the dasyus, of the asuras."

Here we find *ásura–* and *dásyu–* side by side in the same case. At the very least it is clear that the poet is comparing Indra's killing

39. AVP 6.2.6, 7.3.9, 8.12.5, 8.16.8, 11.5.11, 15.23.1, 19.52.15, 20.46.5, 20.48.7, 20.54.2.

40. The quoted text for all verses from books 5-20 of the AVP are Barret's emended text. The manuscript here reads: asurasīndrānāmāyuṣmān śataśārada / sa indrīva deveṣu tviṣīmāṅ viśā vada.

41. The manuscript reads: āyam agaṃ phālgumaṇir balena baladā saha yenendro dasyūnāṃ vīrān asurāṇām avāsṛjat.

the dasyus and his killing the asuras. But the verse seems to do more than just compare these two groups of enemies. The words may even be in apposition, in which case the poet is identifying asuras and dasyus. Such an identification fits perfectly into the history of the development of *ásura–* that I am attempting to establish.

yathendrāyāsurān
  arandhayad vṛhaspatiḥ
evā tvam agne aśvatthān
  amūn amayam ihā naya prāḥ. AVP 9.25.14[42]

"As Bṛhaspati delivered the asuras to Indra, may you, O Agni, bring these sacred fig trees.?.."[43]

Here the asuras are depicted as enemies of Indra.

yad indro agre asurān jaghāna
  tato lakṣmīr ni dadhur martyeṣu
tāsām pāpiṣṭhā nir itaḥ pra hinmaś
  śivā asyai jātavedo ni yaccha. AVP 20.20.3[44]

"When Indra in the beginning killed the asuras, then they placed fortunes among mortals. We drive away from here the most evil of these. Grant to this one the auspicious ones, O Jātavedas."

This verse seems to depict Indra's killing the asuras as a primordial event. We have seen this idea before.

sa vratam acarat so 'nukṛśo bhavati
  tasmād anukṛśo vratacārī bhavati
avaḷuyi kṛśo bhūtvendro
  asurān apāvṛṅkta. AVP 17.28.3[45]

42. The manuscript reads: yathendrāyāsurān arundhayatu vṛhaspatiḥ evā tvam agne aśvatthān amūn amayam ihā naya prāḥ.

43. The last part of the text seems corrupt and is therefore left untranslated.

44. The manuscript reads:...ndro agre asurāṅ jighāna tato lakṣmīn ni dadhur martyeṣu / tāsāṃ pāpiṣthā nudatu pratigmā śivāsye jātavedo ni yaścha.

45. The manuscript reads: sa vratam acārat so nukṛśa bhavati tasmād ananukṛso vratacāri bhavaty avaḷuyi kṛṣo bhūtvendro asurān upāvṛṅktā.

"He performed the vow; he became thin. Thus one who performs the vow becomes thin. Indra becoming thin *avaḷuyi* (?) drove away the asuras."[46]

indra papātha prathamāṃ śataudanāṃ
sapta ṛṣibhyaḥ sumanasyamānaḥ
tayāsurāṇāṃ balam oja ādadhe
tayā ruroha viṣṭhapo devalokān. AVP 14.3.22[47]

"O Indra, you drank the first *śataudanā*, being well-disposed toward the seven seers; with this he took the strength, the power of the asuras; with this he climbed to the high places, the worlds of the gods."

Other verses depict the asuras as a distinct class of beings.

apsarābhyo gandharvebhyo
devebhyo asurebhyaḥ
atho sarvasmāt pāpmanas
tasmān naḥ pāhi jaṅgiḍa. AVP 4.18.4[48]

"From apsarases, gandharvas, gods, asuras—thus from each evil protect us, O Jaṅgiḍa."

The asuras here are depicted as a class of beings from whose evil one needs protection. It is interesting to note that gods are also listed as such a source of evil.

yā ceṣitāsurair
devebhir iṣitā ca yā
atho yā manyor jāyate
'rātiṃ harmi vrahmaṇā. AVP 5.26.9[49]

46. It is unclear what *avaḷuyi* means.

47. The manuscript reads: indra prapātha prathamāś śataudanās sapta ṛṣibhyaḥ / sumanasyamānaḥ bhayāsurāṇāṃ balam oja ādadhe bhayā ruroha viṣṭhapo devalokāṅ.

48. This text is quoted from Bhattacharyya's edition of the Orissan manuscripts.

49. The manuscript reads: yā ceṣitāsurair devebhir iṣitā ca yā / atho yā manyor jāyate rātrīṃ harmi vrahmaṇā.

"I remove with a chant the adversity which is sent by the asuras and which is sent by the gods and that which is born of anger."

This verse depicts asuras much as the last one did. They are a group of beings distinct from the gods who can inflict hardships on men, as can the gods.

One more verse (AVP 11.5.11) mentions the asuras as a group of beings distinct from men and gods in a short list (devān manuṣyān asurān), but the verse itself is untranslatable.[50]

caturdaṃstrān kumbhamuṣkān
dīrghakeśān asṛṅmukhān
alābugandhīn asurān
durṇāmno nāśayāmasi. AVP 17.12.8[51]

"We destroy the asuras who have four tusks, who have jar-shaped scrotums, who have long hair, whose faces are bloody, who smell of the bottle-gourd, who have bad names."

It is unclear whether this is a description of mythological beings or human enemies. Of course, if they are human, the description is exaggerated. However, it is quite clear that these asuras are evil enemies. Some of these same adjectives occur in AV 11.11.17 (11.9.17 in Whitney and Roth's edition) in a hymn for conquering enemies.

sarvā imā oṣadhayaḥ
pṛthivyām adhi niṣṭhitāḥ
athaiva bhadrike tvam
asurebhyo ajāyathāḥ. AVP 1.89.1[52]

"All these plants were put down into the earth. Thus indeed, O Bhadrikā, you were born from the asuras."

This verse seems to go with those we saw in the AV which talked about the asuras burying various herbs and charms, which the gods

50. The manuscript reads: bhadrakṛtaṃ sukṛtam ādiśaṃ bhuva saraṃ bhuvaṃ prati gṛhṇāsy āyatīṃ/ghṛtaśriyaṃ nabhamī saṃvasāno devān manuṣyāṃn asurān atarhi.

51. The manuscript reads: caturdauṣṭrān kumbhamuṣkān dīrghakeśān amunsukhām. alavugandhīn ansurān durnāmno nāśayāmasi.

52. The manuscript reads: sarvā imāṃ uṣadhayaḥ pṛthivyām avi niṣṭhitāḥ athaiva bhadrake tvām asurebhyo ajāyata.

then dug up. Because the herb addressed as Bhadrikā here was planted by the asuras, it is said to be born from them.

yāś ca dāsīr asurāṇāṃ
  manuṣyebhiś ca yāṣ kṛtāḥ
ubhayīs tāṣ parā yanti parā yanti
  parāvato navatiṃ nāvyā ati. AVP 17.15.4[53]

"Both the dāsic (witchcrafts) which are of the asuras and which are made by people, both these go far away across ninety-nine navigable rivers."

This verse seems to be an abridgement of AV 8.5.9, which is quoted and discussed in the next chapter. A comparison with that verse suggests that the noun "witchcrafts" needs to be supplied. (The second *parā yanti* in pāda c should also be omitted in order to translate the verse.) The concurrence of the words *dāsa–* and *ásura–* here is significant. The witchcrafts are simultaneously "dāsic" and "of the asuras."

Conclusions

These verses from the AVP are basically in agreement with what we have already seen. *Ásura–* appears in the AVP in the same variety of meanings it shows in the AV. The first two verses I quoted are of special interest. AVP 10.3.6 speaks of an "asura of indras" (if we can accept Barret's reconstruction of the text). It is hard to see how *ásura–* could mean anything different from "lord" here, although this is rather problematical since it means that *ásura–* is used in an early meaning while *indra–* is used in a late meaning. AVP 19.31.8 seems to equate—or at least compare—asuras and dasyus. This could occur when the connotation of *ásura–* had shifted from "lord" to "enemy lord" to "enemy." The last verse quoted (AVP 17.15.4) is also significant because it speaks of witchcrafts which are "dāsic" and also "of the asuras." Such verses are very suggestive, but this evidence should be accepted cautiously since the texts of the AVP are so corrupt.

53. The manuscript reads: yaś ca dāsīr asurāṇāṃ manuṣyebhyaś ca yāṣ kṛtāḥ ubhe hastās parā yanti parā yanti parāvatiṃ navatiṃ nāvyāti. I made one further emendation that Barret did not suggest. I changed manuṣyebhyas to manuṣyebhis.

CHAPTER VII

DERIVATIVES AND COMPOUNDS OF *ÁSURA–* IN THE ATHARVA VEDA

I turn now to the derivatives and compounds of *ásura–* in the AV and AVP.

The adjective *āsurá–* occurs once.

yát te várco jātavedo
  bṛhád bhávaty ā́huteḥ
yā́vat sū́ryasya várca
  āsurásya ca hastínaḥ
tā́van me aśvínā várca
  ā́ dhattāṃ púṣkarasrajā. AV 3.22.4

"What exalted splendor becomes yours from the oblation, O Jātavedas, however much splendor there is of the sun and of the āsuric elephant, may the lotus-garlanded Aśvins give me that much splendor."

This verse is from a charm for splendor. It is an elephant who is called āsuric. This is quite intelligible if *ásura–* means "lord." The elephant is thus said to be "lordly" or "majestic." Such an interpretation is supported by verse six of this same hymn where the elephant is called the superior of the wild beasts.[1]

The feminine form of this adjective, *āsurī́–*, appears four times —three times as a noun and once as an adjective.

suparṇó jātáḥ prathamás
  tásya tváṃ pittáṃ āsitha
tád āsurī́ yudhā́ jitā́
  rūpáṃ cakre vánaspátīn. AV 1.24.1

"The eagle was born first; you were its gall. Then the āsurī, conquered in battle, made (her) form into trees."[2]

1. hastī́ mṛgā́ṇāṃ suṣádām atiṣṭhā́van babhū́va hí. AV. 3.22.6ab.
2. This corresponds to AVP 1.26.1.

Bloomfield emends *jitā́* to *jitvā́* and translates "The Āsurī having conquered this (gall) gave it to the trees for their colour."[3] The verse is from a charm to cure leprosy performed with the help of a plant. But the nature of the āsurī and her action remains obscure.

āsurī́ cakre prathamā́–
  idáṃ kilāsabheṣajám
  idáṃ kilāsanā́śanam
ánīnaśat kilā́saṃ
  sárūpām akarat tvácam. AV 1.24.2

"The āsurī first made this remedy against leprosy, this remover of leprosy. It has caused the leprous spot to disappear; it made the skin of even color."[4]

This verse follows the preceding one in the AV. The identity of the āsurī is still uncertain, but crediting her with the creation of this herbal remedy is reminiscent of verses we have already seen in the AV which tell of remedies buried by the asuras and later dug up by the gods.[5]

yénā nicakrá āsurī́–
  índraṃ devébhyas pári
ténā ní kurve tvā́m aháṃ
  yáthā té 'sāni súpriyā. AV 7.39.2 (7.38.2)

"By which the āsurī brought Indra down from among the gods, by that I bring you down, so that I may be very dear to you."[6]

This verse is from a charm used by a woman with a certain herb to obtain the love of a man. There is an allusion here to a myth in which an āsurī entices Indra with this herb. The nature of this āsurī is unclear, but the word most likely refers to a female member of the class of beings called asuras, i.e., the late meaning of *ásura*.–

yā́ḥ kṛtyā́ āṅgirasī́r
  yā́ḥ kṛtyā́ āsurī́r

3. Bloomfield, *Atharva-Veda*, pp. 16 and 168-9.
4. This corresponds to AVP 1.26.2.
5. See AV 2.3.3 and 6.109.3, which are quoted and discussed in the last chapter.
6. The first line of this verse corresponds to AVP 20.30.7 c.

yā́ḥ kṛtyā́ḥ svayáṃkṛtā
  yā́ u cānyébhir ā́bhṛtāḥ
ubháyīs tā́ḥ párā yantu
  parāváto navatíṃ nāvyā̀ áti. AV 8.5.9

"The witchcrafts that are Aṅgirasic, the witchcrafts that are āsuric, the witchcrafts that are self-made, and those which are produced by others—let these of both kinds go away to the distances across ninety navigable (rivers)."[7]

This verse is from a hymn to a certain type of amulet. *Āsurī́*- appears as an adjective modifying *kṛtyā*– (witchcraft). It relates to *ásura*– in the late meaning of a class of hostile beings. The verse is very similar to AVP 17.15.4, which was quoted and discussed in the last chapter, and helps us to understand the meaning of that verse.

The compound *asuramāyā́*– occurs once in the AV.

yénā śravasyavaś cáratha
  devā́ ivāsuramāyáyā
śúnāṃ kapír iva dū́ṣaṇo
  bándhurā kābavásya ca. AV 3.9.4

"Since you wander, O ones seeking glory, like gods with asuramāyā, like the ape, the spoiler of dogs, and with the binder of the *kābava*."[8]

This verse is from a charm which is apparently directed against various demons. My translation of the second half of this verse is uncertain. I have followed Whitney. Bloomfield translated instead: "the fastening (of the amulet) is destructive to the kâbava, as the ape to the dog."[9] I find his translation suspect because it ignores the word *ca*. Neither translation makes much sense. The first half of the verse suggests that these beings are able to wander like gods because of their asuramāyā.

The compound *ásurakṣiti*– occurs in only one hymn in the AV.

7. This corresponds to AVP 16.27.9.
8. This corresponds to AVP 3.7.5.
9. Bloomfield, *Atharva Veda*, p. 67.

yám ábadhnād bŕ̥haspátir
devébhyo ásurakṣitim
sá mā' 'yáṃ maṇír ā́gamad
rásena sahá várcasā. AV 10.6.22

"The asura-destroying (amulet) which Bṛhaspati bound on for the gods, that amulet has come here to me together with essence, with splendor."[10]

Ásura– in this compound must mean "demon" or "hostile being."

The compound *asurakṣáyaṇa–* occurs three times in the AV, all in the same hymn.

bŕ̥haspátir āṅgirasá
ŕ̥ṣayo bráhmasaṃśitāḥ
asurakṣáyaṇaṃ vadháṃ
tríṣandhiṃ divy ā́śrayan. AV 11.12.10 (11.10.10)

"Aṅgirasic Bṛhaspati (and) the seers sharpened by brahman set up in the sky Triṣandhi, the asura-destroying weapon."

This verse and the next two verses are from a hymn to *Triṣandhi* which is used as a charm for slaying enemies. *Ásura–* appears in the compound with the meaning "demon" or "hostile being."

sárvaṃl lokā́nt sám ajayan
devā́ ā́hutyānáyā
bŕ̥haspátir āṅgirasó
vájraṃ yáṃ ásiñcata–
asurakṣáyaṇaṃ vadhám. AV 11.12.12 (11.10.12)

"The gods conquered all the worlds by means of that oblation—the vajra, the asura-destroying weapon which Aṅgirasic Bṛhaspati poured out."

Ásura– appears again in the same compound with the same meaning of "demon" or "hostile being."

10. This verse corresponds to AVP 16.44.5. Verses 23-28 repeat the first three lines, but change the fourth, thus increasing the list of things that come with the amulet.

bŕ̥haspátir āṅgirasó
vájraṃ yám ásiñcata-
asurakṣáyaṇaṃ vadhám
ténāhám amū́ṃ sénāṃ
ní limpāmi bṛhaspate-
amítrān hanmy ójasā. AV 11.12.13 (11.10.13)

"With that vajra, the asura-destroying weapon which Aṅgirasic Bṛhaspati poured out, I blot out that army, O Bṛhaspati; I kill the enemies with force."

Half of this verse is identical with the preceding verse, and *ásura–* appears in the same meaning.

These are all the occurrences of derivatives and compounds of *ásura–* in the AV. There are five more verses in the AVP which contain derivatives or compounds of *ásura–* but which do not appear in the AV. Three of these are untranslatable due to the corrupt state of the text.[11] The other two contain the words *āsurá–* and *asuryà–*.

indreṇa dattaṃ balam āsurābhyāṃ
śṛṅga etu śchlāvatā ye ca tubhyam
tvaṃ nudasva kaṇvā aśivā ajuṣṭā
adhā gṛhāṇāṃ gṛhapā tvam eṣām. AVP 19.36.15

"Strength is given to the two āsuras by Indra. . . . May you drive away the two inauspicious unsatisfactory *kaṇvas*. Now you are the house-protector of these houses."[12]

The second line of this verse makes no sense and is therefore omitted from the translation. The remainder is translatable, but the meaning is far from clear. The two āsuras are apparently demons, but it is unclear why Indra gave them strength. (If *indreṇa dattaṃ* is emended to *indreṇādattaṃ*, then it could be translated "Indra took away the strengths. . . .")

11. AVP 15.18.6, 17.13.6, and 17.28.2.

12. The text is given with Barret's emendations. The manuscript reads: indreṇa dattaṃ balam āsurabhyāṃ sṛṅgaituśchālvatāye ca tubhyam. taṃ nūdasya kaṇvā śivāṃ juṣṭādhā gṛhāṇāṃ gṛhapātvam eṣam.

somārudrā dhārayethāṃ suvīryaṃ
pra vām iṣṭvā varam aśnavātai
yuvaṃ no dhattam iha bheṣajāni
pra yacchataṃ vṛṣaṇā jetvāni. AVP 1.109.3

"O Somārudrā, maintain your good heroism. May one worshipping you two acquire a boon. May you give us here remedies. Give us manly things to be gained."

The text quoted here is from the Orissan recension of the AVP and contains no derivative of *ásura–*. However, the Kashmirian recension reads: sómārudrā dhāráyetham asuryáṃ jívāsiṣṭvā́v áram aśnuvā́tai / yuvám no dhattám iha bheṣajā́ni prá yacchataṃ vṛ́ṣaṇā jéttāni. There are obviously some corruptions in this text, but it is basically the same as the Orissan recension, only with *suvīryam* ("good heroism") replaced by *asuryam*. This same pāda (with *asuryam*) also occurs at RV 6.74 1a, MS 4.11.2a, and KS 11.12.1. Thus the Orissan manuscripts reflect an innovation in substituting *suvīryam* for *asuryam*. Such a substitution should have been quite simple for the poets since the words have the same metrical structure and very similar meanings. "Good heroism" is not very different from "lordliness," especially since (as we have seen) this lordliness includes having a fighting force of heroes(*vīrā́ḥ*).

Summary and Conclusions

Many of these verses are obscure, and it is difficult to get any clear picture of the precise connotations of derivatives and compounds of *ásura–* in these texts. Only two verses seem to use the words with a good connotation. AV 3. 22.4 speaks of an āsuric elephant in a complimentary way, and the Kashmirian recension of AVP 1.109.3 has *asuryam* in place of *suvīryam* in the Orissan recension. The remaining occurrences of derivatives and compounds of *ásura–* in the AV and AVP seem to have a generally bad connotation. If the connotation is not clearly bad, it is at least questionable as in AV 1.24.2 in which an āsurī is said to have first made a cure for leprosy. The connotation here may not be bad at all, but it does imply some possible dealings with magical practices, that is, some activities which are at least not clearly good. There is also mention in one verse of asuramāyā as the means by which certain beings (probably demons) are able to wander like gods (AV 3.9.4).

CHAPTER VIII

ÁSURA– IN THE SĀMA VEDA SAṂHITĀ, THE ṚGVEDA KHILA, AND THE MANTRA PORTIONS OF THE YAJUR VEDA

I turn now to the occurrences of *ásura*– in the remaining metrical Vedic texts—the Sāma Veda Saṃhitā, the Ṛgveda Khila, and the mantra portions of the Yajur Veda.

Ásura– occurs with a good connotation four times in these texts.

tánūnápād ásuro viśvávedā
devó devéṣu deváḥ
pathó anaktu mádhvā ghṛténa. VS 27.12

"May Tanūnapāt, asura, all-knower, god, god among gods, anoint the paths with honey (and) with ghee."[1]

This verse is from a hymn to Agni, and he is the asura here. As we have seen Agni is frequently called asura in the older literature.

víbhāti ketúr aruṇáḥ purástād
ādityó víśvā bhúvanāni sárvā
sugáṃ nú pánthām ánveti prajānán
pitā́ devā́nām ásuro vipaścít. MS 4.14.14

"Āditya, the red banner, lightens up the whole world. The knowing, inspired father, asura of the gods, follows indeed the easy-going path."

Āditya has not been called asura in any previous verses, but it is not surprising to find this epithet applied to him. The phrase "asuras of the gods" did occur once before in RV 7.65.2 referring to Mitrāvaruṇā.

1. This verse is found in MS 2.12.6, but with *devébhyo devayā́nān* in place of *devéṣu deváḥ*. It is also in TS 4.1.8.1, but with *pathá ā́nakti* in place of *pathó anaktu*. AV 5.27.ld & 2b also corresponds to this, but with more variations. It is in the Kāṇva recension of the White Yajur Veda at VSK 29. 2.2. The corresponding verses and variations given throughout this and the following chapter are from Bloomfield's *Concordance*, but the wording has been double checked in the texts themselves except for the VSK for which no text was available to me.

várūtrīṃ tváṣṭur váruṇasya nā́bhim
  áviṃ jajñānā́ṁ rájasaḥ párasmāt
mahī́ṁ sāhasrī́m ásurasya māyā́m
  ágne mā́ hiṁsīḥ paramé vyòman. VS 13.44

"O Agni, harm not in the highest heaven the guardian of Tvaṣṭṛ, the navel of Varuṇa, the ewe being born from the highest region, the great thousand (–fold) māyā of the asura."[2]

This is from a hymn to Agni. It is unclear exactly whom the poet is asking Agni not to harm, but the context of the verse in the TS suggests that this refers to some victim used in the fire ritual. It remains uncertain who the asura is.

índraś ca marútaś ca krayā́yopótthitó
  'suraḥ paṇyámāno
  mitráḥ krītó
víṣṇuḥ śipiviṣṭá ūrā́v ā́sanno
  víṣṇur narándhiṣaḥ. VS 8.55

"Both Indra and the Maruts when put up for sale, the asura when being bargained for, Mitra when bought, Viṣṇu *śipiviṣṭa* when seated on the thigh, Viṣṇu the delighter-of-men (?)."[3]

This verse is from a portion of the text dealing with the Soma ritual. It identifies Soma with several different deities. It is unclear which deity *ásura–* refers to here. One might take it to refer to Varuṇa since it occurs in a list next to Mitra, but since Varuṇa, asura, and Mitra occur in the version of this list that occurs in the TS, this is unlikely. However, *ásura–* still should not be taken as a proper name here, since it never seems to be a proper name elsewhere.[4]

2. This verse is also found in VSK 14.4.7, KS 16.17, MS 2.7.17, and TS 4.2.10.3, but the MS has the first two words reversed and the KS has for the fourth pāda: tā́m agne héḍaḥ pári te vṛṇaktu.

3. Pādas *a*, *b*, and *d* correspond to VSK 7.9.2 and 3, but that text has *urā* instead of *urāv*. Similar passages also occur in KS 34.14 and TS 4.4.9.1, but with considerable differences. The KS text reads: bhagaḥ paṇyamāno 'suraḥ krītaś śapiviṣṭa. The TS text reads: váruṇa úpanaddhó 'suraḥ krīyámāṇo mitráḥ krītáḥ śipiviṣṭá ā́sādito narándhiṣaḥ prohyámāṇo.

4. Two verses in the RV that have been interpreted by some scholars as using *ásura*- as a proper name were discussed previously. See the discussions of RV 5.63.3 and 5.83.6 in chapter 2.

devā́nāṃ ca ṛ́ṣīṇāṃ ca–
ásurāṇāṃ ca pūrvajám
mahādevám̐ sahasrākṣám̐
śívam āvā́hayāmy ahám. MS 2.9.1

"I invoke the auspicious thousand-eyed great god, first-born of gods and seers and asuras."

This is from a hymn directed to Rudra. The asuras seems to be a group of beings distinct from gods and seers. We saw similar lists of gods, men, asuras, and seers in AV 8.9.24; gods, men, asuras, pitṛs, and seers in AV 10.10.26; and Ṛbhus, asuras, and seers in AV 6.108.3.

yásyāṃ pū́rve pūrvajanā́ vicakriré
yásyāṃ devā́ ásurān abhyávartayan
yā́ bibhárti bahudhā́ prāṇád éjat
sā́ no bhū́miḥ pūrvapéyaṃ dadhātu. MS 4.14.11

"On whom the people of old formerly spread out, on whom the gods overcame the asuras, who bears in many ways what breathes (and) what moves, may that earth give us the first drink."[5]

The pādas of this verse appear in a slightly different order in the AV in a hymn to the earth. The verse locates the earth as a place where the gods defeated the asuras.

índrasya bāhū́ sthávirau yúvānāv
anādhṛṣyáu supratī́kāv asahyáu
táu yuñjīta prathamáu yóga ā́gate
yā́bhyāṃ jitám ásurāṇām̐ sáho mahát. SV 2.1219

"The two arms of Indra are firm, young, invincible, beautiful, unconquerable. When the conjuncture comes, may he yoke these two excellent ones by which the great power of the asuras has been conquered."

In this verse from the Sāma Veda the asuras appear as a group of hostile beings, enemies of Indra.

5. This verse corresponds to AV 12.1.2ab (which is quoted and discussed in chapter 6), 3d, and 4c.

ekāṣṭakā́ tápasā tápyamānā
jajā́na gárbhaṃ mahimā́nam índram
téna dásyūn vy àsahanta devā́
hantā́ 'surāṇām abhavac chácībhiḥ. TS 4.3.11.3h

"Ekāṣṭakā doing penance with tapas gave birth to a great embryo, Indra; by him the gods overcame the dasyus. He became a slayer of asuras with his strengths."

This verse is interesting because of the close proximity of dasyus and asuras. The gods overcame the dasyus by means of Indra, and he became a slayer of asuras. But the AV version of this verse makes the relation between dasyus and asuras even closer. The first half of AV 3.10.12 is the same as this verse, but the second half reads: téna devā́ vy àsahanta śátrūn hantā́ dásyūnām abhavac chácīpatiḥ ("By him the gods overcame their enemies. The lord of strength became a slayer of dasyus."). Thus this text has *dásyu-* in place of *ásura-*. This suggests that the two words had a very similar meaning for the poets.

yé rūpā́ṇi pratimuñcámānā
ásurāḥ sántaḥ svadháyā cáranti
parāpúro nipúro yé bháranty
agníṣ ṭā́m̐l lokā́t práṇudāty asmā́t. VS 2.30

"May Agni drive from this world these who being asuras roam at will assuming (various) shapes, who bear great bodies (?) or small bodies (?)."[6]

The asuras appear here as demonic enemies of Agni.

agnáye kavyavā́hanāya svā́hā
sómāya pitṛmáte svā́hā
ápahatā ásurā rákṣāṁsi vediṣádaḥ. VS 2.29

"For Agni, who bears what is for the wise (?), *svāhā*! For Soma, accompanied by the fathers, *svāhā*! The asuras are slain, the rakṣases, the ones who sit near the altar."[7]

Here asuras are either very closely compared with or identified with rakṣases.

6. This corresponds to VSK 2.7.2 and is somewhat similar to AV 18.2.28.
7. This corresponds to VSK 2.7.1.

ugrāyudhāḥ pramatinaḥ pravīrā
  māyāvino balino micchamānāḥ
ye devā asurān parābhavan tāṃs
  tvaṃ vajreṇa maghavan ni vāraya. RVKh 2.14.11

"(They) who are gods, having powerful weapons, wise, very heroic, possessing māyā, strong, harming, overcame these asuras. May you destroy (the asuras) with your vajra, O generous one."

Summary and Conclusions

These are all of the occurrences of *ásura–* in the remaining mantra portions of the Saṃhitās. They generally confirm our previous findings. But there are some noteworthy features. TS 4.3.11.3h offers us a verse whose AV variant has *dásyu–* in place of *ásura–*. This suggests a very close connection between these two words. In fact it will be argued later that to a large extent *ásura–* replaces *dásyu–* in the later texts. If the TS verse is later than the AV verse (and there is no way to demonstrate this), then such a development has literally occurred here. Another noteworthy point is that in VS 2.29 asuras are practically identified with rakṣases. Such identification is rare in the texts examined up to this point, but it becomes quite common by the time of the Śatapatha Brāhmaṇa. It is also noteworthy that *ásura–* seems to be used with good connotations in all four of its occurrences in the singular and with a bad connotation in all of its plural occurrences except perhaps MS 2.9.1, in which asuras are simply spoken of as a distinct class of beings with no explicit mention of any hostility.

CHAPTER IX

DERIVATIVES AND COMPOUNDS OF *ÁSURA*- IN THE SĀMA VEDA SAṂHITĀ, THE ṚGVEDA KHILA, AND THE MANTRAS OF THE YAJUR VEDA

I turn next to the derivatives and compounds of *ásura*- in the Ṛgveda Khila, the Sāma Veda Saṃhitā, and the mantras of the Yajur Veda.

There is only one occurrence of the noun *asuryàm*.

agnér ánīkam apá ā́viveśa-
  apā́ṃ nápāt pratirákṣann asuryàm
dámedame samídhaṃ yakṣy agne
  práti te jihvā́ ghṛtáṃ úccaraṇyat svā́hā. VS 8.24

"Apām Napāt has entered the waters, the face of Agni, protecting asuraness. Offer the kindling stick in each house, O Agni. May your tongue stretch out to the ghee, svāhā."[1]

Both Keith and Eggeling translate this verse with a pejorative connotation for *asuryàm* ("protecting from the power of the demons"), but I see no need for this.[2] The phrase *rákṣamāṇā asuryàm* ("protecting asuraness") has already been seen once in ṚV 2.27.4 where it was applied to the Ādityas.

The adjective *asuryà*- occurs once.

asuryā̀ nā́ma té lokā́
  andhéna támasā́vṛtāḥ
tā́ṃs té prétyā́pigacchanti
  yé ké cātmaháno jánāḥ. VS 40.3

1. This verse also occurs in VSK 9.4.2, KS 4.13, MS 1.3.39 and TS 1.4.45. 1-2, but the MS has *pratirákṣad asurayā̀n* in place of *pratirákṣann asuryàm* and the KS, TS, and MS all omit *svā́hā*.

2. Arthur Berriedale Keith, *The Veda of the Black Yajus School entitled Taittiriya Sanhita*, Harvard Oriental Series, vols. 18 and 19, 1914, reprint (Delhi: Motilal Banarsidass, 1967), vol. 1, p. 66. Julius Eggeling, *The Śatapatha- Brāhmaṇa*, 5 vols., Sacred Books of the East, vols. 12, 26, 41, 43, 44; 1882, 1885, 1894, 1897, 1900; reprint (Delhi: Motilal Banarsidass, 1972), vol. 2, p. 381.

"These worlds covered with blind darkness are called asuric to which people who kill themselves go when they die."[3]

This verse states that those who commit suicide go to the world of the asuras (obviously an undesirable place) rather than the world of the Pitṛs. It is from the portion of the VS which is also called Īśā Upaniṣad and is clearly much later than the rest of the VS.

Āsurá– occurs three times in these texts, and always in reference to Namuci.

yám aśvínā námucer āsurā́d
ádhi sárasvaty ásunod indriyā́ya
imám tám̐ śukrám mádhumantam índum̐
sómam̐ rā́jānam ihá bhakṣayāmi. VS 19.34

"I drink here King Soma, this clear, sweet drop, which the Aśvins (took) from āsuric Namuci, (and) Sarasvatī pressed for Indra's strength."[4]

Here *āsurá–* is applied to Namuci. This usage is already found in RV 10.131.4.

aśvínā havír indriyám
námucer dhiyā́ sárasvatī
ā́ śukrám āsurā́d vásu
maghám índrāyājabhrire. VS 20.67

"The Aśvins (and) Sarasvatī with the vision brought the Indraic oblation from Namuci, the clear treasure from the āsuric one, the gift for Indra."[5]

Here again Namuci is called āsuric.

3. This verse appears as VSK 40.1.3, but with *pretyābhigacchanti* instead of *pretyāpigacchanti*.

4. This verse also appears in VSK 21.3.3, MS 3.11.7, KS 38.2, and TB 2.6.3.1, but KS and TB have *ásanod* instead of *ásunod*.

5. This verse appears in VSK 2.7.1, MS 3.11.4, KS 38.9, and TB 2.6.13.1 with the following variations: MS has *madyám* for *maghám* and all four of these texts have *índrāya jabhrire* for *índrāyājabhrire*.

yám aśvínā sárasvatī
havíṣéndram ávardhayan
sá bibheda baláṃ magháṃ
námucāv āsuré sácā. VS 20.68

"Indra, whom the Aśvins (and) Sarasvatī increased with an oblation, split open the strong gift at (the place of) āsuric Namuci."[6]

It is unclear what splitting open the strong gift refers to, and thus the TB reading may be preferable. However, that reading leaves Vala and Namuci associated, and that is not common. Nonetheless, Namuci appears as usual as an āsura opposed to Indra.

The feminine form of the adjective, *āsurī–*, occurs once.

dṛ́ṃhasva devi pṛthivi svastáya
āsurí māyā́ svadháyā kṛtā́si
júṣṭaṃ devébhya idám astu havyám
áriṣṭā tvám úd ihi yajñé asmín. VS 11.69

"Be firm, O goddess earth, for well-being. You are made by nature the āsuric māyā. May this offering be pleasing to the gods. May you go up uninjured in this sacrifice."[7]

Here the earth is said to be āsuric māyā. *Āsurī́–* must have a good connotation in this context.

Asurahán– occurs once in the RVKh.

svastyáyanaṃ tā́rkṣyam áriṣṭanemiṃ
mahádbhūtaṃ vvāyasáṃ devátānām
asuraghnám índrasakhaṃ̐ samátsu
bṛ́had yáśo nā́vam ivā́ ruhema. RVKh 2.4.1

6. This verse appears in VSK 22.7.2, MS 3.11.4, KS 38.9, and TB 2.6. 13.1 with the following variants: MS has *madyam* for *magháṃ*, TB has *valáṃ*, for *baláṃ* and MS, KS, and VSK have *námucā* for *námucāv*. If we take the TB reading and read *valám agháṃ*, then we can translate "Split open evil Vala, " which may make more sense.

7. This verse appears in VSK 12.7.4, MS 2.7.7, KS 16.7, and TS 4.1. 9.2, but *devā́nām* is in place of *devébhya* in TS and *svastáye* in place of *svastáya* in MS.

"May we climb to success, to Tārkṣa Ariṣṭanemi, the great being, bird of the divinities, asura-killer, who has Indra for companion in battles, (and to) great glory, like a ship."

Asurahán– here probably has the same meaning that it did in the RV—that is, "a killer of lords."

Summary and Conclusions

These are all the occurrences of derivatives and compounds of *ásura–* in these texts. They are basically in agreement with our previous findings. It is noteworthy that only two of the seven verses use the term with a good connotation. (VS 8.24. and VS 11.69.)

Chapter X

RAKṢAS– IN THE RV

Ásura– had the basic meaning "lord" in the Indo-Iranian period and continued to have this meaning in the RV. But by the time of the composition of the Brāhmaṇas it had taken on the meaning of "demon" or "anti-god." It is probable that some already extant concept of demon served as a model for at least part of this developing meaning. Therefore, I shall next examine the words *rakṣás*–, *rákṣas*–, *dásyu*–, *dā́sa*–, and *dāsá*– in the RV to see if their meanings show some continuity with the newly developing meaning of *ásura*–. I shall not quote and translate all the occurrences of these words, but shall instead summarize the main facts about them with illustrative quotes and references. In this chapter I shall deal with *rakṣás*– and *rákṣas*–. I do not see much development in the meaning of these terms from the older to the younger parts of the RV, so I shall draw on passages from the whole RV to illustrate the meanings of these words. In my translations and discussions I shall supply the accent mark to make it clear which word is meant.

Rákṣas– is an abstract neuter noun which Grassmann defines as *Beschädigung*. *Rakṣás*– is a masculine derivative of *rákṣas*– and means "having rákṣas." However, the abstract neuter form can be and sometimes is used as a personified form and is then synonymous with the masculine form. Grassmann in fact interprets all but two of the occurrences of the neuter form as equivalent with the masculine form.[1]

Rákṣas– only occurs a few times with a modifying adjective. It is twice said to be growing or increasing (vāvṛdhānám. RV 4.3.14 and 7.104.4), once said to be sneaking up (éṣat RV 10.89.14), once said to be hidden (*grambhīrá*– RV 6.62.9), and once said to have grown great (máhi cid vāvṛdhānáṃ RV 4.3.14).

The operation of rákṣas is also only occasionally made explicit. In RV 3.30.17 rákṣas– seems to refer to the same figure who is called "enemy of brahman" (*brahmadvìṣ*–) later in the verse. In

1. See Grassmann under rákṣas. The exceptions are RV 7.104.23 and 8.60.20

RV 6.62.9 *rákṣase* seems to be in apposition with Ānava of deceitful speech (dróghāya cid vácasa ā́navāya). But RV 7.104.23 gives a better idea of how rákṣas operates. This verse says: "May the rákṣas of the hexing ones not reach us" (mā́ no rákṣo abhí naḍ yātumā́vatām RV 7.104.23). This suggests that the rákṣas is a force which can be sent by a sorcerer to inflict harm on another. RV 7.104.22 links rákṣas with demons (*yātú-*) in various animal forms.

> Kill the yātu in the form of an owl, the yātu in the form of a little owl, the yātu in the form of a dog, the yātu in the form of a cocoo, the yātu in the form of an eagle, the yātu in the form of a vulture. Grind the rakṣas as if with a millstone, O Indra.
>
> (úlūkayātuṃ śuśulū́kayātuṃ jahí śváyātum utá kókayātum / suparṇáyātum utá gṛ́dhrayātuṃ dṛṣádeva prá mṛṇa rákṣa indra. RV 7.104.22)

RV 8.60.20 says: "O one rich in glow, may a rákṣas not enter us, not the yātu of a sorcerer." (mā́ no rákṣa ā́ veśīd āghṛṇīvaso mā́ yātúr yātumā́vatām. RV 8.60.20) It is not certain that *rákṣas-* and *yātú-* are meant to refer to the same being here, but the two at least seem to be closely linked.

It may also help to see what other beings are associated with rákṣas. In some cases these may even be the same as the personified rákṣases. It is often very difficult to determine. If a certain god is invoked to kill X and destroy Y, it is often impossible to tell whether this is two different ways of saying the same thing, and thus X and Y are the same, or whether X and Y are two different types of beings whom the poet wants to be rid of.

Rákṣas is often mentioned along with enemies. Indra is asked to overcome enemies by chopping and smashing them with his hot thunderbolt (*aśani-*) and to kill the rákṣas (sáṃ ghóṣaḥ sṛṇve 'vamáir amítrair jahí ny èṣv aśániṃ tápiṣṭhām / vṛścém adhástād ví rujā sáhasva jahí rákṣo maghavan randháyasva. RV 3.30.16). In RV 5.2.10 after saying that Agni has sharp weapons for killing the rákṣas, the poet says that the adevic enemies do not restrain him (utá svānā́so diví ṣantv agnés tigmā́yudhā rákṣase hántavā́ u / máde cid asya prá rujanti bhā́mā ná varante paribā́dho ádevīḥ. RV 5.2.10). Soma (or possibly Indra) is said to kill the rákṣas and drive away enemies (hánti rákṣo bā́dhate páry árātīr várivaḥ kṛṇván vṛjánasya rā́jā. RV 9.97.10). Soma is asked to purify himself "overcoming the aggressor, warding off rákṣases (and) difficult ways, having a good weapon, (and) having overcome enemies" (sá pavasva sáhamānaḥ pṛtanyū́nt sédhan rákṣāṃsy ápa durgáhāṇi svāyudháḥ sāsahvā́nt soma śátrūn. RV 9.110.12). Agni is invited to strike away scorn and enemies and burn rákṣases everywhere (ghnán mṛdhrā́ny ápa dvíṣo dáhan rákṣāṃsi viśváhā / ágne tigména dīdihi. RV 8.43.26). Scorners are also mentioned along with the rákṣas and enemies in another verse. "(Kill) the rákṣas; kill the scorner. Smash the jawbones of Vṛtra. (Smash) the anger of the enemy lying in wait, O Vṛtra-killer Indra" (ví rákṣo ví mṛ́dho jahi ví vṛtrásya hánū ruja / ví manyúm indra vṛtrahann amítrasyābhidā́sataḥ. RV 10.152.3).

Rákṣas is also sometimes mentioned along with plagues. "Kill the rákṣases (and) ward off plagues" (hatáṃ rákṣāṃsi sédhatam ámīvāḥ. RV 8.35.16. This pāda is also repeated in verses 17 and 18 of this hymn.). "May the plague together with the rákṣas become far away" (ápā́mīvā bhavatu rákṣasā sahá. RV 9.85.1). "Ward off plagues (and) rákṣases" (ápā́mīvām ápa rákṣāṃsi sedha. RV 10.98.12). "Destroying the serpent, wolf, (and) rákṣases, may they keep plagues completely from us" (jambháyantó 'hiṃ vṛ́kaṃ rákṣāṃsi sánemy asmád yuyavann ámīvāḥ. RV 7.38.7). One suspects that rákṣases were thought to cause plagues, but there is no concrete evidence in the RV to prove this.

Rákṣas is found together with sorcerers. "Throw the weapon at the rákṣases, the stone at the sorcerer" (rákṣobhyo vadhám asyatam aśániṃ yātumádbhyaḥ. RV 7.104.25). "May the sorcerer not harm you who are shining against the murderer (and) the rákṣases" (hiṃsráṃ rákṣāṃsy abhí śóśucānaṃ mā́ tvā dabhan yātudhā́nā. RV 10.87.9). "Destroy the sorcerer with heat, O Agni, destroy the rákṣas with flame. Destroy the idol-worshipper (?) with flame, burning up the life-stealer" (párā śṛṇīhi tápasā yātudhā́nān párāgne rákṣo hárasā śṛṇīhi / párārcíṣā mū́radevāñ chṛṇīhi párāsutṛ́po abhí śóśucānaḥ. RV 10.87.14): "May you who have an eye for man spy the rákṣas in the clans. Destroy the three points of this one. O Agni, destroy his ribs with your flame. Chop threefold the root of the sorcerer" (nṛcákṣā rákṣaḥ pári paśya vikṣú tásya trī́ṇi práti śṛṇīhy ágrā / tásyāgne pṛṣṭī́r hárasā śṛṇīhi tredhā́ mū́laṃ yātudhā́nasya vṛśca. RV 10.87.10). This verse is obscure, but it links rákṣas with a sorcerer once again. The rákṣas seems to be the force which the sorcerer sends to inflict harm on others.

Rákṣas also appears occasionally with other evil beings. Indra is asked to smash a demon named Piśāci and each rákṣas (piśáṅga-bhṛṣṭim ambhṛṇáṃ piśā́cim indra sáṃ mṛṇa / sárvaṃ rákṣo ní barhaya. RV 1.133.5). Agni is asked to break up hard distress and kill the great growing rákṣas (práti ṣphura ví ruja vīḍv áṃho jahí rákṣo máhi cid vāvṛdhānáṃ. RV 4.3.14). He is said to overcome the evil adevic māyās and sharpen his horns for piercing the rákṣas (prā́devīr māyā́ḥ sahate durévāḥ śíśīte śṛ́ṅge rákṣase viníkṣe. RV 5.2.9). Indra-Soma are invoked to destroy the rákṣas, the *tamovṛdhaḥ* (those who are increased in darkness or who increase darkness), the witless ones, and the Atrins (índrāsomā tápataṃ rákṣa ubjátaṃ nyàrpayataṃ vṛṣaṇā tamovṛ́dhaḥ / párā sṛṇītam acíto nyòṣataṃ hatáṃ nudéthāṃ ní śiśītam atríṇaḥ. RV 7.104.1). The Soma-pressing stones ward off rákṣases, a bad dream, Nirṛti, (and) each Atrin (grā́vā vádan ápa rákṣāṃsi sedhatu duḥṣvápnyaṃ nírṛtiṃ víśvam atríṇam. RV 10.36.4). Indra-Soma is asked to throw at the evil one the weapon by which he burns down the rákṣas (índrāsomā vartáyataṃ divó vadháṃ sáṃ pṛthivyā́ aghásaṃsāya tárhaṇaṃ / úttakṣataṃ svaryàṃ párvatebhyo yéna rákṣo vāvṛdhānáṃ nijū́rvathaḥ. RV 7.104.4). Soma kills the rákṣas and the liar (hánti rákṣo hánty ā́sad vádantam. RV 7.104.13). Soma is asked to strike away all who err (and) the rákṣases (ápa srídhaḥ / jahí rákṣāṃsi. RV. 9.63.28). The poet of RV 10.89.14 expresses his impatience for the time when Indra will punish the guilty one, break the sneaking rákṣas, and destroy those who bleed friends (?) (kárhi svit sā́ ta indra cetyā́sad aghásya yád bhinádo rákṣa éṣat / mitrakrúvo yác chásane ná gā́vaḥ pṛthivyā́ āpṛ́g amuyā́ śáyante. RV 10.89.14).

All the verses in the RV containing *rákṣas–* have to do with some god destroying or warding off rákṣases or a rákṣas. It is instructive to see which gods are specifically named as enemies of rákṣases. There are forty-five verses containing *rákṣas–* in the RV (excluding RV 8.35.17 and 18 which only repeat 16). Of these, seventeen have Agni opposed to the rákṣases, ten have Soma, seven have Indra, three have Indra-Soma, two have the Aśvins, and one each has Indra-Agni, Mitra-Varuṇa, Vājinaḥ, Vasiṣṭha (according to the Anukramaṇī), the Soma-pressing stones, and the Maruts.

It may also be instructive to see just what each deity is expected to do with rákṣases. Agni is invoked to burn them (daha RV 10. 118.7 and 10.87.19) or destroy them with his flame (rákṣo hárasā śṛṇīhi. RV 10.87.14). He is described as burning rákṣases everywhere (dáhan rákṣāṃsi viśváhā. RV 8.43.26) or as one who burns down rákṣases (yó rákṣāṃsi nijū́rvati. RV 10.187.3). Agni is also asked to kill rákṣases (jahí rákṣāṃsi. RV 6.16.29 jahí rákṣo RV 4.3.14). He is invoked to drive off rákṣases (rákṣāṃsi sedha RV 10.98.12) or said to do so (rákṣāṃsi sedhati RV 1.79.12, 7.15.10, and 8.23.13). He sharpens his horns for killing rákṣases (śíśīte sṛ́ṅge rákṣase viníkṣe. RV 5.2.9) and his cracklings (*svānā́saḥ*) have sharp weapons for killing the rákṣas (tigmā́yudhā rákṣase hántavā́ u RV 5.2.10). He is shining against the murderer and the rákṣases (hiṃsrám rákṣāṃsy abhí śóśucānaṃ RV 10.87.9). He is asked to spy out the rákṣas in the clans (rákṣaḥ pári paśya vikṣú. RV 10.87.10) so that he can destroy them. Agni is the one by whom the rákṣases are smashed (yenā...tṛḷhā́ rákṣāṃsi RV 6.16. 48). In praising Agni a poet pleads, "May a rákṣas not enter us" (mā́ no rákṣa ā́ veśīt RV 8. 60.20).

Soma is described as killing rákṣases in a fixed phrase which occurs three times. Soma "streams into the filter killing rákṣases, longing for the gods" (pavítre arṣati vighnán rákṣāṃsi devayū́ḥ RV 9.17.3, 9.37.1, 9.56.1). He is also said to kill the rákṣas (hánti rákṣo RV 7.104.13 and 9.97.10). His powers (*śuśmāsaḥ.*) are described as breaking the rákṣas (rákṣo bhindántaḥ RV 9.53.1). He is invoked to strike away rákṣases (ápa...jahí rákṣāṃsi RV 9.63. 28) or described as doing so (rákṣāṃsy apajáṅghanat RV 9.49. 5). He is invited to purify himself while warding off rákṣases (sédhan rákṣāṃsy ápa RV 9.110.12). In one verse the poet asks of Soma that the plague together with the rákṣas become far away (ápāmīvā bhavatu rákṣasā sahá RV 9.85.1).

The verses addressed to Indra show the most variety in the treatment of rákṣases. He is invoked to kill the rákṣas (jahí rákṣaḥ RV 3.30.16, ví rákṣo...jahi RV 10.152.3), to burn down the rakṣas (rákṣo ní dhakṣi RV 6.18.10), to break the rákṣas (bhinádo rákṣaḥ RV 10.89.14), to grind the rákṣas (prá mṛṇa rákṣaḥ RV 7. 104.22), and to smash each rákṣas (sárvaṃ rákṣo ní barhaya RV 1.133.5). One poet even says, "O Indra, rip out the rákṣas by the root, chop (his) middle, (and) crush (his) top" (úd vṛha rákṣaḥ sahámūlam indra vṛścā́ mádhyaṃ práty ágraṃ śṛṇīhi RV 3.30.17.

Indra-Soma are requested to burn and subdue the rákṣas (tápataṃ rákṣa ubjátaṃ RV 7.104.1). They are asked to wield the weapon by which they burn down the rákṣas (yéna rákṣo vāvṛdhānáṃ nijū́rvathaḥ RV 7.104.4). And they are asked to throw their weapons at the rákṣases (rákṣobhyo vadhám asyatam RV 7.104.25). The Aśvins are asked to kill the rákṣases (hatáṃ rákṣāṃsi. RV 8.35.16), and one poet says to them, "May the rákṣases be slain" (hatā́ rákṣāṃsi... syuḥ RV 6.63.10). Indra-Agni are asked to subdue the rákṣas (rákṣa ubjatam RV 1.21.5). Mitra or Varuṇa is asked to throw his missile at the hidden rákṣas (gambhīrā́ya rákṣase hetím asya RV 6.62.9). In one verse the *vājínaḥ* (booty-winners) are described as destroying rákṣases (jambháyanto...rákṣāṃsi RV 7.38.7). The poet of one verse (addressed to Vasiṣṭha according to the Anukramaṇī) says, "May the rákṣas of the hexing ones not reach us" (mā́ no rákṣo abhí naḍ yātumā́vatām RV 7.104.23). The Soma-pressing stones are asked to ward off rakṣases (grā́vā vádann ápa rákṣāṃsi sedhatu RV 10.36.4). The Maruts are asked to pierce the rákṣas with lightning (vídhyatā vidyútā rákṣaḥ RV 1.86.9).

Rakṣás– is the masculine derivative of *rákṣas–*. It means "one who has *rákṣas–*." Various adjectives are used to describe rakṣáses in the RV. They are said to be evil (*pāpá–* RV 1.129.11), accursed (*aśás–* RV 4.4.15), repulsive (*ájuṣṭa–* RV 7.1.13), māyā-possessing (*māyín–* RV 8.23.14), greedy (*árāvan–* RV 8.60.10), and tricky (*bhaṅgurā́vat–* RV 10.76.4). They are also twice called *atrín–* (RV 9.86.48 and 9.104.6). This is either a proper name as Geldner and Renou take it, or it is an adjective meaning "voracious."

The evil activities in which rakṣáses engage are not often spelled out, but a few are mentioned. They are said to make fun of Bṛhaspati (yé tvā nidé dadhiré dṛṣṭávīryam RV 2.23.14). Just being a rakṣas seems to imply being guilty of some evil, since Indra is asked to kill a rakṣás who denies his guilt (yó vā rakṣā́ḥ śúcir asmíty ā́ha / índras táṃ hantu mahatā́ vadhéna RV 7.104.16). One verse suggests that they can take on the form of birds at night and disrupt sacrifices. "Spread out, O Maruts, in the clans, seek, grasp the rakṣases, destroy (those) who becoming birds fly by night or who deposit contaminations in the godly sacrifice" (ví tiṣṭhadhvaṃ maruto vikṣv ìcchátа gṛbhāyáta rakṣásaḥ sáṃ pinaṣṭana / váyo yé bhūtví patáyanti naktábhir yé vā rípo dadhiré devé adhvaré RV 7.104.18). There is also some indication in this verse that rakṣáses hide among the people, since they must be sought out in the clans. The ability of a rakṣás to take on a bird form may also be implied in RV 7.104.17, "May she who goes forth like an owl at night hiding herself with deception go down into bottomless pits. May the pressing-stones kill the rakṣáses with their din" (prá yā́ jígāti khargáleva náktam ápa druhā́ tanvàṃ gū́hamāna / vavrā́m̐ anantā́m̐ áva sā́ padīṣṭa grā́vāṇo ghnantu rakṣása upabdáiḥ RV 7.104.17). That rakṣáses are associated with the disruption of sacrifices is found again in RV 1.76.3 where Agni is asked to burn the rakṣáses and become one who protects the sacrifice from curses (prá sú víśvān rakṣáso dhákṣy agne bhávā yajñā́nām abhiśastipā́vā RV 1.76.3). They are enemies of the sacred chant (yé brahmadvíṣaḥ RV 10.182.3).

The company kept by the rakṣáses—that is, the other beings who are named along with them—can also help to illustrate their character. In some cases the other figures mentioned may be intended to be the same as the rakṣáses. But even if they are not identical it will help to understand them if we see what categories of beings they are frequently associated with. They are often associated with (or identified as) beings who are tricky. "O Agni, protect us from the rakṣás, protect from the trickery of the stingy one, protect from the one harming or the one about to kill" (pāhí no agne rakṣásaḥ pāhí dhūrtér árāvṇaḥ / pāhí ríṣata utá vā jíghaṃsato RV 1.36.15). "O Agni, protect us from the repulsive rakṣás, protect from the trickery of the greedy evil one" (pāhí no agne rakṣáso ájuṣṭāt pāhí dhūrtér áraruṣo aghāyóḥ RV 7.1.13). "Think: in fleeting haste destroy the evils, the rakṣáses, the tricky ones. O Indra-Soma, may luck not arise for the ill-doer, who always shows enmity to us with evil" (práti smarethāṃ tujáyadbhir évair hatáṃ druhó rakṣáso bhaṅgurā́vataḥ / índrāsomā duṣkṛ́te mā́ sugáṃ bhūd yó naḥ kadā́ cid abhidā́sati druhā́ RV 7.104.7). These last two verses have also mentioned evil (*ághāyu-* and *drúh-*) in connection with rakṣáses. "Burn back the tricky ones with poison, the rakṣáses" (viṣéṇa bhaṅgurā́vataḥ práti ṣma rakṣáso daha RV 10.87.23).

Rakṣáses are also often mentioned together with magicians and sorcerers. Savitṛ is spoken of as driving away rakṣáses and sorcerers (apasédhan rakṣáso yātudhā́nān RV 1.35.10). Indra is asked to kill the one who is a rakṣás, but refuses to admit it, and the one who falsely accuses the poet of being a sorcerer (yó mā́yātum yā́tudhānéty ā́ha yó vā rakṣā́ḥ śúcir asmíty ā́ha / índras táṃ hantu mahatā́ vadhéna RV 7.104.16). "Shatter completely the strength (and) manliness of the rakṣás (and) the sorcerer" (yātudhā́nasya rakṣáso bálaṃ ví ruja vīryàṃ RV 10.87.25). This verse either identifies the rakṣás and the sorcerer or speaks of their working hand in hand. The following verse helps to clarify this. "Indra became the destroyer of the demons who disturb the offering (and) who are enemies. Śakra goes against the rakṣáses as an axe (against) a tree or as one would break pottery" (índro yātūnā́m abhavat parāśaró havirmáthīnām abhy ā̀vívāsatāṃ / abhíd u śakráḥ paraśúr yáthā vánaṃ pā́treva bhindánt satá eti rakṣásaḥ RV 7.104.21). This verse sounds as if the demons (*yātú–*) are identified with the rakṣáses. Since these *yātus* are said to disturb the sacrifice and the rakṣáses are elsewhere mentioned in this connection, (RV 7.104.18 and 1.76.3) as we have seen, this identification is quite possible. But if *yātus* and rakṣáses are the same, then a sorcerer (*yātu-dhā́na–*, literally "one who impels *yātus*") is one who can control rakṣáses. Such a connection between rakṣáses and black magic seems to be quite basic to an understanding of *rakṣás–*. In another verse the Maruts are asked to attack one who pays attention to the rakṣáses in the sacrifice (yá óhate rakṣáso devávītāv acakrébhis táṃ maruto ní yāta RV 5.42.10). This could also be a reference to rakṣáses connected with black magic.

Rakṣáses also occur in more general lists of evils from which the poet seeks protection. In RV 10.182.3 the poet pleads for destruction of rakṣáses, but also for destruction of the back-biter (*áśasti–*) and evil thought (*durmatí–*). Another poet pleads: "O Agni, abandon us not to a lack of sons, us not to this ill-clothed lack of ideas, us not to hunger, not to a rakṣás, O possessor of ṛta" (mā́ no agne 'vírate párā dā durvā́sasé 'mataye mā́ no asyái / mā́ naḥ kṣudhé mā́ rakṣása ṛtāvo RV 7.1.19). In another verse Agni is asked to drive away "enemies, rakṣáses, and plagues" (dviṣó rakṣáso ámīvāḥ RV 3.15.1). Another verse after asking for salvation from each rakṣás asks for release from "adevic dishonest constriction" (sánemi kṛdhy àsmád ā́ rakṣásaṃ káṃ cid atríṇaṃ / ápā́devaṃ dvayúm áṃho yuyodhi naḥ RV 9.104.6).

In almost every verse containing *rakṣás–* in the RV a deity is asked or said to kill them or to offer protection from them. It is instructive to note which deities are thus designated as enemies of the rakṣáses. There are thirty-three occurrences of *rakṣás–* in the RV. Agni is most often named as their enemy—thirteen times. Indra and Soma are tied for second place with five times each.

Bṛhaspati, the Maruts, and the soma-pressing stones are named in this capacity twice each. Parjanya, Savitṛ, Indra-Soma, and Mitra-Varuṇa appear once each as killers of or defenders from rakṣáses.

Agni is frequently asked to burn the rakṣáses (√dah- RV 1.76.3, 1.79.6, 4.4.15). He is also asked to burn them down (√dah-+ni RV 8.23.14) or to burn them back (√dah-+prati RV 10.87.23). He is asked to protect from the rakṣáses (pāhí RV 1.36.15, 7.1.13, 8.60.10). He is asked to drive away the rakṣáses (ví bādhasva RV 3.15.1), to pierce them with very hot missiles (vídhya rakṣásas tápiṣṭhaiḥ RV 4.4.1), or to shatter the strength and manliness of the rakṣás (rakṣáso bálaṃ ví ruja vīryàm RV 10.87.25). He is once requested not to abandon the poet and his group to a rakṣás (párā dā RV 7.1.19). Only one of these verses mentioning Agni in opposition with the rakṣáses does not contain an imperative. There Agni is simply described as burning rakṣases (tepānó rakṣásaḥ RV 8.60.19).

Soma is invoked to kill all the rakṣáses (jahí víśvān rakṣásaḥ. RV 9.86.48). He is described as slaying rakṣáses (apaghnánt soma rakṣásaḥ RV 9.63.29). He is asked to remove completely each rakṣás (sánemi kṛdhy àsmád ā́ rakṣásaṃ RV 9.104.6). He is invoked to split the firm seats of the rakṣás (rujā́ dṛḷhā́ cid rakṣásaḥ sádāṃsi RV 9.91.4). In one verse he is said to protect from the rakṣás (rakṣásaḥ pāti RV 9.71.1).

Indra is asked to slay the rakṣáses with the stone thrown from heaven (prá vartaya divó áśmānam indra...abhí jahi rakṣásaḥ párvatena RV 7.104.19). He is also called on to kill with his great weapon the rakṣás who denies his guilt (yó vā rakṣā́ḥ śúcir asmíty ā́ha / índras táṃ hantu mahatā́ vadhéna RV 7.104.16). He "goes against the rakṣáses as an axe (against) a tree or as one would break pottery" (abhíd u śakráḥ paraśúr yáthā vánaṃ pā́treva bhindánt satá eti rakṣásaḥ. RV 7.104.21). In one verse he is described as a killer of the evil rakṣás (hantā́ pāpásya rakṣásaḥ RV 1. 129. 11). He is once asked to overcome the glow of the rakṣases which has spread over him and to drive them out (abhí tvā pā́jo rakṣáso ví tasthe máhi jajñānám abhí tát sú tiṣṭha / táva pratnéna yújyena sákhyā vájreṇa dhṛṣṇo ápa tā́ nudasva RV 6.21.7).

Bṛhaspati is called on to burn the rakṣases who ridicule him (téjiṣṭhayā tapaní rakṣásas tapa yé tvā nidé dadhiré dṛṣṭávīryam RV 2.23.14). He is also asked to burn the rakṣáses who are enemies of the sacred chant (tápurmūrdhā tapatu rakṣáso yé brahmadvíṣaḥ śárave hántavā́ u RV, 10.182.3). The Maruts are invoked to go down with their wheelless (chariots ?) on those who pay attention to the rakṣáses in sacrifices to gods (yá óhate rakṣáso devávītāv acakrébhis tám̐ maruto ní yāta RV 5.42.10). Elsewhere they are asked to spread out in the clans, "seek, grasp the rakṣáses, destroy (those) who becoming birds fly by night or who deposit contaminations in the godly sacrifice" (ví tiṣṭhadhvaṃ maruto vikṣv ìccháta gṛbhāyáta rakṣásaḥ sáṃ pinaṣṭana / váyo yé bhūtvī́ patáyanti naktábhir yé vā rípo dadhiré devé adhvaré RV 7.104.18). The soma-pressing stones are invoked to kill the rakṣáses with their din (grā́vāṇo ghnantu rakṣása upabdáih RV 7. 104.17). Elsewhere they are asked to strike away the rakṣáses (ápa hata rakṣáso bhaṅgurā́vataḥ RV 10.76.4). Savitṛ is described as driving away rakṣáses and sorcerers (apasédhan rakṣáso yātudhā́nān RV 1.35.10). It is once said of Parjanya that he kills rakṣáses (hanti rakṣáso RV 5.83.2). Indra-Soma is asked to kill evils, rakṣáses, and tricky ones (hatáṃ druhó rakṣáso bhaṅgurā́vataḥ RV 7.104.7). The singers of one verse invoke Mitra-Varuṇa to aid them in overcoming rakṣáses (yuvóḥ krāṇā́ya sakhyáir abhí ṣyāma rakṣásaḥ RV 10.132.2).

Rákṣas or the rakṣáses have as their main opponents Agni (thirty times), Soma (fifteen times), and Indra (only twelve times). There is no indication that they can ever be human. They are always malevolent and always something to be gotten rid of. They are sometimes associated with plagues, enemies, and various evils. But perhaps most significant is their frequent association with sorcerers. They seem to be the force or the beings by which the evil sorcerer carries out his injuries. That is, the sorcerer sends rákṣas or the rakṣáses to do his bidding against his enemies. Since they are associated with black magic, it is appropriate that Agni and Soma—the gods who can be handled in the ceremonies—should be their adversaries more often than Indra, who is more likely to be pitted against more human warrior figures. Examples of fire fighting off evil spirits could be cited from religious traditions around the world.

The verses containing derivatives and compounds of *rákṣas*– confirm these conclusions about the meaning of the word. Soma is called a rakṣas-killer (*rakṣohán*–) three times in the RV (RV 9.1. 2, 9.37.3, and 9.67.20). This epithet is used once of Indu ("drop"), clearly another term for Soma (RV 1.129.6). Agni is called rakṣas-killer (*rakṣohán–*) twice (RV 10.87.1 and 10.162.1). This epithet occurs once with Bṛhaspati (RV 2.23.3), once of the Aśvins (RV 7.73.4), and once of the poet (*vípra–* RV 10.97.6). Bṛhaspati's chariot is once said to be rakṣas-killing (*rakṣohán–* RV 10. 103.4). And praise is offered to Agni "in order that gleaming, sickness-repelling, rakṣas-killing well-being may arise for the singers (and their) close companion" (śáṃ yát stotṛ́bhya āpáye bhávāti dyumád amīvacā́tanam rakṣohā́ RV 7.8.6).

The verses containing *rakṣasvín–* ("rákṣas-possessor") indicate the link between rákṣas and sorcerers. Agni is invoked to burn against the rákṣas-possessor, the one who causes harm (práti ṣma ríṣato daha / ágne tváṃ rakṣasvínaḥ RV 1.12.5). "Burn together always the rákṣas-possessors, the sorcerers, each Atrin" (rakṣasvínaḥ sádam íd yātumā́vato víśvaṃ sám atríṇaṃ daha RV 1.36. 20). "May you two (Indra-Agni) slay the ill-speaking, ill-thinking, rákṣas-possessing mortal" (tā́v íd duḥśáṃsaṃ mártyaṃ dúrvidvāṃsaṃ rakṣasvínaṃ RV 7.94.12). "May we envision mastery, with good heroes, standing well, desirable, unassailable by a rákṣas-possessor" (suprāvargáṃ suvī́ryaṃ suṣṭhú vā́ryam áṇādhṛṣṭaṃ rakṣasvínā RV 8.22.18). "Blessing is not to come down nor approach here for the rákṣas-possessor" (néhá bhadráṃ rakṣasvíne nā́vayái nópayā́ utá RV 8.47.12). "Do not hand us over to the cheating, rákṣas-possessing mortal, not to the evil-speaking one" (mā́ no mártāya ripáve rakṣasvíne mā́gháśaṃsāya rīradhaḥ RV 8.60.8). These quotes make it clear that a rákṣas-possessor is an evil mortal who is potentially dangerous. He is apparently one who is in control of a force (rákṣas) which he can send to do his bidding. In other words, he is a sorcerer or black magician.

Compounds or derivatives of *rákṣas–* occur three more times in the RV. The Aśvins are invoked against the companion of the rakṣas (*rakṣoyúj–*) (RV 6.62.8). Indra is asked to place the vajra in his arms for killing rakṣases (rakṣohátyāya) (RV 6.45.18). And the Ādityas are addressed as follows: "Whatever mortal wishes to harm us by means of rákṣas-power, may that man harm (his own) life by his own actions" (yó naḥ káś cid rírikṣati rakṣastvéna mártyaḥ / svaíḥ ṣá évai ririṣīṣṭa yúr jánaḥ RV 8.18.13). Here rákṣas-power (rakṣastvá–) seems to be synonymous with black magic.

CHAPTER XI

DÁSYU– IN THE SAMHITĀS AND BRĀHMAṆAS

I turn now to the occurrences of *dásyu–* in the RV.

Dasyus are twice described as vowless (*ávrata–*) (RV 1.175.3 and 9.41.2). They are said to be without brahman (*ábrahman–*) and māyā-possessing (*māyā́vat–*) (RV 4.16.9). If the dasyus were human (as will be indicated by the evidence presented in this chapter), then being without vows and without brahman indicates that they did not practice the same religion as the Aryan poets of the RV. Dasyus are further described as without ritual acts (*akarmán–*), not thinking (*amantú–*), having other vows (*anyávrata–*), and inhuman (*ámānuṣa–*) (RV 10.22.8). Dasyus are also inauspicious (*áśiva–*) and possess tricks (*māyá́–*) (RV 1.117.3). Thus they were considered dangerous and were not trusted. The adjective *ánās–* is used of them once (RV 5.29.10). This word is *hapax* and apparently means "without a mouth," although earlier translators translated it "noseless." This could refer to a physical racial characteristic or their inability to speak the Aryan language, but it is dangerous to put much weight on such slim evidence. The dasyu is once described as rich (*dhanín–*) (RV 1.33.4) and once as greedy (*ápṛṇat–*) (RV 5.7.10). They are once described as strong (*śárdhata–*) (RV 6.23.2). They are described as "desiring to creep upward with tricks" (*māyā́bhir utsísṛpsataḥ*) and "desiring to climb to heaven" (*dyā́m ārúrukṣataḥ*) (RV 8.14.14). Perhaps this means that the Aryans accused the dasyus of attempting to usurp their religion. The prohibitions found in the later *dharmaśāstra* texts against Śūdras participating in practices that belong to the twice born make it quite likely that such usurpation would have been frowned on at an earlier time, too.

Besides these adjectives which occur with *dásyu–*, there are also a few proper names of dasyus that occur in the RV. Navavāstva (RV 1.36.18), Śambara (RV 6.31.4), Cumuri (RV 7.19.4), and Śuṣṇa (RV 8.6.14) are all explicitly called dasyus and all in contexts which make it clear that they are enemies of the poets and their patrons. *Dásyu–* also appears four times as part of the proper name Dasyave Vṛka (RV 8.51.2, 8.55.1, 8.56.1, and 8.56.2). This man, whose name means "one who is a wolf to the dasyu," was friendly to the poets.

There is no mention of evil activities in which the dasyus engage except those noted above in the discussion of adjectives which are found with the word *dásyu–*, and RV 10.22.8 which says: "The dasyu who is without ritual acts, does not think, has other vows, (and) is inhuman (goes) against us" (akarmā́ dásyur abhí no amantúr anyávrato ámānuṣaḥ RV 10.22.8).

Several verses contrast the dasyus with the Aryans. "Distinguish the Aryans and (those) who are dasyus" (ví jānīhy ā́ryān yé ca dásyavo RV 1.51.8). "Blowing on the dasyu with the *bakura*, you made a wide light for the Aryan" (abhí dásyuṃ bákureṇā dhámantorú jyótiś cakrathur ā́ryāya RV 1.117.21). "You opened up the light for the Aryan. The dasyu is seated down to the left, O Indra" (ápāvṛṇor jyótir ā́ryāya ní savyatáḥ sādi dásyur indra RV 2.11.18). "May we win who with your aids are overcoming all enemies, dasyus (together) with the Aryan" (sánema yé ta ūtíbhis táranto víśvāḥ spṛ́dha ā́ryeṇa dásyūn RV 2.11.19). "Having killed the dasyus, he (Indra) aided the Aryan race" (hatví dásyūn prā́ryaṃ várṇam āvat RV 3.34.9). It is also noteworthy that the word for "race" here is *várṇa–*, which also means color and therefore suggests that the Aryan and dasyu races may have been distinguished by their skin pigmentation. "Hurl the weapon at the dasyu. Increase the Aryan strength (and) glory, O Indra" (dásyave hetím asyā́ryaṃ sáho vardhayā dyumnám indra RV 1.103.3). "You indeed now tamed the dasyus. You alone conquered the peoples for the Aryan" (tváṃ ha nú tyád adamāyo dásyūm̐r ékaḥ kṛṣṭī́r avanor ā́ryāya RV 6.18.3). "You drove the dasyus from their dwelling, O Agni, giving birth to broad light for the Aryan" (tváṃ dásyūm̐r ókaso agna āja urú jyótir janáyann ā́ryāya. RV 7.5.6). "I the piercer of Śuṣṇa wielded the weapon, I who did not turn the Aryan name over to the dasyu" (aháṃ śúṣṇasya śnáthitā vádhar yamam ná yó rará ā́ryaṃ nā́ma dásyave RV 10.49.3). In some of these verses the singular of *ā́rya–* must either be understood as a collective term or have a word such as "race" (*várṇa*) supplied in order to make full sense of the verse. *Dásyu–* cannot be an adjective, but is sometimes used in the singular as a collective noun to refer to the race of dasyus. It seems clear from this collection of instances that *dásyu–* referred to a member of a tribe or race distinct from the Aryans and against whom the Aryans often fought.

It may also be instructive to examine what other beings are mentioned along with dasyus. This is especially so since in many cases it is impossible to tell whether these other beings are simply mentioned with dasyus because they are given some sort of similar treatment or whether they are meant to be synonymous. (The situation was the same with *rakṣas*–.) Dāsas seem to be closely related to dasyus. "The dasyu who is without ritual acts, does not think, has other vows, (and) is inhuman (goes) against us. May you outwit the weapon of this dāsa, O enemy-killer" (akarmā́ dásyur abhí no amantúr anyávrato ámānuṣaḥ / tvám̐ tásyāmitrahan vádhar dāsásya daṃbhaya RV 10. 22.8). *Dásyu*– and *dāsá*– seem to be the same in this verse. "O Indra, you made the dasyus lowest of all, the dāsic tribe without praise. You two (Indra-Soma) struck, smashed down the enemy" (víśvasmāt sīm adhamā́m̐ indra dásyūn víśo dā́sīr akṛṇor apraśastā́ḥ / ábādhethām ámṛṇataṃ ní śátrūn RV 4.28.4). The dasyus here are either identified with or closely related to the dāsic tribes. "Possessing a support from birth, putting faith in strength, breaking dāsic fortresses he wanders widely. O one with the vajra, knowing (how), hurl the weapon at the dasyu" (sá jātū́bharmā śraddádhāna ójaḥ pū́ro vibhindánn acarad ví dā́sīḥ / vidvā́n vajrin dásyave hetím asya RV 1.103.3). It is unclear whether or not *dā́sa*– and *dásyu*- refer to the same beings here. One more obscure verse has both *dā́sá*– and *dásyu*–, but the relationship between them is unclear. "What's more, the dāsa made women his weapons. 'What can these his frail weapons do to me?' For Indra discovered the two female breasts of this one. Then he went forth to fight the dasyu" (stríyo hí dāsá ā́yudhāni cakré kím mā karann abalā́ asya sénāḥ / antár hy ákhyad ubhé asya dhéne áthópa práid yudháye dásyum índraḥ. RV 5.30.9). The Āyus are spoken of as "overcoming the dasyu, desiring to conquer the vowless ones with vows" (tū́rvanto dásyum āyávo vratáiḥ sī́kṣanto avratáṃ RV 6. 14.3). The vowless one here is presumably the same as the dasyu. "(He has struck) down the ones who are without spiritual power, knotty (?), ill-speaking, stingy, faithless, not increasing, without sacrifices. Agni drove farther and farther away the dasyus; the first one made the non-sacrificing ones last" (ny àkratū́n grathíno mṛdhrávācaḥ paṇī́m̐r aśraddhā́m̐ avṛdhā́m̐ ayajñā́n / prápra tā́n dásyūm̐r agnír vivāya pū́rvaś cakārā́parām̐ áyajyūn. RV 7.6.3). All of these adjectives quite likely refer to the dasyus, but they could just be terms for other beings who are given similar treatment by the poets in certain contexts. "His own friend the mountain should shake down the one who has other vows, who is non-human, not sacrificing, (and) not striving for the gods; the mountain (should shake down) the dasyu for easy killing " (anyávratam ámānuṣam áyajvānam ádevayuṃ / áva sváḥ sákhā dudhuvīta párvataḥ sughnā́ya dásyuṃ párvataḥ. RV 8.70.11). All of these adjectives apparently refer to the dasyu. In a verse to Indra the poet asks to attain nourishment dispersing the dasyu with the enemies dispersed (índreṇa dásyuṃ daráyanta índubhir yutádveṣasaḥ sám iṣā́ rabhemahi RV 1.53.4). Agni is called "the greatest killer of enemies, who casts away dasyus" (vṛtrahántamaṃ yó dásyū̐r avadhūnuṣé. RV 1.78.4). It is hoped for Indra to "strike down many enemies, dasyus" (purū́ ca vṛtrā́ hanati ní dásyūn RV 6.29.6). Dasyu and enemy seem practically synonymous here. Indra is said to smash down and kill dasyus and śimyus (RV 1.100.18), but since śimyus are mentioned only one other time in the RV, nothing helpful is gained from their mention. Indra is asked to smash Kuyava (and) one thousand dasyus in one day (prapitvé áhnaḥ kúyavaṃ sahásrā / sadyó dásyūn prá mṛṇa kutsyéna. RV 4.16.12). "Agni Vaiśvānara having killed the dasyu shook the barriers (and) chopped down Śambara" (vaiśvānaró dásyum agnír jaghanvā́m̐ ádhūnot kā́ṣṭhā áva śámbaraṃ bhet. RV 1.59.6). Here the dasyu is associated (or identified) with Śambara, who is elsewhere called a dasyu (RV 6.31.4). This frequent mention of dasyus by name is in marked contrast with the treatment of rakṣases, who always remain nameless. There are several other verses in which beings such as Vṛtra are mentioned, but the context is such that these seem to have little relationship with the mention of dasyus, so I have omitted them from this discussion.

As with the preceding words it will be instructive to see which deities are specifically named as being in opposition to the dasyus and what each is asked to do to them. There are sixty-three verses containing *dásyu–* in the RV (excluding four verses in which the word occurs only as part of the name *Dasyave Vṛka*). Indra is by far the one most often called their enemy. He appears in this role forty-two times. Agni is the second most frequently named enemy of the dasyus, but he is so depicted in only eight verses and in one of these Indra is also named as an opponent of dasyus (RV 4.28.3). Soma is mentioned twice in this capacity, and so are the Aśvins. The following appear once each in this role: the eagle, Manyu, the mountain, the Āyus, Rudra, Atri, Earth-Sky, the gods, and the poet and his group. There is one remaining verse in which no enemy is actually named, but Śaramā is probably implied (RV 1.104. 5).

Indra is once invoked to strike down the dasyus (hanati ní dásyūn RV 6.29.6). Twice he is called a killer of the dasyu (hantā́ dásyor RV 8.98.6, yó dásyor hantā́ RV 2. 12.10). But the hymns addressed to him frequently mention that he kills dasyus. "Because you kill the rich dasyu with (your) club, wandering alone with (your) helpers, O Indra, they scatter to all sides from (their) hiding-place (?)" (vádhīr hí dásyuṃ dhanínaṃ ghanénaṁ ékaś cárann upaśākébhir indra RV 1.33.4). "Indra killed, Agni burned, O drop, the dasyus in front before noon" (áhan índro ádahad agnír indo purā́ dásyūn madhyándinād abhíke RV 4.28.3). "The much called one zealously killing dasyus and śimyus with (his) spear smashed (them) down to the ground" (dásyūñ chímyuṃś ca puruhūtá évair hatvā́ pṛthivyā́ṃ śárvā ní barhīt RV 1.100.18). "Having killed the dasyus, he overcame the bronze fortresses" (hatví dásyūn púra ā́yasīr ní tarhīt RV 2.20.8). "Having killed the dasyus, he aided the Aryan race" (hatví dásyūn prā́ryaṃ várṇam āvat RV 3.34.9). "Having covered Cumuri and Dhuni with sleep, you killed the dasyu; you aided Dabhīti" (svápnenābhyúpyā cúmuriṃ dhúniṃ ca jaghánta dásyuṃ prá dabhítim āvaḥ RV 2.15.9). This same theme is expressed elsewhere in different words. "You caused the dasyu Cumuri and Dhuni to sink into sleep (so that they would be) easy to kill for Dabhīti" (tváṃ ní dásyuṃ cúmuriṃ dhúniṃ cā́svāpayo dabhítaye suhántu RV 7.19.4). Indra is said to prepare his vajra for killing the dasyu easily (vájraṃ yáś cakré suhánāya dásyave RV 10.105.7).

Indra is also described as defeating or overcoming dasyus. It is Indra "who defeated the dasyus" (índro yó dásyūm̐r ádharām̐ avā́tirat RV 1.101.5). "Having overcome the vowless dasyu, may you burn (him) like a (wooden) vessel with flame" (sahā́vān dásyum avratám óṣaḥ pā́traṃ ná śocíṣā RV 1.175.3). "May we win who with your aids are overcoming all enemies, dasyus along with the Aryan" (sánema yé ta ūtíbhis táranto víśvāḥ spṛ́dha ā́ryeṇa dásyūn RV 2.11.19). "O Indra, you overcame the strong dasyus" (árandhayaḥ śárdhata indra dásyūn RV 6.23.2).

Indra is sometimes said to smash, crush, or grind the dasyus or is invoked to do so. "He smashed the tricky ones with (his) embrace, the one of excelling strength (smashed) the dasyus with (his) tricks" (vṛjánena vṛjinā́nt sáṃ pipeṣa māyā́bhir dásyūm̐r abhíbhūtyojāḥ RV 3.34.6). "At daybreak smash Kuyava, one thousand dasyus in one day" (prapitvé áhnaḥ kúyavaṃ sahásrā / sadyó dāsyūn prá mṛṇa RV 4.16.12). "You smashed the mouthless dasyus with the weapon" (anā́so dásyūm̐r amṛṇo vadhéna RV 5.29.10). "Easily conquering you chopped up the dasyus in their seat" (ví dásyūm̐r yónāv ákṛto vṛthāṣā́ṭ RV 1.63.4). Indra's tawny steeds are called those by which he smashed down the dasyu before Manu (yébhir ní dásyuṃ mánuṣo nighóṣayo RV 8.50.8).

Indra is sometimes said to disperse or scatter or drive away dasyus. "Going forth at daybreak, you drove away the dasyus" (prapitváṃ yánn ápa dásyūm̐r asedhaḥ RV 5.31.7). "O Indra, you have cast away the dasyus who are desiring to creep upward with tricks (and) desiring to climb to heaven" (māyā́bhir utsísṛpsata índra dyā́m ārúrukṣataḥ// áva dásyūm̐r adhūnuthāḥ RV 8.14. 14). He "blew away the dasyus with a battle" (śū́ro nír yudhā́dhamad dásyūn RV 10.55.8). "You blew away the dasyu with the priests, O Indra" (nír brahmábhir adhamo dásyum indra RV 1. 33.9). One poet also asks that he and his group may succeed against the dasyus with Indra's help. "Dispersing the dasyu, with Indra (and) with the drops (of soma), may we share in nourishment, warding off enemies" (índreṇa dásyuṃ daráyanta índubhir yutádveṣasaḥ sám iṣā́ rabhemahi RV 1.53.4).

There are occasional mentions of other ways in which Indra deals with dasyus. Indra is asked that the dasyu be put down or on the inauspicious left side. "May the māyā-possessing abrahmanic dasyu sink down" (ní māyā́vān ábrahmā dásyur arta RV 4.16. 9). "The dasyu is seated down to the left, O Indra" (ní savyatáḥ sādi dásyur indra RV 2.11.18). "O Indra, you made the dasyu lowest of all, the dāsic tribes without praise" (víśvasmāt sīm adhamā́m̐ indra dásyūn víśo dā́sīr akṛṇor apraśastā́ḥ RV 4.28.4). One rather obscure verse seems to say that Indra attacks the tricks of the dasyus with his own tricks. "Since he attacked the tricks, the dasyu, with these (tricks?), he spread out the darkening mists, the darkness" (ā́bhir hí māyā́ úpa dásyum ā́gān míhaḥ prá tamrā́ avapat támāṃsi RV 10.73.5)[1]. 'The dasyu who is without ritual acts,

1. It is also possible that *māyā́* is a truncated form for *māyā́bhir* with the normal sandhi omitted at the caesura. The translation would then be: "Since he attacked the dasyu with these tricks, he spread out the darkening mists."

does not think, has other vows, (and) is inhuman, (goes) against us. May you outwit the weapon of this dāsa, O enemy-killer" (akarmā́ dásyur abhí no amantúr anyávrato ámānuṣaḥ / tvám̐ tásyāmitrahan vádhar dāsásya dambhaya. RV 10.22.8). He burns the dasyu down from heaven above (ávādaho divá ā́ dásyum uccā́. RV 1.33.7). He is asked to "distinguish the Aryans and (those) who are dasyus. Deliver the vowless ones to the one with barhis, punishing (them)" (ví jānīhy ā́ryān yé ca dásyavo barhíṣmate randhayā śā́sad avratā́n RV 1.51.8). "You fettered the dasyus in what does not consist of ropes for Dabhīti" (arajjáu dásyūnt sám unab dabhítaye. RV 2.13.9). He "cut short the life of the dasyu" (aminād ā́yur dásyoḥ RV 3.49.2). "Indra went forth to fight the dasyu" (áthópa práid yudháye dásyum índraḥ RV 5.30.9). He "subdued the dasyus" (tvám ha nú tyád adamāyo dásyūn RV 6.18.3). He "knocked down one hundred unconquerable fortresses of the dasyu Śambara" (tvám śatā́ny áva śámbarasya púro jaghanthāpratī́ni dásyoḥ RV 6.31.4). He is asked to strike his vajra down on the dasyu Śuṣṇa (ní śúṣṇa indra dharṇasím vájram jaghantha dásyavi RV 8.6.14), and to "hurl the weapon at the dasyu" (dásyave hetím asya RV 1.103.3). He "took the manliness from the dasyus" (ahám dásyubhyaḥ pári nṛmṇám ā́ dade RV 10.48.2). He "did not turn the Aryan name over to the dasyu" (ná yó rará ā́ryam nā́ma dásyave RV 10.49.3). "When, O Indra, the bulls sing a praise-song for you, the bull, (then) the stones (and) Aditi united—who are wheel rims impelled by Indra without horses (and) without chariots—roll forth against the dasyus" (vṛ́ṣṇe yát te vṛ́ṣaṇo arkám árcān índra grā́vāṇo áditiḥ sajóṣāḥ/anaśvā́so yé paváyo 'rathā́ índreṣitā abhy ávartanta dásyūn RV 5.31.5).

Agni also kills dasyus. "Agni Vaiśvānara having killed the dasyu shook the barriers (and) chopped down Śambara" (vaiśvānaró dásyum agnír jaghanvā́m̐ ádhūnot kā́ṣṭhā áva śámbaram bhet RV 1.59.6). "Agni just born shone killing dasyus" (agnír jātó arocata ghnán dásyūn RV 5.14.4). He also drives dasyus away. "Scare away the dasyu with your weapon" (vadhéna dásyum prá hí cātáyasva RV 5.4.6). "You drove the dasyus from their dwelling, O Agni" (tvám dásyūm̐r ókaso agna āja RV 7.5.6). "Agni drove the dasyus farther and farther away" (prápra tā́n dásyūm̐r agnír vivāya RV 7.6.3). "We sing praise with (songs of) splendor to you, the greatest killer of enemies, who casts away the dasyus" (tám u tvā vṛtrahántamam yó dásyūm̐r avadhūnuṣé dyumnáir abhí prá ṇonumaḥ RV 1.78.4). He can also lead an attack against the dasyus. "Agni leads Navavāstva, Bṛhadratha, (and) Turvīti (as) a force against the dasyu" (agnír nayan návavāstvaṃ bṛhádrathaṃ turvítiṃ dásyave sáhaḥ RV 1.36.18). And in a verse already quoted Agni works with Indra against the dasyus. "Indra killed, Agni burned, the dasyus in front before noon, O drop" (áhann índro ádahad agnír indo purā́ dásyūn madhyándinād abhī́ke RV 4.28.3).

Soma also opposes the dasyus and kills them. Soma "made opposition for the dasyu" (dásyave kar abhī́kəm RV 9.92.5). "You are a killer of each dasyu, O Soma" (hantā́ víśvasyāsi soma dásyoḥ RV 9.88.4). The Aśvins are described as "thwarting the tricks of the inauspicious dasyu" (minántā dásyor áśivasya māyā́. RV 1.117.3) and "blowing on the dasyu with the *bakura*" (abhí dásyuṃ bákureṇā dhámantā RV 1.117.21). The *bakura* was apparently a musical instrument used in battle. The gods overcome the dasyus with the help of Agni. "This is the army-conquering, very heroic Agni, by whom the gods overcame the dasyus" (ayám agníḥ pṛtanāṣā́ṭ suvī́ro yéna devā́so ásahanta dásyūn RV 3.29.9). Dyaus-Pṛthivī gave "the land-winning, field-winning, powerful, fearful striker for the dasyus" (kṣetrāsā́ṃ dadathur urvarāsā́ṃ ghanáṃ dásyubhyo abhíbhūtim ugráṃ RV 4.38.1). It is unclear exactly who or what this "striker" is, but it is clear that Dyaus-Pṛthivī are in the struggle against the dasyus. It is also noteworthy that in this verse overcoming dasyus is connected with winning land and fields. It is also hoped that Atri will overcome dasyus. "Then, O Agni, may Atri overcome the greedy dasyus" (ā́d agne ápṛṇató 'triḥ sāsahyād dásyūn RV 5.7.10). The people pray to Rudra: "Let us overcome the dasyus with (our) bodies" (turyā́ma dásyūn tanū́bhiḥ RV 5.70.3). The Āyus oppose dasyus. "The Āyus (are) overcoming the dasyu, desiring to conquer the vowless one with vows" (tū́rvanto dásyum āyávo vrataíḥ síkṣanto avratáṃ RV 6.14.3). One poet asks of Indra that the mountain itself oppose the dasyu. "May his own friend the mountain shake down the ones who have other vows, who are non-human, not sacrificing, not striving for the gods; (may) the mountain (shake down) the dasyu for easy killing" (anyávratam ámānuṣam áyajvānam ádevayuṃ / áva sváḥ sákhā dudhuvīta párvataḥ sughnā́ya dásyuṃ párvataḥ. RV 8.70.11). The singers of one verse speak of overcoming the dasyus themselves. "We remember the fortunate journey beyond the inaccessible dam having overcome the vowless dasyu" (suvitásya manāmahé 'ti sétuṃ durāvyàṃ / sāhvā́ṃso dásyum avratáṃ. RV 9.41. 2). Manyu ("zeal") is opposed to the dasyus. "O Manyu, vajra-bearer, turn toward me. Strike down the dasyus and think of a friend" (mányo vajrinn abhí mā́m ā́ vavṛtsva hánāva dásyūm̐r utá bodhyāpéḥ RV 10.83.6). Since Manyu has the epithet *vajrín–* ("vajra-bearer"), perhaps it refers to the zeal of Indra. The eagle is once said to kill dasyus. "When the eagle having iron claws comes with his body to the juice, he kills the dasyus" (úpa yát sídad índuṃ śárīraiḥ śyenó 'yo' pāṣṭir hanti dásyūn RV 10.99.8). The eagle here is perhaps Indra, who takes the form of an eagle in one myth in order to get soma. There is one other verse in a hymn to Indra in which it is unclear who is depicted as the opponent of the dasyus. "When the trace of the dasyu appeared, (Śaramā) who knows (the ways) came to the seat (of the dasyu) as to (her own) dwelling. Think of us, O generous one. Do not hand us over as a squanderer (does his) wealth" (práti yát syā́ níthā́darśi dásyor óko nā́cchā sádanaṃ jānatī́ gāt / ádha smā no maghavañ cakṛtā́d ín mā́ no maghéva niṣṣapí párā dāḥ. RV 1.104.5). This translation follows Geldner's. According to him the first half of this verse refers to Śaramā's finding the hiding place of the dasyus.

The picture of the dasyu that emerges from these passages is quite different from that of the rakṣas. There is nothing about taking the form of a bird and flying by night, no mention of disrupting sacrifices, and no connection with black magic. The dasyus seem to be human beings of a different race from the Aryans and of a different (adevic and abrahmanic) religion. The mention of the proper names of various dasyus who are defeated for (or by) certain named Aryan princes (e.g. Dabhīti) also makes the dasyus sound more like historical human figures. There are occasional mentions of taking land from the dasyus (RV 4.38.1). The mention of dasyus in connection with fortresses (*púr–*) is also a characteristic which is in contrast to the rakṣases. Rakṣases do not build fortresses and fight from them. It seems quite safe to agree with the general conclusion of Vedic scholars that *dásyu–* refers to the indigenous people of the land whom the invading Aryans conquered or absorbed.

The derivatives and compounds of *dásyu–* are used in ways which present no surprises. *Dasyuhán–* appears ten times—six in connection with Indra, twice in connection with Agni, once with

Manyu, and once with Sūrya. Indra is called dasyu-killer (*dasyuhán–*) four times (RV 1.100.12, 6.45.24, 8.76.11, and 8.77.3). Once he is asked to "come home with a dasyu-killing mind" (ā́ dasyughnā́ mánasā yāhy ástaṃ RV 4.16.10). And one verse speaks of a dasyu-killing treasure. "O Indra, give us a wonderful bullish treasure, winning the prize, consisting of eloquent men, victorious, prize-winning, surpassing, very able, dasyu-killing, fortress-breaking" (sanádvājaṃ vípravīraṃ tárutraṃ dhanaspṛ́taṃ śūśuvā́ṃsaṃ sudákṣaṃ / dasyuhánaṃ pūrbhídam indra satyám asmábhyaṃ citráṃ vṛ́ṣaṇaṃ rayíṃ dāḥ. RV 10.47.4). All the epithets of this bullish treasure have to do with successfully waging war, and dasyus are once again found linked with fortresses (*púr–*). Agni is twice called the best dasyu-killer (*dasyuhántama–*, superlative of *dasyuhán–*) (RV 6.16.15 and 8.39.8). Manyu is called "enemy-killer, vṛtra-killer, and dasyu-killer" (amitrahā́ vṛtrahā́ dasyuhā́ ca RV 10.83.3). It is said of Sūrya: "The high, shining, well taken care of, most vigor-winning, true, set in the base, in the foundation of the sky, enemy-killing, vṛtra-killing, most dasyu-killing, asura-killing, rival-killing light was born" (vibhrā́ḍ bṛhát súbhṛtaṃ vājasā́tamaṃ dhárman divó dharúṇe satyám árpitaṃ / amitrahā́ vṛtrahā́ dasyuhántamaṃ jyótir jajñe asurahā́ sapatnahā́. RV 10.170.2). Dasyus are treated here together with enemies, vṛtras, asuras, and rivals. All five of these terms seem to be very similar.

Dasyuhátya– ("dasyu-killing") occurs seven times in the RV, and six of these refer to Indra. "You blew away the tricky ones with tricks, who offer in their own way over the shoulder. O manly-minded one, you destroyed the fortresses of Pipru. You aided Ṛjiśvan in the dasyu-killing" (tváṃ māyā́bhir ápa māyíno 'dhamaḥ svadhā́bhir yé ádhi súptāv ájuhvata / tváṃ pípror nṛmaṇaḥ prā́rujaḥ púraḥ prá ṛjíśvānaṃ dasyuhátyeṣv āvitha. RV 1.51.5). Here again occurs some link between fortresses (*púr–*) and dasyus. "You aided Kutsa in the slayings of Śuṣṇa; you delivered Śambara to Atithigva. You trampled down even great Arbuda with (your) foot. Even from antiquity you were born for killing the Dasyus" (tváṃ kútsaṃ śuṣṇahátyeṣv āvithā́randhayo 'tithigvā́ya śámbaraṃ / mahā́ntaṃ cid arbudáṃ ní kramīḥ padā́ sanā́d evá dasyuhátyāya jajñiṣe. RV. 1.51.6). This verse addressed to Indra shows again the tendency to mention proper names with dasyus. Indra "broke fortresses in the dasyu-killing as was his right" (púro 'bhinad árhan dasyuhátye RV 10.99.7). He "helped the son of Kutas in the dasyu-killing" (ā́vo yád dasyuhátye kutsaputrám̐ RV 10. 105.11). He is described as "going forth for dasyu-killing" (upaprayán dasyuhátyāya RV 1.103.4). The only other occurrence of *dasyuhátya–* in the RV is in the Purūravas-Urvaśī hymn where Urvaśī says to Purūravas: "the gods increased you for the great battle, for the dasyu-killing" (mahé yát tvā purūravo ráṇāyā́vardhayan dasyuhátyāya devā́ḥ RV 10.95.7).

The compounds *dásyujūta–* ("spurred on by the dasyu") and *dasyutárhana–* ("dasyu-destroying") occur once each in the RV. "Indra being praised does not bow to the tough, nor to the firm, nor to the strong, nor to the one spurred on by the dasyu" (ná vīḷáve námate ná sthirā́ya ná sárdhate dásyujūtāya stavā́n RV 6. 24.8). It is said in a hymn to Soma: "the dasyu-destroyings of this one which are done and will be done are known" (kṛtā́níd asya kártvā cétante dasyutárhaṇā. RV 9.47.2).

Since there are only a few occurrences of *dásyu–* in the other Saṃhitās and the Brāhmaṇas (excluding quotes from the RV), I shall discuss those here, too. I have already discussed AV 9.2.17, 9.2.18, and 10.3.11—all three of which contain reference to Indra or the gods defeating both asuras and dasyus. I have also discussed AV 3.10.12, which appears as a variant of TS 4.3.11.3 and KS 39.10, containing *dásyūnām* where these texts have *ásurāṇām*. AV 18.2.28 also appears as a more remote variant of VS 2.30. The first half of the former reads: "Which dasyus having entered among the fathers wander having the faces of acquaintances (and) eating what is not sacrificed" (yé dásyavaḥ pitṛ́ṣu práviṣṭā jñātímukhā ahutā́daś cáranti AV 18.2.28) while the first half of the latter reads: "Who being asuras wander at will assuming (various) shapes" (yé rūpā́ṇi pratimuñcámānā ásurāḥ sántaḥ svadháyā cáranti VS 2.30). The third pādas of both verses are identical. There are some differences in the fourth pādas, but they are minor. It is worth noting that the activities described here are rather atypical of both asuras and dasyus and would be more natural for rakṣases.

A few more verses of the AV also depict Indra as defeating the dasyus. "Encircling (them) with that (net) the mighty one scattered the army of the dasyus" (ténābhidhā́ya dásyūnāṃ śakráḥ sénām ápāvapat AV 8.8.5). "Encircling the army of the dasyus with that (net) the mighty one slew a hundred, a thousand, ten thousand, a hundred million" (téna śatáṃ sahásram ayútaṃ nyàrbudaṃ jaghnā́na śakró dásyūnām abhidhā́ya sénayā AV 8.8.7). In my translation I followed Whitney in taking the AVP reading of *senām* for *senayā*. In another verse an amulet is asked to "shake down those attacking (us) as Indra (does) the dasyus" (índra iva dásyūn áva dhūnuṣva pṛtanyatáḥ AV 19.46.2). Another verse refers to the Aryan acquisition of the land by saying that the earth abandoned the dasyus and chose Indra. "The earth abandoning the god-despising dasyus (and) choosing Indra, not Vṛtra, kept herself for the mighty virile bull" (párā dásyūn dádatī devapīyū́n índraṃ vṛṇānā́ pṛthivī́ ná vṛtrám / śakrā́ya dadhre vṛṣabhā́ya vṛ́ṣṇe AV 12.1.37). This verse also seems to connect Vṛtra with the dasyus.

Others besides Indra are occasionally opponents of the dasyus in the AV. "The Aṅgirases split the fortresses of the dasyus" (áṅgiraso dásyūnāṃ bibhiduḥ púras AV 10.6.20). Agni is also called a killer of dasyus. "O Agni, bring here the sorcerer, the *kimīdin* who is praising, for you, O god, praised, have become a killer of dasyus" (stuvānám agna ā́ vaha yātudhā́naṃ kimīdínam / tváṃ hí deva vanditó hantā́ dásyor babhū́vitha AV 1.7.1). This verse also suggests some connection of dasyus with black magic. As this brief survey indicates, such a connection is not as often mentioned for dasyus as it is for rakṣases. Perhaps the verse indicates that the indigenous people were among those often suspected of black magic. The verse does not say that the dasyu is the demon sent by the sorcerer as a rakṣas might be sent. Another verse addressed to a type of demon called *sadānvā–* also mentions dasyus. "If you are of those who possess fields or if sent by men (or) if you are born from the dasyus, disappear from here, O *Sadānvās*" (yádi sthá kṣetriyā́ṇāṃ yádi vā púruṣeṣitāḥ / yádi sthá dásyubhyo jātā́ náśyatetáḥ sadānvāḥ AV 2.14.5). Here again the dasyu is not the evil demon, but the one who sends it.

The AVP has a few verses containing *dásyu–* which are not found in the AV, but this text is so corrupt that they are hardly worth more than a brief mention. One poet asks to overcome a certain enemy as Indra did the dasyus (abhi tvām aham ojasendro dasyūn ivā bhuvam AVP 1.60.1). Another requests the one he invokes to act against his rivals as Indra did against the inferior dasyus (indraivo dhasyon adharāṃ kṛṇsvasva. AVP 13.3.8. Barret reads: indra iva dasyūn adharāṃ kṛṇuṣva). An amulet is said to be that "by which Indra hurled (at) the heroes of the dasyus, of the asuras" (AVP 19.31.8). This was quoted and discussed previously.

There are two mentions of the dāsī of the dasyus, but the verses are too corrupt to make much sense of them (AVP 8.16.7 = 20.47.9 and 8.16.5). There are also two references to killing the dasyus (*dasyuhatya–*) (AVP 19.50.13 and 14).

The VVRI Index indicates no other occurrences of *dásyu–* in the remaining Saṃhitās which are not quoted (sometimes with some variations) from the RV. There are also no new verses containing *dásyu–* in the RV Khila. The Brāhmaṇas contain only four new occurrences of *dásyu–*,[2] and one of these is in a *pratīka* of an otherwise unknown mantra (indra iva dasyūn pramṛṇa iti. Sāmavidhāna Brāhmaṇa 3.6.9). In the Aitareya Brāhmaṇa a story is told about Viśvāmitra cursing his sons that their offspring should inherit the ends of the earth. As a result, most of the dasyus are Viśvāmitra's descendents (Aitareya Brāhmaṇa 7.18). In the Śatapatha Brāhmaṇa Indra refers to Vṛtra as a dasyu when he chastises Agni and Soma for supporting Vṛtra against him (ŚB 1.6.3.13). In the Jaiminīya Brāhmaṇa the advice is given that if one is wandering in the woods with a *kṣatriya* and meets a dasyu, one should be friendly (JB 2.423).

There are only two new occurrences of derivatives or compounds of *dásyu–* in the Brāhmaṇas and the Saṃhitās other than RV, AV, and AVP. The one invoked in MS 4.12.3 is asked to "become like Indra the dasyu-killer" (índra iva dasyuhā́ bhava MS 4.12.3). And Indra-Soma are referred to as "the best dasyu-killers in battle" (yudhi dasyuhantamā. Kāṭhaka. Aśītibhadram 61:14)

It is remarkable that *dásyu–* becomes so rare after the AV. One possible reason for this is that by this time the invading Aryans had taken over the land and absorbed the indigenous people and therefore no longer needed to use this term for them. This was one factor in the decline in the use of *dásyu–*, but not the only one. This word drops out of usage about the same time that *ásura–* begins to be used in the pejorative sense. *Ásura–* in this meaning seems to replace *dásyu–*. We have seen how similar the meanings of these two words are in many verses and even one verse in which *ásura–* actually replaces *dásyu–* in some of the variants in other texts.

2. The VVRI Index lists five others. Three of these are slight variations of verses in the RV. TB 3.88 = RV 5.70.3. JB 3.233 = RV 8.98.6. TB 2.5.8.11 = RV 7.19.4. Kāṇvīya - Śatapatha Brāhmaṇa 2.6.1.7 apparently corresponds with ŚB 1.6.3.13 Śāṃkhāyana-Āraṇyaka 12.3 seems to be an error.

Chapter XII

DĀSA– IN THE SAṂHITĀS AND BRĀHMAṆAS

In this chapter I shall consider the occurrences of *dāsá*– and *dā́sa*–. I shall begin with the noun *dāsá*–.

Only a few adjectives are used of dāsas in the RV. Two dāsas are said to be ransom-demanding (*vasnayántā*) (RV 6.47.21), and another is said to think himself immortal (ámartyaṃ cid dāsáṃ mányamānam RV 2.11.2). However, as with *dásyu*–, many dāsas are given proper names. Namuci (RV 5.30.7, 5.30.8, 6.20.6 and 10.73.7), Varcin (RV 4.30.15 and 6.47.21), Śambara (RV 4.30.14 and 6.47.21), Arśasāna (RV 2.20.6), Ahīśuva (RV 8.32.2), and Balbūtha Tarukṣa (RV 8.46.32) are all called dāsas in the RV. Of these Varcin is elsewhere called an asura (RV 7.99.5) and Namuci is called an āsura (RV 10.131.4). Śambara is elsewhere called a dasyu (RV 6.31.4). So the terms *ásura*–, *dásyu*–, and *dāsá*– are at the very least not mutually exclusive.

There are very few mentions of activities of the dāsas by virtue of which they are considered enemies. But there are two verses that suggest such activities.

> What's more, the dāsa made women into his weapons. 'What can these his frail weapons do to me?'
> For Indra discovered the two female breasts of this one.
> Then he went forth to fight the dasyu.
>
> (stríyo hí dāsá ā́yudhāni cakré kím mā karann abalā́ asya sénāḥ/ antár hy ákhyad ubhé asya dhéne áthópa práidyudháye dásyum índraḥ RV 5.30.9)
>
> O generous one, not by my will did Vyaṃsa break both (your) jawbones, wounding you. Then (though) wounded, you got the upper hand. You smashed the head of the dāsa with (your) weapon.
>
> (mámac caná te maghavan vyàṃso nivividhvā́m̐ ápa hánū jaghā́na / ádhā níviddha úttaro babhūvā́n̐ chíro dāsásya sáṃ piṇag vadhéna RV 4.18.9)

It is instructive to see what other beings are associated with or identified with the dāsas. "Giving a gift at birth, you smashed apart well the enemies, being pleased with the cattle, O generous one, when here you caused the head of the dāsa Namuci to roll, desiring a free path for Manu" (ví ṣū́ mṛ́dho janúṣā dā́nam ínvann áhan gávā maghavant saṃcakānáḥ / átrā dāsásya námuceḥ śíro yád ávartayo mánave gātúm icchán RV 5.30.7). In this verse the dāsa Namuci is named with the enemies. "(Indra is) the powerful one freeing the waters, who killed Sṛbinda, Anarśani, Pipru, (and) the dāsa Ahīśuva" (yáḥ sṛ́bindam ánarśaniṃ píprum dāsám ahīśúvaṃ / vádhīd ugró riṇánn apáḥ RV 8.32.2). Although *dāsá-* appears only with the last of these four names, it is quite likely that the other three are dāsas as well. This is significant since Pipru is elsewhere called an asura. "The Aryan found a counterweight for the dāsa. Indra shattered the fortifications of the magical asura Pipru, working with Ṛjiśvan" (vidád dāsā́ya pratimā́nam ā́ryaḥ / dṛḷhā́ni pípror ásurasya māyína índro vy àsyac cakṛvā́m̐ ṛjíśvanā RV 10.138.3). This verse not only calls Pipru an asura, but also seems to identify him again as a dāsa. "O Indra, you caused the great (waters) to flow, which you caused to swell, the many (waters) enclosed by the serpent, O hero. You struck down even the dāsa thinking (himself) immortal (when you were) being increased by praises" (sṛjó mahī́r indra yā́ ápinvaḥ páriṣṭhitā áhinā śūra pūrvī́ḥ / ámartyaṃ cid dāsáṃ mányamānam ávābhinad uktháir vāvṛdhānáḥ RV 2.11.2). If the two halves of this verse refer to the same event, then Vṛtra seems to be called a dāsa here. One should recall in this connection AV 12.1.37, which connects Vṛtra with the dasyus. "The dasyu who is without ritual acts, does not think, has other vows, (and) is inhuman, (goes) against us. May you outwit the weapon of this dāsa, O enemy-killer" (akarmā́ dásyur abhí no amantúr anyávrato ámānuṣaḥ / tváṃ tásyāmitrahan vádhar dāsásya dambhaya RV 10.22.8). This verse (which was discussed in the last chapter) apparently identifies the dāsa and the dasyu. "He made the earth a cushion for the dāsa; the generous one made the three (rivers) gleaming with drops; he threw Kuyavāc down into a bad dwelling place, into need" (kṣā́ṃ dāsā́yopabárhaṇīṃ kaḥ / kárat tisró maghávā dā́nucitrā ní duryoṇé kúyavācaṃ mṛdhí śret RV 1.174.7). This verse adds Kuyavāc to the list of dāsas. "(It is you Indra) who releases from constriction, from the bear, or who bends down the weapon of the dāsa from the

Aryan among the seven rivers, O very strong one" (yá ṛ́kṣād áṃhaso mucád yó vā́ryāt saptá síndhuṣu / vádhar dāsásya tuvinṛmṇa nīnamaḥ RV 8.24.27). The translation of this verse is uncertain, but if this translation is correct, the dāsa is lumped together with other evils (constriction and the bear) and distinguished from the Aryan.

Every verse in the RV which speaks of the dāsas (*dāsá-*) as enemies has Indra as the one opposed to them. He causes the head of the dāsa Namuci to roll (dāsásya námuceḥ śíro yád ávartayo RV 5.30.7). He is twice described as "churning the head of the dāsa Namuci" (śíro dāsásya námucer mathāyán RV 5.30.8 and 6.20.6). He killed Sṛbinda, Anarśani, Pipru, and the dāsa Ahiśuva (yáḥ sṛ́bindam ánarśanim píprum dāsám ahīśúvam / vádhīd. RV 8.32.2). He made the earth a cushion for the dāsa Kuyavāc and threw him down into a miserable place (kṣā́ṃ dāsā́yopabárhaṇīṃ kaḥ / kárat tisró maghávā dā́nucitrā ní duryoṇé kúyavācaṃ mṛdhí śret RV 1.174.7). He "slew one thousand one hundred five (men) of the dāsa Varcin like fellies" (utá dāsásya varcínaḥ sahásrāṇi śatā́vadhīḥ / ádhi páñca pradhī́m̐r iva RV 4.30.15). He "slew the ransom-demanding dāsas Varcin and Śambara in Udavraja" (áhan dāsā́ vṛṣabhó vasnayántodávraje varcínaṃ śámbaraṃ ca RV 6.47.21). He "struck down the dāsa Śambara, son of Kulitara, from the high mountain" (utá dāsáṃ kaulitaráṃ bṛhatáḥ párvatād ádhi / ávāhann indra śámbaraṃ RV 4.30.14). He carried down the head of the dāsa Arśasāna (áva priyám arśasānásya sāhvā́ñ chíro bharad dāsásya svadhā́vān RV 2.20.6). He put 30,000 dāsas to sleep for Dabhīti with māyā and blows (ásvāpayad dabhítaye sahásrā triṃśátaṃ háthaiḥ / dāsā́nām índro māyáyā. RV 4.30.21). When Indra shattered the fortifications of the asura Pipru, the Aryan (either Indra or his ally) found a counterweight for the dāsa (vidád dāsā́ya pratimā́nam ā́ryaḥ / dṛḷhā́ni píപror ásurasya māyína índro vy ā́syac cakṛvā́m̐ ṛjíśvanā RV 10.138.3). Indra is invoked to outwit the strength of the dāsa (ójo dāsásya dambhaya RV 8.40.6) or to outwit the weapon of the dāsa (vádhar dāsásya dambhaya RV 10.22.8). Indra also "bends down the weapon of the dāsa from the Aryan among the seven rivers" (yó vā́ryāt saptá síndhuṣu / vádhar dāsásya tuvinṛmṇa nīnamaḥ RV 8.24.27). This translation is uncertain. He "struck down even the dāsa thinking (himself) immortal" (ámartyaṃ cid dāsáṃ mányamānam ávābhinad RV 2.11.2). As we saw before, this dāsa is apparently Vṛtra. Even though wounded, he smashed the head of the dāsa Vyaṃsa (mámac-caná te maghavan vyàṃso nivividhvā́m̐ ápa hánū jaghā́na / ádhā níviddha úttaro babhūvā́ñ chíro dāsásya sáṃ piṇag vadhéna RV 4.18.9). Indra went forth to fight the dasyu when the dāsa made women into his weapons (stríyo hí dāsá ā́yudhāni cakré kíṃ mā karann abalā́ asya sénāḥ / antár hy ákhyad ubhé asya dhéne áthópa práid yudháye dásyum índraḥ RV 5.30.9). He is asked to put on protective armor and strike down the dāsa with blows (mádhye vasiṣva tuvinṛmṇorvór ní dāsáṃ śiśnatho háthaiḥ. RV 8.70.10). "Increasing in strength, having much strength, the enemy (Indra) gives fear to the dāsa" (vāvṛdhānáḥ śávasā bhū́ryojāḥ śátrur dāsā́ya bhiyásaṃ dadhāti RV 10. 120.2). "He curtailed the name even of the sun in his own house, the bull (curtailed) even the name of the dāsa in battles" (tatakṣé sū́ryāya cid ókasi své vṛ́ṣā samátsu dāsásya nā́ma cit RV 5.33.4). This translation follows Geldner's. The translation of this last half verse and its meaning are very uncertain, but it does seem clearly to be in agreement with the other verses cited which name Indra as the opponent of the dāsas.

There are a few more verses containing *dāsá–* in the RV in which the word seems clearly to mean "slave" or "servant." "May blameless I be servile to the impatient god as a dāsa to his benefactor" (áraṃ dāsó ná mīḷhúṣe karāṇy aháṃ devā́ya bhū́rṇayé 'nāgāḥ RV 7.86.7). "(He gave) to me one hundred asses, one hundred wooly (sheep), one hundred dāsas, (and) further garlands" (śatáṃ me gardabhā́nāṃ śatám ū́rṇāvatīnām / śatáṃ dāsā́m̐ áti srájaḥ RV 8.56.3). "And Yadu and Turva gave two dāsas for service, proportionally trained, together with plenty of cows" (utá dāsā́ parivíṣe smáddiṣṭī góparīṇasā / yádus turváś ca māmahe RV 10.62.10).

There are two more verses in which the sense of *dāsá–* is unclear. "I the poet received one hundred by the dāsa Balbutha Tarukṣa" (śatáṃ dāsé balbūthé vípras tárukṣa ā́ dade RV 8.46.32). It is unclear whether *dāsá–* is part of the name, but this looks very much like a non-Aryan name. "The most motherly rivers should not devour me when the dāsas put this well-bound one down. When Traitana splits the head of this one, the dāsa himself eats up the breast and shoulders" (ná mā garan nadyò mātṛ́tamā dāsā́ yád īṃ súsamubdham avā́dhuḥ / śíro yád asya traitanó vitákṣat svayáṃ dāsá úro áṃsāv ápi gdha RV 1.158.5). Geldner suggests that *dāsá–* here refers to a servant and not the dāsa who is an enemy of the Aryans. I have no suggestions for clarifying the verse.

Dāsas appear to be much more like dasyus than like rakṣases. They do not fly by night, take on various shapes, disrupt sacrifices, or carry out the bidding of sorcerers as do rakṣases. However, like the dasyus they are often given names, have warriors fighting for them, and have Indra, not Agni, as their main opponent. In short, *dāsá–* also seems to be used to refer to the indigenous people whom the invading Aryans conquered. The occurrences of *dāsá–* which must mean "servant" or "slave" are also consistent with this. The Aryans would quite naturally take conquered people as slaves. But there is another tendency in evidence here, too. The appearances of Vṛtra and Namuci as dāsas show that the term is also used for figures who are not historical, but mythological.

Dā́sa– is the adjectival form of *dāsá–*. The usages of this term will confirm the conclusions just drawn concerning the meaning of *dāsá–*. Although *dā́sa–* is an adjective, it is sometimes used without any noun to qualify and is then virtually equivalent to *dāsá–*. Nevertheless, for clarity I shall translate such occurrences here by "dāsic one."

Since *dā́sa–* is rarely used as a noun, there is only one verse in which adjectives appear modifying it. "The houselord overcame the six-eyed, three-headed, loud-roaring dāsic one" (sá íd dā́saṃ tuvīrávaṃ pátir dán ṣalakṣáṃ triśīrṣā́ṇam damanyat RV 10.99.6). This verse is also atypical in describing the dāsa in terms which are definitely not human.

Although *dā́sa–* is seldom modified, it often modifies other words. It will be instructive to look at these. Dāsic fortresses (*púr–*) are mentioned twice (RV 1.103.3 and 4.32.10) and implied once (RV 2.20.7). Dāsic tribes (*víś–*) are mentioned four times (RV 2.11.4, 4.28.4, 6.25.2, and 10.148.2) and the dāsic race or color (*várṇa–*) once (RV 2.12.4). Five verses mention dāsic enemies (*vṛtrá–*) (RV 6.22.10, 6.33.3, 6.60.6, 7.83.1, and 10.69.6). *Dā́sa–* occurs with three proper names—Śambara (RV 6.26.5), Śuṣṇa (RV 7.19.2), and Vṛṣaśipra (RV 7.99.4). *Dā́sa–* occurs once modifying nourishment (*íṣ–*) (RV 8.5.31), once with the godless one (*ádeva–*) (RV 10.38.3), and once modifying power (*ójas–*) (RV 10.54.1).

Several verses distinguish Aryans and dāsas. "Throw down the dāsic tribes for the Aryan" (ā́ryāya víśó 'va tārīr dā́sīḥ RV 6.25.2). "The Aryan leads the dāsic one at will" (yathāvaśáṃ nayati dā́sam ā́ryaḥ RV 5.34.6). "I go observing, distinguishing (between) the dāsic one (and) the Aryan" (ayám emi vicā́kaśad vicinván dā́sam ā́ryam RV 10.86.19). "Hold distant the weapon either of the dāsic one or of the Aryan, O generous one" (dā́sasya vā maghavann ā́ryasya vā sanutár yavayā vadhám RV 10.102.3). "May we conquer the dāsic one (and) the Aryan" (sāhyā́ma dā́sam ā́ryaṃ RV 10.83.1). There are several references to dāsic and Aryan enemies (dā́sā vṛtrā́ṇy ā́ryā RV 6.33.3 and 10.69.6, ható vṛtrā́ṇy ā́ryā ható dā́sāni RV 6.60.6, dā́sā ca vṛtrā́ hatám ā́ryāṇi ca RV 7.83.1, dā́sāny ā́ryāṇi vṛtrā́ RV 6.22.10). Another verse also draws this racial distinction without naming the Aryans. "The gods should make harmless the anger of the dāsic one. They should help our race to well-being" (devā́so manyúṃ dā́sasya ścamnan té na ā́ vakṣant suvitā́ya várṇaṃ RV 1.104.2).[1]

The dāsic one is often associated with or identified with enemies or those causing harm. Several such references to Aryan and dāsic enemies were just listed. But there is one more verse that does not mention the Aryans. "Indra the fort-breaker overcame the dāsic one with chants, the finder-of-goods dispersing the enemy" (índraḥ pūrbhíd ā́tirad dā́sam arkáir vidádvasur dáyamāno ví śátrūn RV 3.34.1). The dāsic race is once associated with *ari*–. "By whom all these exploits are done, who has defeated and put into hiding the dāsic race, who has taken the riches of the *ari* as a game winner, who won the stakes, he O people, is Indra" (yénemā́ víśvā cyávanā kṛtā́ni yó dā́saṃ várṇam ádharaṃ gúhā́kaḥ / śvaghnī́va yó jigīvā́ṃ lakṣám ā́dad aryáḥ puṣṭā́ni sá janāsa índraḥ RV 2.12.4). Another verse compares the killing of the dāsic one to the killing of Vṛtra. "It is I who (protecting) Navavastva (and) Bṛhadratha smashed the dāsic one like Vṛtra, I the Vṛtra-killer, (as then) as I transformed the growing, thoroughly spreading out (Vṛtra) at the far end of the realm into heavenly lights" (ahám sá yó návavāstvaṃ bṛhádrathaṃ sáṃ vṛtréva dā́saṃ vṛtra-

1. There is one more verse in the RV containing the word *dā́sa*- which seems to contrast Aryan and dāsa, but I have not been able to translate it adequately. It is in a hymn to Indra. yásāyáṃ viśva ā́ryo dā́saḥ śevadhipā́ / aríḥ tirā́ś cid aryé rúśame pávīravi túbhyét só ajyate rayíḥ RV 8.51.9. The first part seems to mean "He (Indra) of whom every Aryan (or) dāsic miser is an enemy. . . ."

hārujaṃ / yád vardháyantaṃ pratháyantam ānuṣág dūré pāré rájaso rocanā́karaṃ RV 10.49.6). My translation follows Geldner's. Two more verses mention dāsic tribes and fortresses in connection with dasyus, but these were discussed in the last chapter (RV 1. 103.3 and 4.28.4).

Of those who are named as being in opposition to the dāsic ones, Indra is by far the most frequent. Indra is so named twenty-four times. None of the other six named opponents of the dāsic ones are so named more than once, and three of these six are dvandva compounds containing *índra–*. These six are: Indra-Varuṇa, Indra-Aśvins, Indra-Agni, Agni, the devas, and "we" with Manyu as companion.

Indra defeated the dāsic tribes. "Indra the fort-breaker overcame the dāsic one with chants" (índraḥ pūrbhíd ā́tirad dā́sam arkáir RV 3.34.1). It is he "who defeated and put into hiding the dāsic race" (yó dā́saṃ várṇam ádharaṃ gúhā́kaḥ RV 2.12.4). He "overcame the six-eyed, three-headed, loudroaring dāsic one" (sá íd dā́saṃ tuvīrávaṃ pátir dán ṣaḷakṣám triśīrṣā́ṇaṃ damanyat RV 10.99.6). He is requested to "conquer the dāsic tribes with the sun" (asmé dā́sīr víśaḥ sū́ryeṇa sahyāḥ RV 2.11.4, dā́sīr víśaḥ sū́ryeṇa sahyāḥ RV 10.148.2). He "overcame the dāsic power" (ā́tiro dā́sam ójaḥ RV 10.54.1). "He slew the dāsic (tribes)" (hán dā́sīḥ RV 6.20.10). "He made the dāsic tribes to be without praise" (víśo dā́sīr akṛṇor apraśastā́ḥ RV 4.28.4). He is asked to "throw down the dāsic tribes for the Aryan" (ā́ryāya víśó 'va tārīr dā́sīḥ RV 6.25.2). One poet also prays to Indra that "the dāsic or Aryan godless one who intends to fight us be enemies easily overcome by us for you" (yó no dā́sa ā́ryo vā puruṣṭutā́deva indra yudháye cíketati / asmā́bhiṣ ṭe suṣáhāḥ santu śátravas RV 10.38.3).

Indra also destroys the fortresses of the dāsas. "Breaking dāsic fortresses he wanders widely" (púro vibhindánn acarad ví dā́sīḥ RV 1.103.3). "We would proclaim your heroic deeds, the dāsic fortresses which you attacked and broke open, being intoxicated (with soma)" (prá te vocāma vīryā̀ yā́ mandasānā́ ā́rujaḥ / púro dā́sīr abhī́tya RV 4.32.10). "The Vṛtra-killer Indra split the dāsic (fortresses) which had the black race in their wombs, the fort-breaker" (sá vṛtrahéndraḥ kṛṣṇáyonīḥ purandaró dā́sīr airayad ví RV 2.20.7). This verse also makes it clear that the dāsas were a dark-skinned race.

There are also some more explicit descriptions of Indra's treatment of the dāsas. "I (Indra) the Vṛtra-killer smashed the dāsic one like Vṛtra" (sáṃ vṛtréva dā́saṃ vṛtrahā́rujaṃ RV 10. 49.6). "O Indra, strike both enemies, dāsic and Aryan enemies, O hero, like trees" (tváṃ tā́m̐ indrobháyām̐ amítrān dā́sā vṛtrā́ṇy ā́ryā ca śūra / vádhir váneva RV 6.33.3). "I (Indra) got rid of the powerful dāsic one with blows" (ŕ̥dhak kṛṣe dā́saṃ kŕ̥tvyaṃ háthaiḥ RV 10.49.7). Indra "struck down dāsic Śambara from the mountain" (áva girér dā́saṃ śámbaraṃ han RV 6.26.5). Indra helped Kutsa in battle by handing over dāsic Śuṣṇa, the Kuyava, to him (tváṃ ha tyád indra kútsam āvaḥ śúśrūṣamāṇas tanvā̀ samaryé / dā́saṃ yác chúṣṇaṃ kúyavam ny àsmā árandhaya ārjuneyā́ya śíkṣan RV 7.19.2).

There are a few other miscellaneous ways in which Indra deals with the dāsas. He goes "observing (and) distinguishing (between) the dāsic one and the Aryan" (ayám emi vicā́kaśad vicinván dā́sam ā́ryaṃ RV 10.86.19). Indra is asked to "hold distant the weapon either of the dāsa or of the Aryan" (dā́sasya vā maghavann ā́ryasya vā sanutár yavayā vadhám RV 10.102.3). Indra is asked to grant great, continuous, untiring luck for conquering the enemy, by which he makes the dāsic, Aryan, and Nāhuṣic enemies flee (ā́ saṃyátam indra ṇaḥ svastíṃ śatrutū́ryāya bṛhatím ámṛdhrāṃ / yáyā dā́sāny ā́ryāṇi vṛtrā́ káro vajrint sutúkā nā́huṣāṇi RV 6.22.10). "The Aryan (Indra) leads the dāsic one at will" (yathāvaśáṃ nayati dā́sam ā́ryaḥ RV 5.34.6). This verse also seems to be referring to *dā́sa–* in the meaning of "servant" or "slave." "I (Indra) exterminate even the name of the dāsic one" (áva kṣṇaumi dā́sasya nā́ma cit RV 10.23.2). In his notes Geldner interprets the "name of the dāsic one" here to mean everything that is called dāsic.[2] Indra also "slew Namuci who wished to appear noble, making the dāsic one without māyā for the ṛṣi" (tváṃ jaghantha námuciṃ makhasyúṃ dā́saṃ kṛṇvāná ŕ̥ṣaye vímāyaṃ RV 10.73.7).

The other gods interact with the dāsic ones in about the same way. "You (Agni) conquered riches of the plain (and) of the mountain, dāsic enemies (and) Aryan" (sám ajryā̀ parvatyā̀ vásūni dā́sā vṛtrā́ṇy ā́ryā jigetha RV 10.69.6). Indra-Viṣṇu "struck (down) the māyās even of the dāsic Vṛṣaśipra in battles" (dā́sasya

2. Geldner, *Der Rig-Veda*, Vol. 3, p. 160.

cid vṛṣaśiprásya māyā́ jaghnáthur narā pṛtanā́jyeṣu RV 7.99.4). Indra-Varuṇa are asked to "kill the enemies, both dāsic and Aryan" (dā́sā ca vṛtrā́ hatám ā́ryāṇi ca RV 7.83.1). It is said of Indra-Agni: "You two kill the Aryan enemies; you two lords of the clan kill the dāsic (ones)" (ható vṛtrā́ṇy ā́ryā ható dā́sāni sátpatī RV 6.60.6). "The gods should make harmless the anger of the dāsic one" (devā́so manyúṃ dā́sasya ścamnan RV 1.104.2). "May we conquer the dāsic one, the Aryan, with you (Manyu) as companion" (sāhyā́ma dā́sam ā́ryaṃ tváyā yujā́ RV 10.83.1).

There is one more verse containing *dā́sa–* which clearly contrasts the dāsas with the Aryan poets. It is in a hymn to the Aśvins. "O immortal Aśvins, bring here from the distance the many dāsic nourishments, eating (them)" (ā́ vahethe parākā́t pūrvír aśnántāv aśvinā / íṣo dā́sīr amartyā RV 8.5.31).

There are only two compounds containing *dāsa–* in the RV. *Dāsápravarga–* occurs once meaning "provided with a troop of slaves" and modifying the wealth (*rayí–*) that the poet wishes to obtain from Uṣas (úṣas tám aśyāṃ yaśásaṃ suvíraṃ dāsápravargaṃ rayím áśvabudhyam RV 1.92.8). Dāsápatnī occurs four times. "O Indra-Agni, you shook together with a single action the ninety forts which had the dāsa as master" (índrāgnī navatím púro dāsápatnīr adhūnutam / sākám ékena kármaṇā RV 3.12.6). "The waters, which had the dāsa as master, protected by the serpent, stood blocked up like the cows of Paṇi. Having killed Vṛtra, he (Indra) opened up the orifice of the waters which was enclosed" (dāsápatnīr áhigopā atiṣṭhan níruddhā ā́paḥ paṇíneva gā́vaḥ / apā́ṃ bílam ápihitaṃ yád ā́sīd vṛtráṃ jaghanvā́m̐ ápa tád vavāra RV 1.32.11). Vṛtra is referred to as a dāsa here.[3] Two other verses also say that Indra conquered the waters which had the dāsa as master (víśvā apó ajayad dāsápatnīḥ RV 5.30.5, tvám apó ajayo dāsápatnīḥ RV 8.96.18).

Since there are only a few new occurrences of *dāsá–*, *dā́sa–*, and their derivatives and compounds in the remaining Saṃhitās and Brāhmaṇas, I shall discuss them here also.

Some of the mentions of *dāsá–* in the AV are much like those in the RV. Thus a poet asks that the dāsas may creep downward to the earth (nīcáir dāsā́ / úpa sarpantu bhū́mim AV 5.11.6). Another verse draws a contrast between Aryan and dāsa when Agni

3. Perhaps this is a way of saying in mythological terminology that the dāsas built dams which Indra smasned.

says, "neither Aryan nor dāsa damages by his might the vow which I shall maintain" (ná me dāsó nā́ryo mahitvā́ vratáṃ mīmāya yád aháṃ dhariṣyé AV 5.11.3). *Dāsā́-* occurs in the meaning "slave" when the power of a particular ointment is expressed by saying that fever, a disease called *balāsa*, and the snake are slaves to it (tráyo dāsā́ ā́ñjanasya takmā́ balā́sa ā́d áhiḥ AV 4.9.8).

The feminine form of *dā́sa-* occurs four times in the AV. In one verse a fever is sent to afflict the dāsī (tákman vyāla ví gada vyàṅga bhū́ri yāvaya / dāsī́ṃ niṣṭákvarīm iccha tā́ṃ vájreṇa sám arpaya AV 5.22.6). There are several uncertainties about the exact translation of this verse. Two other verses refer to the polluting effects of the dāsī. "Or when a dāsī with wet hands smears (it), cleanse the mortar (and) pestle, O waters" (yád vā dāsy ā̀rdráhastā samaṅktá ulū́khalaṃ músalaṃ śumbhatāpaḥ AV 12.3.13). "If a dāsī throws together the urine (and) dung of her (a cow), then a deformity which does not disappear is born" (yád asyā́ḥ pálpūlanaṃ śákṛd dāsī́ samásyati / tátóparūpaṃ jāyate tásmād ávyeṣyad énasaḥ AV 12.4.9). The other verse containing *dāsī́-* is too obscure and makes no sense without some emendation (AV 5.13.8. See Whitney's comments on this verse.). There are further occurrences of this word in the AVP, but this text is so corrupt that it is hardly worthwhile to examine them.[4]

Dāsa- occurs four times in new verses in the RV Khila—twice referring to enemies and twice to slaves. "Indra helped the Aryan race; he stopped the dāsic clans" (indra ud āryaṃ vvarṇam atirad ava dāsīd viśo astabhnāt RVKh 5.5.11). The translation is uncertain. Another poet asks his god to "make the dāsas distant" (párān kṛṇuṣva dāsā́n RVKh 3.16.5). One poet claims to have been given a hundred asses, a hundred sheep, and a hundred female slaves (śatáṃ me gardabhā́nāṃ śatám ū́rṇāvatīnām / śatán dāsā́m̐ ádhi srajaḥ RVKh 3.8.3). Another asks that he may find men and female slaves (dāsyó vindéyaṃ púruṣān ahám RVKh 2.6.15). *Dāsa-* occurs five more times in the remaining Saṃhitās and Brāhmaṇas—four of these in the feminine meaning "female slave" (TS 7.5.10.1, JB 2.352, AB 2.19, KB 12.3)[5] and one in the masculine

4. If the reader wishes to examine them, they can be found at AVP 4.21.1, 5.26.5, 6.14.5, 6.14.7, 9.22.17, 13.1.9, 19.37.1, and 20.38.4.

5. The unclear passage is from JB 2.196 and reads: pañcānāṃ ha vai puruṣāṇāṃ rājyāyābhiṣicyamāno 'bhiṣicyate—rājñe rājanyāya sūtāya grāmaṇye śūdrāya dāsāya. The problem with this passage is that it speaks of five persons and then lists six, making it uncertain which two (if any) are meant to be synonymous. Also, two of the manuscripts have *mārayā* instead of dāsāya.

is a passage whose meaning is not quite certain. The compounds *dāsīśata–* and *dāsīsahasra–* also occur once each meaning "hundreds of female slaves" and "thousands of female slaves" (Svidh 3.5.3 and AB 8.22).

These occurrences of *dā́sa–* and its compounds and derivatives in the RV and *dāsá–*, *dā́sa–*, and their compounds and derivatives in the remaining Saṃhitās and Brāhmaṇas confirm what was suggested earlier about the meaning of *dāsá–*. Dāsas are indigenous people as are the dasyus, but *dāsá–* has the further connotation of being inferior and thus slaves or servants. It is even clearer than it was with the dasyus that Indra and not Agni was the chief opponent of these people. This is quite significant for an understanding of the newly developing meaning of *ásura–*. In most of the verses examined in previous chapters, when an enemy of the asuras was specifically named, that enemy was Indra. A comparison of the characteristics of the evil asuras discussed in previous chapters with the characteristics of rakṣases, dasyus, and dāsas makes it clear that if any of the later three served as a model for the evolving concept of the former, it was the dāsas and dasyus and not the rakṣases. The asuras have much more in common with these human enemies than with the non-human rakṣases. The distribution of the words *dāsa–*, *dásyu–*, and *ásura–* in the "demonic" sense is also quite remarkable. The texts in which the last of these three appear are almost devoid of the first two. It looks very much as if *ásura–* in its new meaning replaced the other two terms. But, of course, the process was not quite that simple. As these terms were being replaced the concept denoted by them was gradually shifting from a more human-like figure to a less human-like figure until by the time of the Śatapatha Brāhmaṇa an asura was practically the same as a rakṣas.

CHAPTER XIII

ÁSURA– IN THE BRĀHMAṆAS

The Brāhmaṇas (including the brāhmaṇa portions of the Black Yajur Veda) contain little material that is of any help in understanding the early shift in the meaning of *ásura–*. By the time of the composition of these texts, the word had come to be used almost exclusively to indicate a class of beings opposed to the gods. I have examined every passage in these texts which contains the word *ásura–* or its derivative or compounds, but since there are about six hundred such passages, it does not seem advisable to cite them all here. I shall instead discuss some of the general characteristics of these passages and give references to a few of the passages that illustrate these characteristics. However, unlike the references in the preceding chapters, these will *not* be exhaustive. Of course, I shall discuss a few of the more interesting passages in greater detail.

In virtually all the passages containing *ásura–* in the brāhmaṇa portions of the TS, the asuras are a class of beings who are in conflict with the gods. The word does not occur in the singular in the brāhmaṇa portion of the text. When an individual member of this class is named, he is called an āsura (See TS 2.1.2.2, 2.5.11.1, 2.6.9.4-5). It is usually the gods as a group who oppose the asuras, but when an individual god is mentioned as being opposed to them, it is equally likely to be Indra or Agni (See TS 6.2.2.7 and TS 6.2.4.3). Nearly all the occurrences of *ásura–* in these portions of the text are in stories about a battle between the gods and the asuras. The reason for the battle is seldom given. Instead, the story begins by simply stating that the gods and the asuras were in conflict. (TS 3.4.4.1, 5.3.11.1, etc.). Sometimes the story begins by saying that the gods and asuras contended for these worlds (TS 2.6.1.3). Rarely some other motivation is given—for example, the asuras steal the wealth of the gods (TS 1.5.9.2) or the sacrifice is with the asuras and the gods wish to have it (TS 6.3.7.2). The gods always win these conflicts. Thus they conquer these worlds or win the wealth of the asuras or gain control of the sacrifice (TS 2.1.3.1, 1.7.4.6, 6.3.7.2). Some stories begin by saying that the asuras mimicked the sacrifices of the gods (TS 2.5.4.1, 3.2.2.2, 3.4.6.1). The gods then do something that the asuras cannot mimic, and thus the asuras are defeated. Some passages make it clear that asuras and rakṣases are different by naming both in a list of beings (TS 2.4.1.1), but other passages seem to interchange the words and thus treat them as synonyms (TS 6.3.7.1-2, 6.2.1.5, 6.2.11.1). In the TS it is common for the gods to win the conflict by using some special rite (TS 1.7.3.3, 1.7.4.2). It is also quite common for one of these stories to end by saying that the sacrificer who knows of it can defeat his enemies in the same way that the gods defeated their enemies, the asuras (TS 3.4.6.3, 6.4.6.1, etc.). Prajāpati also emerges as a key figure in these passages. He is said to have created the gods and the asuras (TS 3.3.7.1). He is also often instrumental in helping the gods win the conflict (TS 3.3.7.1, 2.5. 11.8-9). It should be noted how similar the conflict of gods and asuras is to the conflict of the Aryans and the dasyus. In both cases the conflict seems to arise because the asuras or dasyus have something which the gods or Aryans want, such as land or wealth. Of course, in the case of the gods and asuras, everything is put on a cosmic scale and ritualized. The gods take the worlds from the asuras and not just the land of India, and the deciding factor in the conflict is often the proper use of some ritual.

The passages in the MS are quite similar to those of the TS. Virtually all deal with conflicts between gods and asuras, which the gods always win, often by means of some rite. About half also contain a final statement to the effect that the sacrificer can employ this same technique to become prosperous or overcome his rivals. *Āsurá–* rather than *ásura–* is still used to refer to any of these beings who are given a proper name and are spoken of in the singular rather than plural (MS 2.1.5, 2.5.2, 3.8.10, 4.1.10, 4.2.9, 4.5. 7). There is also a tendency to associate asuras with various inauspicious things such as the night (MS 1.8.6) or the black in a person's eye (MS 3.6.6). One passage links gods with the first half of the lunar month, day, truth, and the right hand and links asuras with the second half of the lunar month, night, untruth, and the left hand (MS 1.9.3). An etymology of *ásura–* is offered by the suggestion that Prajāpati created asuras from his *asu* (MS 4.2.1). Another passage gives an interesting variation of the Indra-Vṛtra myth. Vṛtra declares that he is the best of the asuras and Indra is the best of the gods, so the two of these make a non-aggression pact. But the other gods kill Vṛtra (MS 4.3.4). This is the earliest passage in which Vṛtra is explicitly called an asura, although he is referred to as a dasyu and a dāsa in earlier texts, as we have seen. Apparently these epithets were appropriate to him in the earlier texts, but as *ásura–* more or less replaced these terms in the later texts, it became an appropriate epithet for Vṛtra here, too.

The KS continues the same themes as the TS and MS. Nearly every passage containing *ásura–* deals with a conflict between gods and asuras which the gods win, and there is frequently a statement that the sacrificer can achieve his goals by similar means. *Āsurá–* rather than *ásura–* is still used for the singular. But there are a few passages of special interest. One tells the story of an asura named Ghoṣa, who fled to the trees, but was caught and bound by the gods. Then he growled in an asuric voice, and the rakṣases responded by attacking the sacrifice (ghoṣo vai nāmāsura āsīt sa vanaspatīn prāviśat taṃ devā gṛhītvobhayato 'badhnat kṣveded asuryā vāg yajñam avavaded rakṣāṁsi yajñam anvavetya hanyur KS 25.8. Similar text in KpS 40.1). Perhaps this passage only reflects the late idea of the near equation of asuras and rakṣases, but it does present both these figures in their older roles. The āsura or asura[1] is in a position of leadership (over the rakṣases), and the rakṣases act at someone's command to do evil by attacking the sacrifice. In another passage the gods and asuras are fighting as usual and decide to settle the fight by each sending a "bull" to fight with brahman as weapons. (Apparently this means they had a debate.) The one whose speech was on top (that is, the winner of the debate) was fit to be a priest, but the loser was unfit to be a priest because he is the asuric race (or color) (tasmād yasyāvācī vāk so 'nārtvijīno 'suryo hi sa varṇas tasmād yasyordhvā vāk sa ārtvijīno devatreva hi sa bārhaspatyam KS 13.4). Perhaps the asuric *varṇa* here is the indigenous people who are not twice-born and are unworthy of becoming priests. The other noteworthy usage of *ásura–* occurs in a passage which deals with the proper way for a householder to obtain a properly consecrated fire for use in his home. The text says, "He should take (the fire) from the house of one who is a brāhmaṇa or a vaiśya (who is) wealthy like an

1. The text is in fact ambiguous because of the sandhi, but all clear cases in the KS have *āsurá-* rather than *ásura-* when the singular is used. Thus *āsurá-* seems to function as the singular of *ásura-* in this text, too.

asura" (yó brāhmaṇó vā váiśyo vā puṣṭó 'sura iva syā́t tásya gṛhā́d ā́haret KS 8.12. See also KpS 7.7. Von Schroeder notes that two of his manuscripts read 'eva' instead of 'iva'. This would change the translation to "one who is indeed a wealthy asura"). This seems to be the latest clear usage in Vedic literature of *ásura–* with the old meaning "lord" applied to a human.

The KpS is basically a condensed version of the KS containing many of the same passages as that work with only slightly different wording. But there is one noteworthy difference concerning *ásura–*. KpS 7.7 repeats the passage from KS 8.12 quoted above, but in the only other occurrences of this word in the singular in which the length of the initial vowel is not ambiguous due to the sandhi, the word is *ásura–* and not *āsurá–* as in the other texts (KpS 42.2 and 43.4). Perhaps this is an indication of the lateness of the KpS.

The Taittirīya Brāhmaṇa (TB) continues the same general themes as the brāhmaṇa portions of the Saṃhitās. The gods and asuras are in conflict, and the gods win, often by discovering a new ritual or performing a ritual correctly while the asuras perform it incorrectly. The sacrificer is frequently advised that he too can prosper by acting as the gods did. When a specific protagonist of the asuras is mentioned, it is sometimes Indra and sometimes Agni. *Āsurá–* rather than *ásura–* is used for the singular. An interesting phrase does occur three times. Three episodes begin by saying that Indra first killed Vṛtra and defeated the asura (índro vṛtrám̐ hatvā́/ ásurān parābhā́vya TB 1.2.3.3, 1.3.10.1, and 1.7.1.6). Vṛtra seems seems to be a personification of the indigenous forces overcome by the Aryans who invaded India.[2] In a previous chapter several verses were quoted which mentioned the dāsic enemies (*dāsā vṛtrā*). If *ásura–* replaced *dāsa–* and *dásyu–* in the later texts, it is quite natural to find the killing of Vṛtra mentioned together with the killing of the asuras. There is one more passage in the TB which is quite interesting for this study. It reads:

> The gods and asuras fought. They contended for the sun. The gods won it. Both a brāhmaṇa and a śūdra fight for a piece of leather. Indeed the brāhmaṇa is the daivic varṇa, the śūdra the

2. This is, of course, only one of the several meanings attached to this multivalued mythological symbol .

asuric. The one should say, 'These prospered; these made good prosperity.' The other (should say), 'These making it inhabited, these made bad prosperity.' Thus what is done well of these, what is success, the one causes that. What is badly done, what is failure, the other strikes that. The brāhmaṇa wins. Thus they find the sun of the rival.

devāsurā́ḥ sáṃyattā āsan / tá ādityé vyāyacchanta / táṃ devā́ḥ sámajan (6) brāhmaṇáś ca śūdráś carmakarté vyā́yacchete / dáivyo vái várṇo brā́hmaṇaḥ / asuryàḥ śūdrā́ḥ / imè 'rātsur imé subhūtám akrann íty anyataró brūyāt / imá udvāsīkāríṇa imé durbhūtám akrann íty anyatarā́ḥ / yád eváiṣām̐ sukṛtáṃ yā́ rā́ddhiḥ / tád anyatarò 'bhíśrīṇāti / yád eváiṣāṃ duṣkṛtáṃ yā́rāddhiḥ / tád anyatarópahanti / brāhmaṇā́ḥ sáṃjayati / amúm evā́ ''dityáṃ bhrā́tṛvyasya sáṃvindante. (TB 1.2.6.6-7)

The commentary to this passage explains that the brāhmaṇa and the śūdra perform a ritual in which they act out the battle of the gods and asuras over the sun, which is represented in the ritual by a round piece of leather. The brāhmaṇa plays the part of the gods and the śūdra the part of the asuras. Hence this passage says that the śūdra is the asuric varṇa. But this statement could also be a recognition that the śūdra varṇa consists of the descendants of the original inhabitants of the land, the dasyus, who in later texts were called asuras. Thus the śūdra, who is a descendant of the historical human asuras plays the role of a mythological asura in a rite which acts out the mythological conflict between the gods and the asuras—a conflict which itself seems to be a mythologized version of the historical conflict between Aryans and historical human asuras (or dasyus).

The Tāṇḍya Mahābrāhmaṇa or Pañcaviṃśa Brāhmaṇa (PB) presents about the same picture of asuras as the brāhmaṇa portions of the Black Yajur Veda and the TB. They are mentioned in passages which speak of their struggle with the gods, and this struggle is always won by the gods. There is a slight but predictable difference in the means by which the gods win these struggles. In the Yajur Veda Brāhmaṇas they often won by discovering and using some rite, but in this Brāhmaṇa of the Sāma Veda they are much more likely to win by discovering and using some sāman. As in the other texts there is frequently a statement at the end of these tales stating that he who knows this can similarly confound his rivals. Also, as in the previous texts *ásura–* is used for the plural and *āsurá–* for the singular.

The theme of rivalry between gods and asuras continues to be prevalent in the Jaiminīya Brāhmaṇa (JB). Of course, the gods always win. There is usually a conclusion to the effect that one who knows this can defeat his rival as well. But there are two passages of special interest. Although *āsurá–* is normally used for the singular and *ásura–* in the plural in this text, JB 3.72 uses *ásura–* in the singular to refer to a being named Akhaga. In JB 1.135 the compound *asurarakṣasa–* occurs. This word is a dvandva compound and occurs in the plural when it is said that the asuras and rakṣases surrounded the gods in heaven. It is significant because it is an early example of an increasing tendency for the asuras and rakṣases to become more and more alike in the later Brāhmaṇas.

The Kauṣītaki Brāhmaṇa, or Śāṃkhāyana Brāhmaṇa (KB), continues these same general themes. The asuras are almost exclusively mentioned in passages which tell of a fight between them and the gods, which the gods win. (An exception is KB 6.15, which simply says that Prajāpati created seed, gods, men, asuras, and Indra and mentions no rivalry.) There is still the usual tag line advising sacrificers to employ similar techniques against their rivals who hate them. When Svarbhānu is mentioned in the singular, *āsurá–* rather than *ásura–* is used (KB 24.3). One passage tells of Indra's being charmed by the asuramāyā of an asurī with whom he had an affair and his escaping by the use of certain verses (KB 23.4). (The translation "charmed" is not certain. See Keith, *Rigveda Brahmanas*, p. 477, n. 2.) More importantly, two passages say that the priests or sacrificer can smite away or obstruct the asuras (KB 12.4 and 17.8). Thus in these two passages the asuras appear to be more like rakṣases than like the opponents of the gods they usually are. In a similar vein *asurarakṣas–* occurs three times in the plural, thus treating these two classes of beings as if they were not really distinct (KB 10.2, 17.9, 28.2). One of these passages begins by saying that asurarakṣases used to impede the sacrifices and ends by saying that Agni smote away the rakṣases, so that *rakṣāṃsi* at the end of the passage seems to be synonymous with *asura rakṣāṃsi* at the beginning (KB 28.2). The Śāṃkhāyana Āraṇyaka has two occurrences of *ásura–*. One says that Indra slew the asuras after gaining mastery over his self (ŚāṃĀ 6.20), and the other says that neither rakṣas, piśāca, jambhaka, asura, nor yakṣa can harm one who has a bilva amulet (ŚāṃĀ 12.5).

The Aitareya Brāhmaṇa (AB) has many of the same basic themes. The asuras are usually mentioned as a group of beings in conflict with the gods, and the gods always win this conflict. There is frequently a tag line to the effect that the sacrificer can likewise prosper or defeat his rivals. The compound *devāsura–* appears a few times, but always in phrases such as "The gods and asuras strove for these worlds" (devāsurā vā eṣu lokeṣu samayatanta AB 1.14). *Asurarakṣas–* occurs in three passages (AB 2.11, 2.36, 6.4). In two more passages asuras and rakṣases also act together, but this is expressed by two separate words rather than a compound (AB 2.11, 5.1). Both of these passages begin by saying that the asuras tried to disturb the sacrifices (an activity more commonly associated with rakṣases in older texts) and end by saying that both asuras and rakṣases were driven away. Thus the two classes of beings appear to be virtually identified. Another passage says that the asuras tried to disrupt the sacrifice, but with no mention of rakṣases (AB 2.31). Since there are less than thirty passages in this text which mention asuras, having six that virtually identify them with rakṣases is rather significant. AB 6.36 also has an interesting passage:

> The Asura folk were rebellious towards the gods; Indra with Bṛhaspati as companion smote away the Asura hue when attacking; verily thus also the sacrificers by means of Indra and Bṛhaspati as aid smite away the Asura hue when attacking.[3]

> asuraviśaṃ ha vai devān abhyudācārya āsīt / sa indro bṛhaspatinaiva yujāsuryaṃ varṇam abhidāsantam apāhan / tathaivaitad yujamānā indrā– bṛhaspatibhyām eva yujāsuryaṃ varṇam abhidāsantam apaghnate. (AB 6.36)

The uses of *asuraviś–* and *asurya– varṇa–* sound very much like references to dasyus. There is one new occurrence of *ásura–* in the Aitareya Āraṇyaka, but it is in a very standard looking passage and is of little importance to this study (AA 2.1.8).

3. Translation quoted from Keith, *Rigveda Bruhmanas*, p. 288.

The Śatapatha Brāhmaṇa (ŚB) continues many of the same themes. The gods and asuras are normally fighting each other, and the gods win. These tales are often introduced by the phrase, "The gods and asuras, both sprung from Prajāpati, were contending" (devā́ś ca vā 'ásurāś ca / ubháye prājāpatyā́ḥ paspṛdhire. ŚB 3.5. 4.2 and several other places). Sometimes the formula is augmented by adding what they contend for. Thus they contend for superiority (ŚB 1.2.4.8), the sacrifice (ŚB 1.5.3.2), or the regions (ŚB 9.2.3.8) or they contend with each other (ŚB 2.2.2.8). There is sometimes a tag line at the end of the tale recommending that the sacrificer do as the gods did. But the extent to which the asuras are identified with the rakṣases is quite striking in this Brāhmaṇa. About one third of the passages containing *ásura–* or a compound or derivative of this word in fact have the compound *asurarakṣasá–*. (Note that this word has now been transferred to the thematic declension.) These asura-rakṣasas often fight against the gods as asuras would have done in older texts, but equally often attack or disrupt the sacrifice as rakṣases would have done in older texts. A frequent formula is: "The gods indeed performing the sacrifice feared attack from the asura-rakṣases" (devā́ ha vái yajñáṃ tanvānā́s te 'surarakṣébhya āsaṅgā́d bibhayā́ṃ cakrur. ŚB 1.2.1.6 etc.). The merger of these two terms for demon and anti-god into one concept is complete in two passages which contain *asurarakṣasá–* in the singular (ŚB 1.2.4.17, 6.8.1.14). In these passages the compound cannot be a dvandva, and thus must refer to a single being who is both a rakṣas (or rakṣasa) and an asura. One passage says that asuras have barbarian speech (ŚB 3.2.1.24). Another says that āsuryas make round graves (ŚB 13.8.1.5). And yet another says that āsuryas make sepulchres above the earth (ŚB 13.8.2.1). These could be interpreted as indications that the asuras were originally people of a different language and culture from the composers of the text, but since this text is so late they could just be attempts to describe the asuras in terms that are as bizarre and foreign as possible. One other occurrence of *ásura–* in the ŚB deserves mention. ŚB 12.6.1 gives a list of thirty three oblations that can be performed with accompanying mantras to various deities in order to correct certain errors in the soma ritual. One of these mantras is given as *ásurāya svā́hā* (ŚB 12.6.1.10). Since one of these gods is Śukra (ŚB 12.6.1.24), and Śukra is the name of the preceptor of the asuras in the Brāhmaṇas, this could refer to a demonic asura. However, it is much more likely that both *śukra*– and *ásura*– here refer to gods. Since these words are part of mantras, they can have meanings which are much older than those standard at the time of the composition of the surrounding texts. However, since this mantra is not quoted from a known source, it contains a very late new occurrence of *ásura*– in a very old meaning. There are no other new occurrences of *ásura*– in the singular in this text—*āsurá*– is still used for the singular (ŚB 5.3. 2.2, 5.4.1.9, 12.7.1.10, 12.7.3.1).

The Mantra Brāhmaṇa has two typical passages mentioning asuras. The Ṣaḍviṃśa Brāhmaṇa has a few typical mentions of asuras and asura-rakṣases. The Gopatha Brāhmaṇa also has a few typical stories of gods defeating the asuras and a few passages which speak of asura-rakṣases. *Ásura*– is used for the singular to refer to Svarbhānu (GB 2.3.19). The "Lost Brāhmaṇas" also contain a number of typical gods-versus-asuras stories. Some of these are variations of stories found in the JB. One is a version of the famous story of the churning of the milk ocean (Amā Brāhmaṇa 22:1). There are also a few passages that deal with asura-rakṣases in these texts.

The relative chronology of the Brāhmaṇa texts is very uncertain. However, I have tried to discuss them in more or less chronological order. Certain patterns do emerge. Asuras and rakṣases begin as two distinct sorts of beings, but by the end of the Brāhmaṇa period they are practically indistinguishable. Along with this increasing identification of asuras and rakṣases is an increasing tendency for asuras to be driven off by people or sacrificers instead of fighting only against the gods. Tag lines enjoining the sacrificer to do as the gods did in order to overcome enemies continue throughout, but are somewhat less frequent later. Occurrences of *ásura*– in the singular are extremely rare (except in quotations from the Saṃhitās). When the singular is needed, *āsurá*– is used instead with the exception of the Kapiṣṭhala-Kaṭha Saṃhitā, which does use *ásura*– in the singular.

CONCLUSION

As indicated in Chapter I many scholars have tried to reconstruct for the Indo-Iranian period a group of gods called asuras whose worship was distinct from that of the devas. These scholars then go on to suggest that in Iran asura worship prevailed, culminating in the worship of Ahura Mazdā and the degradation of the daēvas to the status of demons, while in India the devas were worshipped and the asuras became demons. Of course, some of the scholars suggest certain modifications of this basic scheme. But any theory that involves an early cult of asuras is unacceptable.

There are several problems with such a reconstruction. On the Iranian side the evidence for a cult of ahuras (in the plural) is very meagre. The only evidence seems to be the occurrence of *ahura–* in the plural twice in the Gāthās, and in both of these passages this word could just as well refer to those beings who were later called Aməša Spəntas.[1] In addition to this *ahura–* is used several times of people in the Avesta.

On the Indic side there is also nothing to support this theory. First, the word *ásura–* does not occur as a designation for any specific group of gods—that is, the word itself does not define a certain group of gods. In fact *ásura–* does not even appear in the plural in the Family Books of the RV. Secondly, the usage of *ásura–* is never restricted to gods. People are already called asuras in the Family Books in the RV, and since people are also called ahuras in the Avesta, there is no reason to doubt that the word could be used of people in the Indo-Iranian period. Thirdly, there is no being in Vedic literature who is called an asura in the godly sense in the early literature and is later called an asura in the demonic sense. Hence the change that occurs in India is in the usage of the word and not in the nature of a group of beings to which that word applies. Fourthly, two or three of the verses we have examined use the words *ásura–* and *devá–* in such a way that they could not refer to two mutually exclusive groups. Thus, I suggest that there is a more satisfactory explanation for the shift in the meaning of *ásura–*.

1. See the discussion of Y. 30.9 and Y. 31.4 in the appendix.

In its earliest occurrences in the RV *ásura–* meant something like "lord." Such a lord could be human or divine, but since the RV consists of hymns to gods, it occurs much more often referring to gods. We have seen some of the characteristics of these lords. They normally command some force of fighting men (*vīra–*), should have keen planning ability or insight (*krátu–*), and in general should have the characteristics that would make one a good leader. This "rank" of asura does not seem to have been an inherent quality, but was assigned or bestowed or established. (The uses of √*dhṛ* with *asuryàm* suggest this.) Quite significantly the usage of this word was not restricted to friendly leaders and gods. An enemy leader could and sometimes was called an asura.

With this as a starting point the development of the usage of *ásura–* to refer to evil beings can be understood. One such usage was just mentioned—an asura could be an enemy lord. It is significant that in Books One, Eight, and Ten of the RV plural occurrences of *ásura–* first appear and that most of these refer to humans. Perhaps this reflects an increased tendency to use the word for humans, but it is perhaps more likely that the word was always in common use for some sort of human leaders and only occurs more often of gods in the RV because the hymns of the RV speak so much more about gods than about men. In any case this sets the stage for the further development of the word, because soon after this the use of *ásura–* in the singular becomes extremely rare, and the plural is used only to refer to evil beings. The phrase *ásurā adevā́ḥ* first occurs in RV 8.96.9. In this phrase *ásura–* is used with exactly the same meaning that it had in its earliest Vedic occurrences. It means "lord." The adjective *adevá–* here indicates that these asuras were non-Aryan human enemy leaders who did not worship the Aryan gods.

In the AV the plural usage is much more common than the singular usage.[2] Most of the singular occurrences there use the word with a good connotation, and most of the plural occurrences use it with a bad connotation. The asuras there are often enemies. In several of these verses the asuras appear as they do throughout the Brāhmaṇas as a group of beings who are enemies of the gods. But in several other verses they appear as a group of enemies who are opposed by Indra. These verses seem important for under-

2. There are twenty-seven plural occurrences and only eight occurrences of the singular.

standing the development of the meaning of *ásura–*. In the RV the struggle between the Aryans and the indigenous people is often mentioned, but it is normally expressed by saying that Indra fought these people. Thus when a verse in the AV says that Indra fought the asuras, the asuras referred to could easily be indigenous enemy lords.

A comparison of the usages of *ásura–* with the usages of *dāsá–* and *rakṣás–* supports this last point. *Rakṣás–* clearly refers to non-human, demonic beings. These beings are more often opposed by Agni or Soma than by Indra. However, *dásyu–* and *dāsá–* are used to refer to human enemies of the Aryans, and these are usually opposed by Indra. Thus when Indra is opposed to the asuras, the asuras are likely to be human. There also seems to be another connection between *ásura–* and *dásyu–* and *dāsá–*. *Dásyu–* and *dāsá–* become extremely rare in the same texts in which *ásura–* begins to be used often with a bad connotation. Perhaps the plural usage of *ásura–* for enemies was virtually synonymous with *dásyu–* and *dāsá–* and replaced these words in later texts. There are also several verses in which *dásyu–* and *ásura–* appear in close connection—perhaps even in apposition in some cases

There was another development in the concept of asura that occurred during this period of the composition of the late parts of the Saṃhitās. There is never a clear distinction between history and mythology in the Vedic literature, but as the period of the Aryan invasion drew to a close there was even less reason to refer to historical human enemies of the people. Thus the adevic asuras, the human enemies of the Aryan people, who were described by the texts as enemies of the god Indra, became mythologized into a class of beings who opposed the class of beings called gods. Several occurrences of *ásura–* in the AV use this word to refer to a distinct class of beings and in several more occurrences this class of beings is opposed to the gods.

The occurrences in the mantra portions of the Yajur Veda and the remaining Saṃhitās reflect the same meanings found in the AV. However, a further development appears in the Brāhmaṇas. In the oldest Brāhmaṇas and the brāhmaṇa portion of the Black Yajur Veda, asuras appear as a group of beings opposed to the gods and distinct from the rakṣases. But by the time of the Śatapatha Brāhmaṇa, asuras and rakṣases are practically identical in many passages.

Although I have only examined a small part of the Avestan material and then only to use it to support my conclusions about the Indic situation, the results of this study of a certain aspect of Indian religious history still has some implications for the study of the history and prehistory of Iranian religion. The Indic material can no longer be used to support the idea of a group of gods called asuras in the Indo-Iranian period. If some group of gods of whom Ahura Mazdā was only one became the primary gods worshipped before Ahura Mazdā became the one God, this group was not an already extant group called ahuras. Any author who denies the radical nature of Zaraθuštra's reform by arguing that the elevation of Ahura Mazdā was preceded by the elevation of a group of gods which included him owes it to his readers to define exactly what group was so elevated and explain how they form a coherent group. *Devá–* meant god in the Indo-Iranian period. The development of the meaning "demon" for this word in Iran is not connected with the change in meaning of *ásura–* in India.

APPENDIX

AHURA- IN THE AVESTA

I shall look now at some occurrences of *ahura-* in the Avesta to see how well they agree with the picture of *ásura-* that appears in the Vedic literature. *Ahura-* is the exact Avestan cognate of *ásura-*. Both words are derived from the same Indo-Iranian word. *Ahura-* occurs hundreds of times in the Avesta as part of the name of Zaraθuštra's God—Ahura Mazdā. These occurrences are much too numerous to consider here and are also not likely to give much indication of the meaning of *ahura-*. However, *ahura-* does occur a few times in the Avesta without *mazdā-*. These are the occurrences I shall examine.

I shall begin with the oldest occurrences—those in the Gāthās. The translations will be quoted from Stanley Insler's recent edition of these hymns.

adā tašā gə̄uš pərəsat̰ ašəm kaθā tōi gavōi ratuš
hyat̰ hīm dātā xšayantō hadā vāstrā gaodāyō θwaxšō
kə̄m hōi uštā ahurəm yə̄ drəgvō. dəbīš aēšəməm vādāyoit̰.
Y. 29.2

"Thereupon the fashioner of the cow asked the truth: 'Is thy judgement for the cow to be in this way? If ye ruling ones placed her (on earth), there should always be cow-caring zeal by a pastor. Whom do ye wish to be her master [*ahura-*], one who might destroy the fury (caused) by the deceitful?'"[1]

Here the ahura exercises his authority over the cow. Even if the verse is highly metaphorical, the translation "lord" here is quite appropriate. The metaphor of a herdsman to refer to a king or leader of people is very common and has appeared, for example, in ancient Egypt, ancient Israel, and in modern America in the use of *pastor* to refer to a clergyman.

1. Text and translation from Stanley Insler, *The Gāthās of Zarathustra*, *Acta Iranica*, third series, vol. 1 (Leiden: E. J. Brill, 1975), pp. 28-9. The transliteration system used is that of Bartholomae except for å, c, and j for å, č and ǰ.

at̰ hī ayå fravarətā vāstrīm ahyāi fšuyantəm
ahurəm ašavanəm vaŋhə̄us fšənghīm manaŋhō
nōit̰ mazdā avāstryō davąscinā humərətōis baxštā. Y. 31.10

"And, of these two, she chose for herself the cattle-breeding pastor to be her truthful master [*ahura*] (and) the cultivator of good thinking. Wise one, never did the non-pastor share the friendship of her who requires good attention."[2]

Insler remarks in a footnote that *davąscinā* in the text is written for *duvąscinā* and in another footnote that *she* refers to the cow, which he interprets as the good vision.[3] Thus this verse also speaks of the ahura as a herdsman.

yadā ašəm zəvīm aŋhən mazdåscā ahuråŋhō
ašicā ārmaitī vahištā išasā manaŋhā
maibyō xšaθrəm aojōnghvat̰
yehyā vərədā vanaēmā drujim. Y. 31.4

"(to the adherents). When I might call upon truth, the Wise One and the other lords [*ahura–*] shall appear; also reward and piety. (And) through the very best thinking I shall seek for myself their rule of strength, through whose growth we might conquer deceit."[4]

This is one of four occurrences of *ahura–* in the plural in the Avesta. Insler interprets the "other lords" to mean truth and good thinking.[5] Y. 33.11 may offer some support for this. "This Wise One who is the Mightiest Lord, and piety, and truth which prospers the creatures, and good thinking, and (good) rule—listen to us, have mercy on me, when there is any requital" (yə̄ səvištō ahurō mazhåscā ārmaitiščą / ašemcā frādat̰. gaēθəm manascā vohū xša-θrəmcā / sraotā mōi mərəždātā mōi ādāi kahyācit̰ paitī.).[6] The phrase "who is the Mightiest Lord" suggests that there are other lords, and perhaps those other lords are the others named here—

2. Insler, *Gāthās*, pp. 38-9.
3. *Ibid.*, pp. 38 and 39.
4. *Ibid.*, pp. 36-7. Insler reads *zevyā* for original *zuviyā* where the text has *zəvim*, and *išā* for *išasā* in the text.
5. *Ibid.*, note 4.
6. *Ibid.*, pp. 52-53.

piety, truth, good thinking, and (good) rule—who come to be part of a group called Aməša Spəntas in later portions of the Avesta. This verse by no means proves conclusively that these Aməša Spəntas are called lords, but it at least makes the assumption quite plausible. I have no better alternative to offer.

> atcā tōi vaēm hyāmā yōi īm fərašə̄m kərənaon ahūm
> mazdåscā ahuråŋhō ā. mōyastrā baranā ašācā
> hyat haθrā manå bvat yaθrā cistiš aŋhat maēθā. Y. 30.9

> "Therefore may we be those who shall heal this world! Wise One and ye other lords [*ahura–*] be present to me with support and with truth, so that one shall become convinced even where his understanding shall be false."[7]

The same vocative phrase that occurred in the last verse occurs again here. It is not quite so easy to interpret *ahuråŋhō* as meaning truth and good thinking here since *aša–* occurs later in the sentence. But it could refer to the other Aməša Spəntas. The question is whether or not one can justifiably assume that this refers to some previous worship of a cult of gods called Asuras as some have maintained. I think that these two verses offer far too little evidence to justify such an assumption. It seems to fit much better with Zaraθuštra's teaching to interpret these vocatives as referring to the Aməša Spəntas. I see no reason why it would have been a problem for him to call them lords. However, it might have been a problem for him to call any earlier group of gods lords.

Bartholomae takes *ahurō ašā* in Y. 51.3 to be vocative dual referring to Ahura Mazdā and Aša,[8] but Insler instead takes *ahurō* as nominative singular and *ašā* as instrumental singular.[9] The lack of any other occurrences of *ahurā ašā* in the dual supports Insler here. One could also argue, as does Bartholomae,[10] that *ahurō* in Y. 53.9 refers to an earthly ruler. But it seems more likely that it here refers to Ahura Mazdā. (Either interpretation fits quite well with the interpretation of *ásura–* presented above.)

7. *Ibid.*, pp. 34-5. Insler emends *ā.mōyastrā* to *ā mōi (a)stā* and takes *haθrā manå* as a compound.

8. Christian Bartholomae, *Altiranishes Wörterbuch*, 1904, reprint(Berlin: Walter de Gruyter & Co., 1961), col. 286.

9. Insler, *Gāthās*, p. 103.

10. Bartholomae, *Wörterbuch*, col. 293.

These are all of the occurrences of *ahura–* in the Gāthās in which the word does not refer to Ahura mazdā. But it will be instructive to consider briefly how the name *ahura–* mazdā– emerged in the literature. In Younger Avestan these two words appear together and in that order with very few exceptions.[11] The reverse is true in the Gāthās. There *ahura–* and *mazdā–* appear together and in that order only five times (and in one of these—Y. 33.11.—the two words are actually in different clauses). They appear together, but in reversed order twenty-four times. *Ahura–* alone is used to designate Ahura Mazdā nineteen times. *Mazdā–* alone appears in this usage sixty-seven times. The words *ahura–* and *mazdā–* appear in the same verse but separated with *ahura–* coming first forty times. (In eighteen of these they are in separate sentences or clauses.) The words *ahura–* and *mazdā–* appear in the same verse separated by other words but with *mazdā–* coming first forty-eight times. (In nine of these the words are in separate sentences or clauses.)[12] Thus it is quite clear that *ahura– mazdā–* was not a proper name of God for Zaraθuštra. At least one or perhaps both of these words was used as an epithet by him. *Ahura–* meant "lord" and *mazdā–* seems to have meant "wise." Thus Zaraθuštra could refer to God as the Lord, the Wise One, the Wise Lord, or the Lord (Who is) Wise. The name *ahura– mazdā–* developed only later.

I turn next to some occurrences of *ahura–* in the Yašts. In my transliterations of the texts I shall not attempt to separate the metrical parts into verse units.

miθrəm vouru. gaoyaoitīm...yazamaide...
ahurəm gufrəm amavantəm dātō. saokəm vyāxanəm
vahmō. səndaŋhəm bərəzantəm ašahunarəm tanumą̄θrəm
bāzuš. aojaŋhəm raθaēštąm. Yt. 10.25.

"Grass-land magnate Miθra we worship...the profound, strong lord [*ahura–*], the profit-bestowing champion, the exalted gratifier of prayers, the much-talented personification of the divine word, the warrior endowed with strength of arm."[13]

11. See *Ibid.*, col. 286, for exceptions.

12. The statistics given here were compiled from Insler's translation of the Gāthās.

13. Translation quoted from Gerschevitch, *Avestan Hymn to Mithra*, p. 85. The texts for the remainder of the Appendix are from Geldner's edition.

In this verse Miθra is clearly called ahura. No substantial information is given here about the precise meaning of the word, but the basic concepts of the verse seem very much in line with the Ṛgvedic verses containing *ásura–*.

> taδa nō jamyāt̰ avaiŋhe miθra ahura bərəzanta
> yat̰ bərəzəm barāt̰ aštra vācim aspanąmca srifa
> xšufsąn aštrå kahvąn jyå naviθyąn tigγråŋhō
> aštayō taδa hunavō gouru. zaoθranąm jata
> paiθyånte frā.vərəsa. Yt. 10.113.

"may he therefore come to our assistance, O exalted Mithra and Ahura! When loudly resound the whip and the neighing of horses, when the whips are tossing, the bow-strings twanging (?), the sharp arrows darting, then the evil sons of those who have offered viscid (*lit.* heavy) libations (=libations of blood), having been struck, will go down writhing."[14]

Here occurs the phrase *miθra ahura bərəzanta*—all vocative dual. Apparently this phrase refers to Miθra and Ahura Mazdā. *Ahura–* occurs in the dual in the Avesta only in conjunction with *miθra*. This is very significant because the only occurrences of *ásura–* in the dual in the Vedic Saṃhitās or Brāhmaṇas are in connection with Mitrā-varuṇā. This restriction of the dual usage of *ásura– / ahura–* to Mitrāvaruṇā in the Vedas and Miθra and Ahura Mazdā in the Avesta offers strong support for those who argue that Varuṇa and Ahura Mazdā derive from the same Indo-Iranian god. This verse tells us little else about the meaning of *ahura.–*

> miθra ahura bərəzanta aiθyejaŋha ašavana
> yazamaide; strəušca måŋhəmca hvarəca urvarå
> paiti barəsmanyå miθrəm vīspanąm daŋyunąm
> daiŋhupaitīm yazamaide. Yt 10.145.

"(Standing) by the Barsman plant we worship Mithra and Ahura—the two exalted owners of Truth that are removed from danger—, as well as the stars, the moon, and the sun. We worship Mithra, who in (*lit.* of) all countries is the head of the country."[15]

14. *Ibid.*, p. 131.
15. *Ibid.*p., 147.

Here again the dual compound *miθra ahura* occurs. Also later in the verse Miθra is called *daiŋ̊hupaiti–*. It is unclear here whether this relates directly to his being an ahura, but we shall see later a more explicit connection between these terms.

mōi. tū iθra ahurahe grantahe vaēγāi jasaēma yeŋ̊he hazaŋ̊rəm vaēγanąm paiti hamərəθāi jasaiti yō baēvarə. spasānō sūrō vīspō. viδvå aδaoyamnō. Yt. 10.69.

"Let us not meet here with the charge of the wrathful lord [*ahura–*] who comes with a thousand batterings (*lit.* whose thousand batterings come) to the opponent, the strong, all-knowing, undeceivable master of ten thousand spies."[16]

The ahura here is Miθra.

(aməm) yim vašånte ahuråŋ̊hō vašånte āhuiryåŋ̊hō vašånte haosravaŋ̊hanō təm vašata kava usa. yim aspō arša baraiti yim uštrō vaδairiš baraiti yim āfš nāvaya baraiti. Yt. 14.39.

"Kavi Usa controlled that (power) which ahuras will carry (?), ahuric ones (= descendents of lords?) will carry (?), the Haosravaŋ̊hans will carry (?), which a male horse bears, which a rutting he-camel bears, which a navigable water bears."

The power under discussion here is that provided by a certain magic feather. For our purposes it is useful to see what kind of power is appropriate for ahuras. The description here seems to be basically that of strength.

vərəθraγnəm ahuraδātəm yazamaide. asānəm siγūire ciθrəm abarə ahurō puθrō puθråŋ̊hō baēvarə. patayō. amava ās vərəθrava nąma vərəθrava ās amava nąma. Yt. 14.59.

"We worship Vərəθragna, who is created by Ahura (Mazdā). The ahura, (his) son, (his) sons, the lords of ten thousand bore (?) the stone of Siγurian descent. The powerful one was Victorious by name; the victorious one was Powerful by name."[17]

16. *Ibid.*, p. 107. He emends *mōi.tū* to *moiṯ ū.*

17. In my translation I have taken *siγūire ciθrəm* as a compound.

This translation is very uncertain. The corrupt nature of the text and the lack of context make it impossible to use this verse for understanding the meaning of *ahura–*.

> ašāunąm...fravašayō yazamaide yå ahurahe xšayatō dašinąm upa yūiδyeinti yezi aēm bavaiti ašava. xšnus yezi. šē bavainti anāzərətå xšnūtå ainitą̊ aṯbištå uγrå ašāunąm fravašayō. Yt. 13.63.

> "We worship...the fravašis of the righteous, who fight at the right of the ruling ahura when this one becomes one-who-pleases-the-righteous, when the strong fravašis of the righteous become of him not angered, pleased, not offended, not alienated."

The ahura here is a ruling prince, who is aided by the spirits of the departed righteous when he fights in accordance with righteousness. The key points for us here are that the ahura rules and leads a group of fighting men.

> ...vīspe bavaṯ aiwi. vanyå ahurō kava haosrava. Yt. 19.77.

> "The ahura Kavay Haosravah conquered all."

I have quoted only the portion of this passage that looks relevant. The significance of this passage is that Kavay Haosravah, who is called an ahura here, is definitely human.[18]

> yahmya ahurō mazdå hvapō nivaēδayat āiδi paiti ava.jasa arədvī sūre anåhite haca avaṯbyō stərəbyō aoi ząm ahuraδātąm. θwam yazånte aurvaŋhō ahuråŋhō dainhu patayō puθråŋhō dainhu.paitinąm. Yt. 5.85

> "Whom Ahura Mazdā, who does good works, informed: 'Come, come back down here, O Arədvī Sūrā Anāhitā, from those stars to the earth created by Ahura (Mazdā). The brave ahuras, the masters of the land, the sons of the lords of the land will worship you.' "

The problem in interpreting this verse is deciding whether or not *daiŋhu.patayō* is meant to be in apposition with *ahuråŋhō*.

18. For a brief discussion of some of his exploits see Boyce, *History of Zoroastrianism*, vol. 1, p. 106.

The question is undecidable here, but it is still significant to find these two terms together both used to refer to humans.[19]

> tå ahurō sāstranam dąiŋhupaitiš nōit̰ satəm jainti viraja. Yt. 14.37.
>
> "Then (?) the lord of commanders, the master of the land, does not kill one hundred, he the killer of men."

This passage is from a section of the text that discusses the use of a certain feather as a talisman. Here its protective power is described. The ahura again appears to be human. *Ahurō* and *daiŋhupaitiš* are in all likelihood in apposition.

> tištrīm...yazamaide yim yārə.caršō mašyehe ahuraca xratugūtō aurunaca gairišācō sižδraca ravascarātō uzyōrəntəm hispōsəntəm huyāiryāca daiŋhave uzjasəntəm dužyāiryāca. Yt. 8.36.
>
> "We worship...Tištrya who when he rises watches over a year's crops of man and the insight-increasing ahuras and the wild (animals) moving in mountains and timid and roaming the plains and who comes up with either a good year for the land or a bad year."

Ahura here refers to human lords. It is noteworthy that *ahura* is modified by *xratugūtō*. The first member of this compound is the Avestan form of Sanskrit *krátu–* which we have already seen to be an important characteristic for an asura.

I turn now to occurrences of *ahura–* in the Yasna.

> nivaēδayemi hankārayemi uzayeirinãi ašaone ašahe raθwe. nivaēδayemi hankārayemi frādat̰.vīrāi dāhyumāica ašaone asāhe raθwe. nivaēδayemi hankārayemi bərəzatō ahurahe nafəδrō apąm apasca mazdaδātayå. Y. 1.5.

19. Although *daiŋhu-* is the Avestan form of Sanskrit *dasyu-* and *paiti-* is the Avestan form of Sanskrit *pati-*, it would certainly be an error to take this as evidence that *ásura-* originally meant "master of the dasyus." Avestan *daiŋhu* means "land" while *dasyu-* is a designation for one of the indigenous inhabitants of India. The appearance of *daiŋhu.paiti-* in apposition with *ahura-* only indicates that *ahura-* could be used to mean "master of the land" in Avestan This is consistent with the idea that *ásura-* meant "lord" in the Indo-Iranian period, but says nothing about the connection of *ásura-* with Sanskrit *dasyu-*.

"I dedicate (and) carry out (the prayer) for truth-possessing Uzayeirina, judge of Truth. I dedicate (and) carry out (the prayer) for Frādatvīra (and) truth-possessing Daȟyuma, judge of Truth. I dedicate (and) carry out (the prayer) for the exalted ahura Napāt Apąm and for the waters created by Mazdā."

Here we find Apąm Napāt—but with the order of the words reversed—referred to as an exalted ahura.

nivaēδayemi hankārayemi ahuraēibya miθraēibya bərəzanbya aiθyajaŋhaēibya ašavanaēibya...hvarəca xšaētahe aurvat̰.aspahe dōiθrahe ahurahe mazdå. Y. 1.11.

"I dedicate (and) carry out (the prayer) for the Ahura and Miθra—exalted, free from danger, truth-possessing—and for the sun—possessing fast horses, eye of Ahura Mazdā."[20]

I have omitted most of this verse and retained only what is most relevant for us. (The part omitted just extends the list of deities invoked.) Here again *ahura–* and *miθra–* appear with dual endings and thus form a *dvandva* compound. The other phrase which calls the sun the eye of Ahura Mazdā is interesting because the sun is also said to be the eye of Varuṇa (RV 1.50.6.). This gives some support to the theory that Varuṇa and Ahura Mazdā derived from the same Indo-Iranian deity.

ahmya zaoθre barəsmanaēca uzayeirinəm ašavanəm ašahe ratūm āyese yešti. frādat̰.vīrəm dāȟyuməmca ašavanəm ašahe ratūm āyese yešti. ahmya zaoθre barəsmanaēca bərəzantəm ahurəm xšaθrīm xšaētəm apąm napātəm aurvat̰.aspəm āyese yešti. apəmca mazdaδātąm ašaonīm āyese yešti. Y. 2.5.

"I fetch for worship to this oblation and barəsman truth-possessing Uzayeiri, judge of Truth. I fetch for worship Frādatvīra and truth-possessing Daȟyuma judge of Truth. I fetch for worship to this oblation and barəsman the magnificent ruling exalted ahura Apąm Napāt, who has fast horses. And I fetch for worship the truth-possessing water created by Mazdā."

20. I have followed Bartholomae's suggestion to take *hvarə.xšaētahe* as a compound in spite of the intervening *ca.* Bartholomae, *Wörterbuch*, col. 1848.

A comparison of this fifth verse of the second Yasna with the fifth verse of the first Yasna shows that it names the same deities who are invoked, but as part of a slightly different formula with a different verb. Thus Apąm Napāt is mentioned once again, and again called ahura. It is noteworthy that he is also said to be ruling (*xšaθrya*– = Sanskrit *kṣatríya*–).

ahmya zaoθre barəsmanaēca ahura miθra barəzanta aiθya-jaŋha ašavana āyese yešti. Y. 2.11.

"I fetch for worship to this oblation and barəsman the Ahura and Miθra—exalted, free from danger, truth-possessing."

I have omitted most of the verse since it merely repeats this same basic formula with the same list of deities found in Y. 1.11. (However, in this list the sun is not glossed as the eye of Ahura Mazdā.) We find here once again *miθra*– and *ahura*– with dual endings indicating that they are to be taken as a *dvandva* compound.

imat̰ vō āpō jaiδyemi...imat̰ bərəza ahura xšaθrya apąm napō aurvat.aspa. Y. 65.12.

"Therefore I ask you, O waters...therefore, O exalted ruling ahura Apąm Napāt, who has fast horses..."

I have omitted most of this verse, but the part omitted only extends the list of names and epithets in the vocative case. We find here once again Apąm Napāt called an exalted ruling (*xšaθrya*–) ahura. We have not seen an explicit connection between *ásura*– and *kṣatríya*– in the RV, but given the nature of the asura as described there such a connection should not be surprising in the Avestan counterparts of these words.

Conclusions

These are all the occurrences of *ahura*– in the Avesta where the word does not refer to Ahura Mazdā and is not part of that name plus a few where it does seem to refer to Ahura Mazdā that nonetheless look instructive. It occurred in the singular referring to Apąm Napāt three times, Miθra twice, the lord of the cow twice, Kavay Haosravah once, and an unnamed earthly ruler twice. It occurred in the plural three times of earthly lords and twice of "other lords" who are addressed together with Mazdā by Zaraθuštra. It occurs in the dual four times—all in *dvandva* compounds of *ahura–* and *miθra–*, apparently referring to Ahura Mazdā and Miθra. All the occurrences referring to human rulers are from the Yašts.

The things said of ahuras in the Avesta are very much like those said of asuras in the RV. Both seem to be powerful, respected lords with some kind of military force in their command. The term *xratu–* was found associated with ahuras as *krátu–* is associated with asuras. The term *xšaθrya–* was also found in connection with ahuras. Even though we have not seen *kṣatriya–* associated with asuras in the RV, it would not be at all surprising to find such an association.[21] Ahuras also appeared in connection with *daiŋ́hupaiti–*, "master of the land." But there is one way in which ahuras seem to differ from asuras. Asuras seem to have been selected by the people and installed in their position. Ahuras are often mentioned together with sons of ahuras who also rule. Thus the ahura lordship may have been passed down from father to son in Iran. We have seen no evidence of such a succession in India. There are two verses in the Gāthās which refer to "other lords" whom Zaraθuštra addresses with Ahura Mazdā, but since these "other lords" could quite easily just be the Aməša Spəntas, these verses offer little to support the theory that there once was a cult of ahuras in Iran.

21. The rarity of *kṣatríya*- in the RV probably accounts for the lack of appearance of such an association. *Kṣatrám* does appear with *asuryàm* in RV 5.66.2., and *kṣatrá*- is modified by *asuryà*- in RV 7.21.7.

INDEX OF VERSES

This index lists all the verses quoted in whole or in part or discussed plus those verses which are noted in the footnotes as variants of verses quoted or discussed in the body of the text. The numbers for the AV references are according to the edition by Vishva Bandhu. When the numbering of the Whitney-Roth edition differs, that number is given in parentheses immediately below the other number.

BIBLIOGRAPHY

TEXTS

Aitareya Āraṇyaka. *The Aitareya Āraṇyaka.* Ed. and trans. by Arthur Berriedale Keith. Oxford: The Clarendon Press, 1909.

Aitareya Brāhmaṇa. *Aitareya Brāhmaṇa with the Vṛtti of Sadguruśiṣya.* Ed. by R. Anantakṛṣṇa Śāstri and P.K. Narayana Pillai. 3 vols. (incomplete). Travancore Sanskrit Series ncs. 149, 167, and 176. Trivandrum: Bhaskara Press, 1942, 1952, 1955.

Atharvaveda. *Atharvaveda (Śaunaka) with the Pada-pāṭha and Sāyaṇācārya's Commentary.* Ed. by Vishva Bandhu. 5 vols. Hoshiarpur: Vishveshvaranand Vedic Research Institute, 1960-1964.

Avesta. *Avesta, die heilige Bücher der Parsen.* 3 vols. Ed. by Karl F. Geldner. Stuttgart: W. Kohlhammer, 1886, 1889, 1895.

Gopatha Brāhmaṇa. *Gopath Brahmana (of Atharva-Veda).* Ed. by Rajendra Lal Mitra. Delhi: Indological Book House, 1972.

Jaiminīyārṣeya-Jaiminīyopaniṣad-Brāhmaṇas. Ed. by Bellikoth Ramachandra Sharma. Tirupati: Kendriya Sanskrit Vidyapeetha, 1967.

Jaiminīya Brāhmaṇa. *Jaiminiya-Brahmana of the Samaveda.* Ed. by Raghu Vira and Lokesh Chandra. Nagpur: Sarasvatī-Vihāra, 1954.

Kapiṣṭhala-Kaṭha-Saṃhitā. Ed. by Raghu Vira. Delhi: Meharchand Lachhmandas, 1968.

Kāṭhaka Saṃhitā. *Die Saṃhitā der Kaṭha-Śākhā.* Ed. by Leopold von Schroeder. 4 vols. 1900-1910. Reprint. Wiesbaden: Franz Steiner Verlag, 1970-1972.

Kāṭhaka-Saṃkalana: Extracts from the Lost Kāṭhaka-Brāhmaṇa, Kāṭhaka-Śrautasūtra and Kāṭhaka-Gṛhyasūtras. Ed. by Sūryakānta. Lahore: Mehar Chand Lachhman Das, 1943.

Kauṣītaki Brāhmaṇa...*Śāṅkhāyana-Brāhmaṇa.* Ed. by Harinarayan Bhattacharya. Calcutta Sanskrit College Research Series, no 73. Calcutta: Sanskrit College, 1970.

Lost Brāhmaṇas. *Collection of the Fragments of Lost Brāhmaṇas.* Ed. by Batakrishna Ghosh. Calcutta: Modern Publishing Syndicate.

Maitrāyaṇī Saṃhitā. *Die Saṃhitā der Maitrāyaṇīya-Śākhā.* Ed. by Leopold von Schroeder. 4 vols. 1881-1886. Reprint. Wiesbaden: Franz Steiner Verlag GmbH., 1970-1972.

Mantra Brāhmaṇa.

Das Mantrabrāhmaṇa, first Prapāṭhaka. Ed. and trans. by Heinrich Stönner. Halle, 1901.

Das Mantrabrāhmaṇa, second Prapāṭhaka. Ed. and trans. by Hans Jorgensen. Darmstadt: C.F. Wintersche Buchdruckerei, 1911.

Paippalāda Saṃhitā.

"The Kashmirian Atharva Veda, Book One." Ed. by L.C. Barret. *Journal of the American Oriental Society* 26 (1905): 197-295.

"The Kashmirian Atharva Veda, Book Two." Ed. by L.C. Barret. *Journal of the American Oriental Society* 30 (1910): 187-258.

"The Kashmirian Atharva Veda, Book Three." Ed. by L.C. Barret. *Journal of the American Oriental Society* 32 (1912). 343-390.

"The Kashmirian Atharva Veda, Book Four." Ed. by L.C. Barret. *Journal of the American Oriental Society* 35 (1915): 42-101.

"The Kashmirian Atharva Veda, Book Five." Ed. by L.C. Barret. *Journal of the American Oriental Society* 37 (1917): 257-308.

"The Kashmirian Atharva Veda, Book Six." Ed. by Franklin Edgerton. *Journal of the American Oriental Society* 34 (1914): 374-411.

"The Kashmirian Atharva Veda, Book Seven." Ed. by L.C. Barret. *Journal of the American Oriental Society* 40 (1920): 145-169.

"The Kashmirian Atharva Veda, Book Eight." Ed. by L.C. Barret. *Journal of the American Oriental Society* 41 (1921): 264-289.

"The Kashmirian Atharva Veda, Book Nine." Ed. by

L.C. Barret. *Journal of the American Oriental Society* 42 (1922): 105-146.

"The Kashmirian Atharva Veda, Book Ten." Ed. by L.C. Barret. *Journal of the American Oriental Society* 43 (1923): 96-115.

"The Kashmirian Atharva Veda, Book Eleven." Ed. by L.C. Barret. *Journal of the American Oriental Society* 44 (1924): 258-269.

"The Kashmirian Atharva Veda, Book Twelve." Ed. by L.C. Barret. *Journal of the American Oriental Society* 46 (1926): 34-48.

"The Kashmirian Atharva Veda, Book Thirteen." Ed. by L.C. Barret. *Journal of the American Oriental Society* 48 (1928): 34-65.

"The Kashmirian Atharva Veda Book Fourteen." Ed. by L.C. Barret. *Journal of the American Oriental Society* 47 (1927): 238-249.

"The Kashmirian Atharva Veda, Book Fifteen." Ed. by L.C. Barret. *Journal of the American Oriental Society* 50 (1930): 43-73.

The Kashmirian Atharva Veda, Books Sixteen and Seventeen. Ed. by L.C. Barret. American Oriental Series, vol. 9. New Haven: American Oriental Society, 1936.

"The Kashmirian Atharva Veda, Book Eighteen." Ed. by L.C. Barret. *Journal of the American Oriental Society* 58 (1938): 571-614.

The Kashmirian Atharva Veda, Books Nineteen and Twenty. Ed. by L.C. Barret. American Oriental Series, vol. 18. New Haven: American Oriental Society, 1940.

Paippalāda Saṃhitā of the Atharvaveda. 2 vols. (Books 1-4.) Ed. by Durgamohan Bhattacharyya. Calcutta Sanskrit College Research Series, 26; Texts, 14; and 62; Texts, 20. Calcutta: Sanskrit College Calcutta, 1964 and 1970.

Ṛg Veda Khila. *Die Apokryphen des Ṛgveda.* Ed. by Isidor Scheftelowitz. 1906. Reprint. Hildesheim: Georg Olms Verlagsbuchhandlung, 1966.

Ṛg Veda Saṃhitā. *The Hymns of the Rig-Veda in the Saṃhitā and Pada Texts.* By F. Max Müller. The Kashi Sanskrit Series, 167. 2 vols. Reprint. Varanasi: The Chowkhamba Sanskrit Series Office, 1965.

Ṣaḍviṃśa-Brāhmaṇa. Ed. and trans. by Willem Boudewijin Bollée. Utrecht: A. Storm, 1956.

Sāmaveda-Saṃhitā. Pāraḍī: Svādhyāya-Maṇḍala, 1946.

Sāmavidhāna Brāhmaṇa. *The Sāmavidhānabrāhmaṇa of the Sāma Veda*. Ed. by A.C. Burnell. London: Trübner & Co., 1873.,

Saṃhitopaniṣad Brāhmaṇa. *The Saṃhitopanishadbrāhmaṇa of the Sāma Veda*. Ed. by A. C. Burnell. Mangalore: Basel Mission Press, 1877.

Śatapatha Brāhmaṇa. *The Çatapatha-Brāhmaṇa*. Ed. by Albrecht Weber. The Chowkhamba Sanskrit Series, 96. Reprint. Varanasi: The Chowkhamba Sanskrit Series Office, 1964.

Taittirīya Āraṇyaka. *Kṛṣṇayajurvedīyaṃ taittirīyāraṇyakam*. 2 vols. Ānandāśrama, 1967.

Taittirīya Brāhmaṇa. *Kṛṣṇayajurvedīyam Taittirīyabrāhmaṇam*. Ed. by Nārāyaṇa Śāstri. 4 vols. Ānandāśrama Sanskrit granthāvali 37. Poona: Apte, 1898.

Taittirīya Saṃhitā. *Die Taittirīya-Saṃhitā*. Ed. by Albrecht Weber. Indische Studien, vols. 11-12. 1871-1872. Reprint. Hildesheim: Georg Olms Verlag, 1973.

Vājasaneyi Saṃhitā. *Vājasaneyi-Mādhyandina-Śukla-Yajurveda-Saṃhitā*. Ed. by Jagdishlal Shastri. Delhi: Motilal Banarsidass, 1971.

BIBLIOGRAPHY

SECONDARY WORKS AND TRANSLATIONS

Bandhu, Vishva, ed. *A Vedic Word Concordance*. 16 vols., second ed. of vols. 1, 7, and 8. Hoshiarpur: Vishveshvaranand Vedic Research Institute, 1955-1973.

Banerji-Sastri, A. "Asura Expansion by Sea." *The Journal of the Bihar and Orissa Research Society* 12 (1926): 334-360.

———. "Asura Expansion in India." *The Journal of the Bihar and Orissa Research Society* 12 (1926): 243-285.

———. *Asura India*. Patna, 1926.

———. "Asura Institutions." *The Journal of the Bihar and Orissa Research Society* 12 (1926): 503-539.

———. "The Asuras in Indo-Iranian Literature." *The Journal of the Bihar and Orissa Research Society* 12 (1926): 110-139.

Barnett, L.D. "Review of *Asura India* by A. Banerji-Sastri." *Journal of the Royal Asiatic Society of Great Britain and Ireland*, July 1928, pp. 669-70.

Barth, A. "Review of *Dyāus Asura, Ahura Mazdā und die Asuras* by P. von Bradke." *Revue de L'histoire des Religions* 11 (1885): 47-48.

Bartholomae, Christian. "Der Abhinihitasandhi im Ṛgveda," *Studien zur indogermanische Sprachgeschichte* 1(1890): 81-116.

———. *Altiranisches Wörterbuch*. 1904. Reprint. Berlin: Walter de Gruyter & Co., 1961.

Benveniste, Emile. *The Persian Religion according to the Chief Greek Texts*. Paris: Libraire Orientaliste Paul Geuthner, 1929.

Benveniste, E., and Renou, L. *Vṛtra et Vṛϑragna, étude de mythologie indo-iranienne*. Paris: Imprimerie Nationale, 1934.

Bergaigne, Abel. *Vedic Religion according to the Hymns of the Ṛgveda*. 3 vols. Translated by V. G. Paranjpe. Poona: Ārya-saṁskṛti-Prakāśana, 1969, 1971, 1973.

Bhandarkar, R. G. "The Aryans in the Land of the Assuras." *The Journal of the Bombay Branch of the Royal Asiatic Society* 25 (1918): 76-81.

Bloomfield, Maurice. *Hymns of the Atharva Veda,* Sacred Books of the East Series, vol. 42, 1897. Reprint. Delhi: Motilal Banarsidass, 1973.

———. *A Vedic Concordance.* Harvard Oriental Series, vol. 10. 1906. Reprint. Delhi: Motilal Banarsidass, 1964.

Boyce, Mary. *A History of Zoroastrianism.* Vol. 1. Handbuch der Orientalistik, division 1, vol. 8, section 1, part 2. Leiden/Koln: E.J. Brill, 1975.

von Bradke, P. "Beiträge zur altindischen Religions– und Sprachgeschichte." *Zeitschrift der Deutschen Morgenländischen Gesellschaft* 40 (1886): 347-79.

———. *Dyāus Asura, Ahura Mazdā und die Asuras.* Halle: Max Niemeyer, 1885.

Brown, W. Norman. "The Creation Myth of the Rig Veda." *Journal of the American Oriental Society* 62 (1942): 85-98.

———. "Proselyting the Asuras." *Journal of the American Oriental Society* 39 (1919): 100-103.

Burrows, T. "The Proto-Indoaryans." *Journals of the Royal Asiatic Society of Great Britain and Ireland,* 1973, no. 2, pp. 123-140.

———. *The Sanskrit Language,* 2nd ed. London: Faber and Faber, 1965.

Caland, W., ed. and trans. *Das Jaiminīya-Brāhmaṇa in Auswahl.* 1919. Reprint. Wiesbaden: Dr. Martin Säding, 1970.

Caland, W., trans. *Pañcaviṃśa-Brāhmaṇa. The Brāhmaṇa of Twenty Five Chapters.* Calcutta: Baptist Mission Press, 1931.

Coomaraswamy, Ananda K. "Angel and Titan: An Essay in Vedic Ontology." *Journal of the American Oriental Society* 55 (1935): 373-419.

Dandekar, R.N. "Asura Varuṇa." *Annals of the Bhandarkar Oriental Research Institute* 21 (1941): 157-191.

———. *Vedic Bibliography.* 3 vols. Poona: Bhandarkar Oriental Research Institute, 1946, 1961, 1973.

———. *Der Vedische Mensch.* Heidelberg: Carl Winter's Universitätsbuchhandlung, 1938.

Darmesteter, James. *Ormazd et Ahriman, leurs origins et leur histoire.* Bibliothèque de l'école des hautes études, 29th fascicle. Paris: F. Vieweg, 1877.

Delbrück, Bertold. *Altindische Syntax.* 1888. Reprint. Darmstadt: Wissenschaftliche Buchgesellschaft, 1976.

Dillon, Myles. "Celt and Hindu." The Osborn Bergin Memorial Lecture III. Dublin: University College, 1973.

Dumont, Paul Emile. "The Horse-Sacrifice in the Taittirīya-Brāhmaṇa: The Eighth and Ninth Prapāṭhakas of the Third Kāṇḍa of the Taittirīya Brāhmaṇa with Translation." *Proceedings of the American Philosophical Society* 92 (1948): 447-503.

———. "The Special Kinds of Agnicayana (or Special Methods of Building the Fire-Altar) According to the Kaṭhas in the Taittirīya-Brāhmaṇa: The Tenth, Eleventh, and Twelvth Prapāṭhakas of the Third Kāṇḍa of the Taittirīya-Brāhmaṇa with Translation." *Proceedings of the American Philosophical Society* 95 (1951): 628-667.

———. "The Iṣṭis to the Nakṣatras (or Oblations to the Lunar Mansions) in the Taittirīya-Brāhmaṇa: The First Prapāṭhaka of the Third Kāṇḍa of the Taittirīya Brāhmaṇa with Translation." *Proceedings of the American Philosophical Society* 98 (1954): 204-223.

———. "The Full-Moon and New Moon Sacrifices in the Taittirīya-Brāhmaṇa (First Part): The Second Prapāṭhaka of the Third Kāṇḍa of the Taittirīya-Brāhmaṇa with Translation." *Proceedings of the American Philosophical Society* 101 (1957): 216-243.

———. "The Full-Moon and New Moon Sacrifices in the Taittirīya-Brāhmaṇa (Second Part): The Third Prapāṭhaka of the Third Kāṇḍa of the Taittirīya-Brāhmaṇa with Translation." *Proceedings of the American Philosophical Society* 103 (1959): 584-608.

———. "The Full-Moon and New-Moon Sacrifices in the Taittirīya-Brāhmaṇa (Third Part): The Part of the Hotar in the Full-Moon and New-Moon Sacrifices. The Fifth Prapāṭhaka of the Third Kāṇḍa of the Taittirīya Brāhmaṇa with Translation." *Proceedings of the American Philosophical Society* 104 (1960): 1-10.

———. "The Full-Moon and New-Moon Sacrifices in the Taittirīya-Brāhmaṇa (Fourth Part): The Anuvākas 1-6 and 11 of the Seventh Prapāṭhaka of the Third Kāṇḍa of the Taittirīya-Brāhmaṇa with Translation." *Proceedings of the American Philosophical Society* 105 (1961): 11-36.

———. "The Animal Sacrifice in the Taittirīya Brāhmaṇa: The

Part of the Hotar and the Part of the Maitrā-varuṇa in the Animal Sacrifice: The Sixth Prapāṭhaka of the Third Kāṇḍa of the Taittirīya-Brāhmaṇa with Translation." *Proceedings of the American Philosophical Society* 106 (1962): 246-63.

———. "The Human Sacrifice in the Taittirīya-Brāhmaṇa: The Fourth Prapāṭhaka of the Third Kāṇḍa of the Taittirīya-Brāhmaṇa with Translation." *Proceedings of the American Philosophical Society* 107(1963): 177-182.

———. "Taittirīya-Brāhmaṇa 3.7.7-10 and 3.7.12.-14: Seven Anuvākas of the Seventh Prapāṭhaka of the Third Kāṇḍa of the Taittirīya-Brāhmaṇa with Translation." *Proceedings of the American Philosophical Society* 107(1963): 446-460.

———. "The Agnihotra (or Fire-God Oblation) in the Taittirīya-Brāhmaṇa: The First Prapāṭhaka of the Second Kāṇḍa of the Taittirīya-Brāhmaṇa with Translation." *Proceedings of the American Philosophical Society* 108 (1964): 337-353.

———. "The Kaukilī-Sautrāmanī in the Taittirīya-Brāhmaṇa: The Sixth Prapāṭhaka of the Second Kāṇḍa of the Taittirīya Brāhmaṇa with Translation." *Proceedings of the American Philosophical Society* 109 (1965): 309-341.

———. "The Kāmya Animal Sacrifices in the Taittirīya-Brāhmaṇa: The Eighth Prapāṭhaka of the Third Kāṇḍa of the Taittirīya-Brāhmaṇa with Translation." *Proceedings of the American Philosophical Society* 113 (1969): 34-66.

Eggeling, Julius. *The Śatapatha-Brāhmaṇa*, 5 vols. Sacred Books of the East, vols. 12, 26, 41, 43, 44; 1882, 1885, 1894, 1897, 1900. Reprint. Delhi: Motilal Banarsidass, 1972.

Fausböll, V. *Indian Mythology according to the Mahābhārata.* London: Luzac & Co., 1902.

Geldner, Karl Friedrich. *Der Rig-Veda aus dem Sanskrit ins Deutsche Übersetzt und mit einem Laufenden Kommentar versehen*, 3 vols., Harvard Oriental Series, vols. 33-5. Cambridge: Harvard University Press, 1951.

Gershevitch, Ilya. *The Avestan Hymn to Mithra.* Cambridge: University Press, 1967.

Gonda, Jan. *The Dual Deities in the Religion of the Veda.* London: North-Holland Publishing Company, 1974.

———. *Epithets in the Ṛgveda.* 's-Gravenhage: Mouton & Co., 1959.

———. *Die Religionen Indiens.* Vol. 1. Stuttgart: W. Kholhammer Verlag, 1960.

———. *The Vedic God Mitra.* Leiden: E. J. Brill, 1972.

Grassmann, Herman. *Wörterbuch zum Rigveda.* Reprint. Wiesbaden: Otto Harrassowitz, 1964.

Hillebrandt, Alfred. "Review of *Dyāus Asura, Ahura Mazdā und die Asuras* by P. von Bradke." *Theologische Literaturzeitung* 22 (1885): cols. 527-530.

———. *Varuṇa und Mitra: ein Beitrag zur Exegese des Veda.* Breslau: G. P. Anderholz' Buchhandlung, 1877.

———. *Vedische Mythologie.* 3 vols. Breslau: Verlag von M. & H. Marcus, 1902.

Insler, Stanley. *The Gāthās of Zarathustra.* Acta Iranica, third series, vol. 1. Leiden: E. J. Brill, 1975.

Kaegi, Adolf. "Review of *Dyāus Asura, Ahura Mazdā und die Asuras* by P. von Bradke." *Deutsche Litteraturzeitung* 36 (1885): cols. 1268-9.

Keith, Arthur Berriedale. "Mitanni, Iran and India," in *Dr. Modi Memorial Volume.* Bombay: Fort Printing Press, 1939, pp. 81-94.

———. *The Religion and Philosophy of the Veda and Upanishads.* 2 vols. Harvard Oriental Series, vols. 31 and 32. Reprint. Delhi: Motilal Banarsidass, 1970.

Keith, Arthur Berriedale, trans. *Rigveda Brāhmaṇas: The Aitareya and Kauṣītaki Brāhmaṇas of the Rigveda.* Harvard Oriental Series, vol. 25. Reprint, Delhi: Motilal Banarsidass, 1971.

Keith, Arthur Berriedale, trans. *The Śāṅkhāyana Āraṇyaka.* 1908. Reprint. New Delhi: Oriental Reprint, 1975.

Keith, Arthur Berriedale. *The Veda of the Black Yajus School entitled Taittiriya Samhita.* Harvard Oriental Series, vols. 18 and 19, 1914. Reprint. Delhi: Motilal Banarsidass, 1967.

Konow, Sten. "Zur Frage nach den Asuras." In *Beiträge zur Literaturwissenschaft und Geistesgeschichte Indiens, Festgabe Hermann Jacobi zum 75. Geburtstag*, edited by Willibald Kirfel, pp. 259-64. Bonn: Kommissions-verlag Fritz Klopp, 1926.

Kuiper, F. B. J. "Ahura Mazdā 'Lord Wisdom?'" *Indo-Iranian Journal* 18 (1976): 25-42.

———. "The Basic Concept of Vedic Religion." *History of Religion* 15 (1975): 107-120.

———. "Cosmogony and Conception: A Query." *History of Religion* 10 (1970): 91-138.

———. *Varuṇa and Vidūṣaka: On the Origin of the Sanskrit Drama.* Amsterdam: North-Holland Publishing Co., 1979.

Lommel, Herman. *Religion und Kultur der Alten Arier.* Vol. 1. Frankfurt am Mein: Vittorio Klostermann, 1935.

Lord, Albert B. *The Singer of Tales.* 1960. Reprint, 5th printing. New York: Atheneum, 1973.

Lüders, Heinrich. *Varuṇa.* Edited by Alsdorf Ludwig. 2 vols. Göttingen: Vandenhoeck & Ruprecht, 1951 and 1959.

Macdonell, Arthur A. *A. History of Sanskrit Literature.* Reprint. Second Indian Edition. Delhi: Motilal Banarsidass, 1971.

———. *Vedic Mythology.* 1898. Reprint. Delhi: Motilal Banarsidass, 1974.

Mayrhofer, Manfred. *Kurzgefasstes etymologisches Wörterbuch des Altindischen,* 3 vols. Heidelberg: Carl Winter Universitätsverlag, 1953-1976.

Meringer, Rudolf. "Review of *Dyāus Asura, Ahura Mazdā und die Asuras* by P. von Bradke." *Oesterreichische Monatsschrift für den Orient* 4 (1885): 95-97.

Müller, Max, trans. *Vedic Hymns,* Part 1. Sacred Books of the East, vol. 32, 1891. Reprint. Delhi: Motilal Banarsidass, 1973.

Nobel, Johannes. *Der Rig-Veda,* vierter Teil, *Namen- und Sachregister zur Übersetzung.* Harvard Oriental Series, vol. 36. Cambridge: Harvard University Press, 1957.

Oertel, Hanns. "Contributions from the Jaiminīya to the History of the Brāhmaṇa Literature: First Series." *Journal of the American Oriental Society* 18 (1897): 15-48.

———. "Contributions from the Jaiminīya to the History of the Brāhmaṇa Literature: Second Series." *Journal of the American Oriental Society* 19 (1898): 97-125.

———. "The Jaiminiya Brahmana Version of the Dirghajihvi Legend." *International Congress of Orientalists, Third Series.* Paris, 1897, pp. 225-239.

———. "Contributions from the Jaiminīya to the History of the Brāhmaṇa Literature: Fourth Series." *Journal of the American Oriental Soceity* (1902): 23 (1 325-349.

———. "Contributions from the Jaiminīya to the History of the Brāhmaṇa Literature: Fifth Series." *Journal of the American Oriental Society* 26 (1905): 176-196.

———. "Additions to the Fifth Series of Contributions from the Jaiminīya Brāhmaṇa.—" *Journal of the American Oriental Society* 26 (1905): 306-314.

———. "Contributions from the Jaiminīya to the History of the Brāhmaṇa Literature: Sixth Series." *Journal of the American Oriental Society* 28 (1907): 81-98.

———. "Contributions from the Jaiminīya to the History of the Brāhmaṇa Literature: Seventh Series." *Connecticut Academy of Arts and Sciences, Transactions* 15 (1909): 155-216.

———. "Extracts from the *Jaiminīya-Brāhmaṇa* and *Upaniṣad-Brāhmaṇa*." *Journal of the American Oriental Society* 15 (1892): 233-51.

Oldenberg, Hermann. "Ākhyāna-Hymnen im Ṛgveda." *Zeitschrift der Deutschen Morganländischen Gesellschaft* 39 (1885): 52-90.

———. *Die Religion des Veda.* 1917. Reprint. Darmstadt: Wissenschaftliche Buchgesellschaft, 1970.

———. "Ṛgveda VI, 1-20." *Zeitschrift der Deutschen Morgenlandischen Gesellschaft* 55 (1901): 267-330.

———. *Ṛgveda. Textkitische und exegetische Noten.* 2 vols. Berlin: Weidmannsche Buchhandlung, 1909-1911.

———. "Varuṇa und die Ādityas." *Zeitschrift der Deutschen Morgenländischen Gesellschaft* 50 (1896): 43-68.

———. "Zarathustra." *Deutsche Rundschau* 12 (1898): 402-437.

Otto, Rudolf. *Das Gefühl des Überweltlichen.* Munich: C. H. Beck'-sche Verlagsbuchhandlung, 1932.

———. *Gottheit und Gottheiten der Arier.* Giessen: Alfred Topelmann, 1932.

———. *The Kingdom of God and the Son of Man.* Translated by F. V. Filson and B. L. Woolf. London: Lutterworth Press, 1938.

Padmanabhayya, A. "Ancient Bhṛgus." *The Journal of Oriental Research Madras.* 5 (1931): 55-100.

Pischel, Richard and Geldner, Karl F. *Vedische Studien.* 2 vols. Stuttgart: Verlag von W. Kohlhammer, 1889, 1897.

Polome, E. "L'etymologie du terme germanique *ansuz 'dieu soverain.' " *Étude Germanique* 8 (1953): 36-44.

Przyluski, Jean. "Deva et asura." *Rocznik Orjentalistyczny* 8 (1931-2): 25-39.

Raja, K. R. V. "Asura Maya." *Journal of the Royal Asiatic Society of Great Britain and Ireland*, January 1917, pp. 131-2.

Rajwade, V. K. "Asurasya Māyā in Ṛgveda." In *Proceedings and Transactions of the First Oriental Conference, Poona.* Poona: Bhandarkar Oriental Research Institute, 1920.

Rao, U. Venkatakrishna. "The Romance of Words." *The Aryan Path* 14 (1943): 204-207.

Renou, Louis. *Bibliographie Vedique*. Paris: Librairie d'Amerique et d'Orient, 1931.

———. *Études Vedique et Pāninéennes.* 17 vols. Publications de l'institute de civilisation indienne. Paris: E. de Boccard, 1955-1969.

Roy, Rai Bahadur S. C. "The Asuras—Ancient and Modern." *The Journal of the Bihar and Orissa Research Society* 12 (1926): 147-152.

Sarup, Lakshman. *The Nighaṇṭu and the Nirukta.* Delhi: Motilal Banarsidass, second reprint 1967.

Schindler, H. Jochim. *Das Wurzelnomen im Arischen und Griechischen.* Unpublished dissertation, Würzburg, 1972.

Schlerath, Bernfried. "Altindisch *asu*–, Awestisch *ahu*– und ähnlich klingende Wörter." In *Pratidānam: Indian, Iranian and Indo-European Studies presented to Franciscus Bernardus Jacobus Kuiper on his Sixtieth Birthday*, edited by J. C. Heesterman, G.H. Schoker, and V.I. Subramoniam. The Hague: Mouton, 1968.

von Schroeder, Leopold. *Arische Religion.* 2 vols. Leipzig: H. Haessel Verlag, 1914.

———. *Mysterium und Mimus im Rigveda.* Leipzig: H. Haessel Verlag, 1908.

Seebold, Elmar. *Das System der indogermanischen Halbvokale.* Heidelberg: Carl Winter, Universitätsverlag, 1972.

Segerstedt, T. "Les Asuras dans la religion védique." *Revie de l'histoire des religions* 57(1908): 157-203.

———. "Les Asuras dans la religion védique (Suite et fin)." *Revue de l'histoire des religions* 57 (1908): 293-316.

Shamasastry, R. "Vedic Gods." In *B.C. Law Volume*; edited by

D. R. Bhandarkar, K.A. Nilakanta Sastri, B. M. Barua, B. K. Ghosh, P. K. Gode; pp. 277-81. Calcutta: The Indian Research Institute, 1945.

Sköld, Hannes. "Were the Asuras Assyrians?" *The Journal of the Royal Asiatic Society of Great Britain and Ireland*, April 1924, pp. 265-267.

Spiegel, F. "Review of *Dyāus Asura, Ahura Mazdā und die Asuras* by P. von Bradke." *Berliner Philologische Wochenschrif.* 5 (1885): cols. 1076-1080.

Taraporewala, I. J. S. "Some Vedic Words Viewed in the Light of the Gathas and Other Avesta Texts." *Journal of the Bombay Branch of the Royal Asiatic Society* 26 (1951): 121-128.

———. "The Word अहुर (*ahura*) in Sanskrit and the Gobhilas." In *Indo-Iranian Studies.* London: Kegan Paul, Trench, Trubner & Co., 1925.

Thieme, Paul. "The 'Aryan' Gods of the Mitanni Treaties." *Journal of the American Oriental Society* 80 (1960): 301-317.

Vendryes, J. "Les correspondances de vocabulaire entre l'indo-iranien et l'italo-celtique." *Mémoires de la Societé de Linguistique de Paris* 20 (1918): 265-285.

Venkatesvaran, C. S. "The Vedic Conception of 'Asura.'" *The Poona Orientalist* 13 (1948): 57-60.

Wackernagel, Jakob and Debrunner, Albert. *Altindische Grammatik*. 3 vols. 1896, 1930. Reprint. Göttingen: Vandenhoeck & Ruprecht, 1957, 1954, 1975.

Watkins, Calvert. "Studies in Indo-European Legal Languages, Institutions, and Mythology." In *Indo-European and Indo-Europeans*; edited by George Cardona, Henry M. Hoenigswald, and Alfred Senn; pp. 321-354. Philadelphia: University of Pennsylvania Press, 1970.

Whitney, William Dwight. *Atharva-Veda-Saṁhitā*, 2 vols., Harvard Oriental Series, vols. 7-8. Reprint, Delhi: Motilal Banarsidass, 1971.

Wolff, Fritz, trans. *Avesta: die heiligen Bücher der Parsen.* 1910. Reprint. Berlin: Walter de Gruyter & Co., 1960.

Wüst, Walter. Über das Alter des Ṛgveda und die Hauptfragen der indo-iranischen Frühgeschichte," *Wiener Zeitschrift fur die Kunde des Morgenlandes* 34: 165ff.

INDEX

ERRATA

p. 4, line 1 of footnote 18. Change "of derivative" to "of a derivative"

p. 6, line 25. Change "but in the" to "but the"

p. 8, line 5 of footnote 44. Change "or alcomposition" to "oral composition"

p. 15, line 4. Change "'*ονϱανος*" to "'*ουϱανος*"

p. 16, line 6. Change "." to ","

p. 19, line 6. Omit period after "'*ηώς*".

p. 33, line 2 of footnote 216. Change "Morgenlandischen" to "Morgenländischen"

p. 36, line 2 of footnote 236. Change "Morgenlandischen" to "Morgenländischen"

p. 47, line 26. Change "varcíṇaḥ" to "varcínaḥ"

p. 50, line 20. Change "tiṣṭhath" to "tiṣṭhatho"

p. 55, line 2 of note 2. Change "Morgenlandischen" to "Morgenländischen"

p. 57, line 11. Change "*asuryám*" to "*asuryàm*"

p. 70, line 19. Change "śaraṇā" to "śaraṇā́"

p. 89, line 15. Change "Asuras" to Asura"

p. 93, line 20. Change "RV 10.54.5" to RV 10.54.4"

p. 99, line 2 of note 1. Change "4 vols." to "5 vols."

p. 106, line 23. Change "práinān" to "práiṇān"

p. 108, line 22. Change "bhū́yobhūyeḥ" to "bhūyobhūyaḥ"

p. 109, line 13. Change "jitāḥ" to "jitā́ḥ"

p. 110, line 4. Change "RV" to "AV"

p. 112, line 3. Change "téna" to "ténā"

p. 131, line 22. Change "nāma" to "nā́ma"

p. 133, line 24. Change "svastyáyanaṃ" to "stvastyáyanaṃ"

p. 133, line 27. Change "bṛ́had" to "bṛhád"

p. 138, line 24. Change "śrídhaḥ" to "srídhaḥ"

p. 141, line 6. Change "gū́hamāna" to "gū́hamānā"

p. 146, line 13. Change "ánās-" to "anā́s-"

p. 150. line 19. Change "tarhīt" to "tārīt"

p. 150, line 23. Change "jaghánta" to "jaghántha"

p. 151, line 4. Change "dās-" to "dás-"

p. 161, line 32. Change "ásyac" to "àsyac"
p. 164, line 3 of Footnote 1. Change "yásāyáṃ" to "yásyāyáṃ"
p. 164, line 3 of footnote 3. Change "śevaḍhipá/" to "śevadhipá"
p. 164, line 4 of footnote 1. Change "aríḥ" to "aríḥ/"
p. 168, line 16. Change "asyā́ḥ" to "asyāḥ"
p. 171, line 11. Change "TS 3.4.6.3" to "TS 3.4.6.2."
p. 173, line 27. Omit "seems"
p. 184, line 2. Change "fšənghīm" to "fšə̄nghīm".
p. 184, line 3. Change "davąscinā humərətōis" to "davąscinā humərətoiš".
p. 187, line 5. Change "avaiŋhe" to "avaiŋ́he".
p. 187, line 27. Change "strəušca" to "strə̄ušca".
p. 187, line 29. Change "daiŋhupaitīm" to "daiŋ́hupaitīm".
p. 188, line 2. Change "daiŋhupaiti-" to "daiŋ́hupaiti-.."
p. 188, line 5. Change "yeŋhe" to "yeŋ́he" .
p. 189, line 23. Change "aurvaŋho" to "aurvåŋho".
p. 189, line 23. Change "dainhu patayō puθrånho" to "daiŋ́hu. patayō puθråŋho".
p. 189, line 24. Change "dainhu.paitinam" to "daiŋ́hu.paitinąm".
p. 189, line 31. Change "dainhu.patayō" to "daiŋ́hu.patayō".
p. 189, line 31. Change "ahuranhō." to "ahuråŋhō."
p. 190, line 3, Change "daiŋhupaitiš" to "daiŋ́hupaitiš.."
p. 190, line 13. Change "daiŋhave" to "daiŋ́have".
p. 192, line 18. Change "aurvat.aspa" to aurvaṯ.aspa".
p. 209, line 34. Change "Assuras" to "Assurs".
p. 210, line 24. Change "Säding" to "Sändig".
p. 212, line 10. Change "3.7.12.-14" to "3.7.12-14".
p. 214, line 12. Change "Alsdorf Ludwig" to "Alsdorf, Ludwig".
p. 214, line 14. Change "*A.*" to "*A*".
p. 214, last line. Change "(1902):23 (1 325-349." to "23 (1902): 325-349."
p. 217, line 33. Change "Reprint," to "Reprint."